Hans Küng

A REVALUATION

Edited by
Paul Lakeland

Paulist Press
New York / Mahwah, NJ

Cover image by Manfred Grohe / Süeddeutsche Zeitung Photo / Alamy Stock Photo
Cover and design by Lynn Else

Copyright © 2024 by Paul Lakeland

All rights reserved. No part of this publication may be reproduced, stored in a retrieval system, or transmitted in any form or by any means, electronic, mechanical, photocopying, recording, scanning, or otherwise, without either the prior written permission of the Publisher, or authorization through payment of the appropriate per-copy fee to the Copyright Clearance Center, Inc., www.copyright.com. Requests to the Publisher for permission should be addressed to the Permissions Department, Paulist Press, permissions@paulistpress.com.

Library of Congress Cataloging-in-Publication Data
Names: Lakeland, Paul, 1946– editor. | Küng, Hans, 1928-2021, honouree.
Title: Hans Küng: a revaluation / edited by Paul Lakeland.
Description: New York, Mahwah, NJ: Paulist Press, [2024] | Includes bibliographical references. | Summary: "This book explores the theological legacy of the Swiss theologian Hans Küng"—Provided by publisher.
Identifiers: LCCN 2024001819 (print) | LCCN 2024001820 (ebook) | ISBN 9780809156184 (paperback) | ISBN 9780809187799 (ebook)
Subjects: LCSH: Küng, Hans, 1928-2021.
Classification: LCC BX4705.K76 H35 2024 (print) | LCC BX4705.K76 (ebook) | DDC 230/.2092—dc23/eng/20240726
LC record available at https://lccn.loc.gov/2024001819
LC ebook record available at https://lccn.loc.gov/2024001820

ISBN 978-0-8091-5618-4 (paperback)
ISBN 978-0-8091-8779-9 (e-book)

Published by Paulist Press
997 Macarthur Boulevard
Mahwah, New Jersey 07430
www.paulistpress.com

Printed and bound in the
United States of America

CONTENTS

Preface: The Küng Enigma v
   Paul Lakeland

1. On the Death of Hans Küng on April 6, 2021:
   An Appreciation 1
      Karl-Josef Kuschel

2. Trust That Endures: Hans Küng on Justification 7
      Hermann Häring

3. God, the Foundation of Life 32
      Anthony J. Godzieba

4. Revisiting Küng's Christology 53
      Roger Haight, SJ

5. Infallibility and the Vatican 74
      Mary McAleese

6. Priesthood 95
      Susan A. Ross

7. Hans Küng: A Transitional Ecumenist 114
      Jakob Rinderknecht

8. Hans Küng's Global Ethics Project: A Revaluation 136
      Hille Haker

9. Hans Küng Visits the World Religions 156
      Frank X. Clooney, SJ

10. Küng and the Secular World 174
       Johanna Rahner

11. Does Hans Küng Still Matter? 196
    Jonathan Keir

List of Contributors 209

Hans Küng: Works in English 213

PREFACE
The Küng Enigma

Looking along the shelves of my theological library, no author occupies more space than Hans Küng. Admittedly, I don't have the complete works of Karl Barth or Rahner's *Theological Investigations* in their entirety, but Küng's footage on the shelves is still impressive. And this is only those of his books translated into English. There are several more, as you will see from the endnotes to some of this distinguished collection of essays in the present volume. All the chapters have been written for this volume, and in their different ways all of them recognize the complexity of assessing Küng's lasting impact on the Catholic world. Jonathan Keir's punchy title for the final piece—"Does Küng Still Matter?"—is a question that might haunt at least some of the authors here, perhaps those particularly from the English-speaking world. I have all those Küng books on my shelves, and if I have turned to them in recent years less than I used to, well, this could be a reflection on me and not on Küng. But my own anecdotal research in compiling this volume has to conclude that his work does not figure largely in the coursework even of graduate theology, and in consequence, very few younger Catholic theologians are aware of his immense contributions to postconciliar theology. This, I think, is a shame, and invites an explanation. Hence the current volume.

Hans Küng's theological writings have been of enormous importance and are not now merely of historical interest. Only this can explain the willingness of the distinguished slate of authors gathered here. What you will see in the chapters that follow is a sustained argument for continuing to read Küng, though one that does not shy away from recognizing that some of the work is dated and some of it less essential than might once have been thought to be the case. In fact, the greater part of his writing is either, in the best possible senses, "occasional" or of the genre of *haute vulgarization*. Küng was in many respects a pastoral theologian, concerned for the good of people more than for the good of the institutional church, and critical of the self-referentiality of the body ecclesiastic. After the early and more traditionally scholarly work in *Structures of the Church* and *The Church*, Kung turned to lengthy volumes clearly not directed at fellow academics, but rather at the general public: *On Being a Christian* and *Does God Exist?* are prime examples of this shift to more popular writing, and while they were worldwide best-sellers at the time, they now naturally show their age. In more recent times Küng moved out beyond the Christian audience into what looks like a kind of second (or maybe third) career, in his writing and his entrepreneurship in the twin fields of global ethics and interreligious dialogue. Whether or not this move was a result of becoming tired of wrangling ecclesiastical disputes or of frustration with his continued official isolation from Catholic theology, the results seem to have constituted a new lease on life, and one that carried him through the remainder of his days until his death in April 2021.

While the authors gathered here in this volume may or may not agree with the intellectual movement described in the previous paragraph, each of their essays addresses one or two steps in Küng's career as a writer and teacher. All the writers here are distinguished academics who have either worked extensively on Küng's oeuvre, or known him personally, or both. They include a number of Americans, a sprinkling of Germans, and one New Zealander. Each essay was written without cooperation with or knowledge of what other contributors were going to say, but the reader will find a large measure of agreement about the particular strengths of Küng's work, and perhaps somewhat more disagreement over whatever weaknesses they may have discerned.

The book begins with a kind of cross between an obituary and an overview, written by Karl-Josef Kuschel, one of the scholars who over the years worked mostly closely with Küng. In his aptly entitled "Appreciation," Kuschel offers the most personal tribute in this collection, writing movingly of Küng's many public roles eventually being

Preface

displaced by illness and age, and stressing above all that "a critic of the church and the papacy is dead," but that "reducing him to this cliché is an oversimplification." The second essay by Hermann Häring, another of his closest collaborators, rehearses the vitally important role of the idea of "justification" in Küng's early academic work written in dialogue with Karl Barth. Häring outlines the relationship between the older and much more senior Protestant theologian and the very young Catholic, making clear the close affinities while pointing out that where Barth was focused more on the justification of the individual before God, Küng showed a characteristically Catholic preference for the role of justification in the *community* of faith.

The following four chapters examine discrete topics of importance in the more ecclesially focused writings in the first half of Küng's career. Anthony Godzieba's essay explores Küng's foundational or natural theology, showing how Küng sought existential security through trust in God. While we are free to accept or reject God, any fundamental trust in reality is unjustified, thought Küng, if we take the latter step. We all seek such fundamental trust, but only the decision to trust in God can justify such a conviction. Roger Haight picks up the role of Christology in Küng's work, showing how a focus on the Christian life moves theology away from preconciliar abstractions to something much more experiential. Küng's historicist approach eschews dogmatism and places Christology squarely in dialogue with the signs of the times. Mary McAleese takes up the issue of Küng's challenge to the common understanding of papal infallibility, surely the one part of his thinking that everyone has heard of and, equally undeniably, the principal cause of the Vatican's move to dismiss him from the ranks of orthodox Catholic theologians. She places Küng's *Infallible? An Inquiry* in the context of his larger concerns with what he saw to be growing ecclesial unwillingness to concretize the teaching of Vatican II, and as a text that had its impact in part because of the controversies over Paul VI's ban on artificial birth control swirling around the Catholic world at this time. Susan Ross discusses Küng's thought on priesthood as anticipatory of the present synodal direction of the church, while noting that its apparent farsightedness suffers at the same time from its historical location prior to public awareness of the scandal of clerical sexual abuse.

Jakob Rinderknecht's essay on Küng's ecumenical theology provides a nice bridge to his later work on interreligious dialogue and global ethics. Rinderknecht places Küng's contribution in dialogue initially with Karl Barth but goes on to show how the development of the ecumenical process has moved on in a direction neither Barth nor Küng anticipated, with a recognition that the ecumenical future will celebrate the contributions of different traditions rather than any effort to further reunite the churches.

If the loss of his *missio canonica* in 1979 precipitated Küng's turn to ecumenism, only ten years later he moved still further, beginning work on the global ethics project that would become so important to him. Hille Haker takes a critical but appreciative look at the four principles grounding his project, from the first, that there can be "no peace among the nations without peace among the religions," to the last, that there can be "no survival of the earth without a global ethic, connecting religious and non-religious people." This is followed by Frank Clooney's chapter "visiting" Küng's work on world religions, where he appreciates the intent and the popular appeal of the books on Judaism, Hinduism, and Islam, while recognizing that they are not and are not intended to be scholarly treatments of these great religious traditions.

The final two chapters of the book represent a couple of ways of summing up what has gone before. Johanna Rahner's overview of Küng's work takes its starting point from his intense awareness of the modern world, his commitment to validating the idea of "the signs of the times" so central to Vatican II, and his lifelong effort to make the dogmatic categories of Christian theology accessible to a wider population. Küng, she argues, sought to show how faith might be possible to those who seem untouched by it. Then, in a final chapter, Jonathan Keir explores how someone who is not part of the theological establishment could encounter and, indeed, come to appreciate the work of Hans Küng. In a more personal essay that mirrors in some ways Karl-Josef Kuschel's opening "appreciation," Keir positions Küng as a welcoming presence for those outside the narrow confines of Catholicism, or even Christianity, or even religion at all. Surely Küng would have valued this understanding of his lifework, bringing people together on the strength of experience rather than allowing different ideas and ideologies to keep them apart.

Paul Lakeland

1

ON THE DEATH OF HANS KÜNG ON APRIL 6, 2021

An Appreciation

Karl-Josef Kuschel

It fills me with sadness to finally have to say goodbye to a person with whom I have walked a common path for a good fifty years. Hans Küng was my teacher from the year I moved to study in Tübingen in 1970, not least because of him; he already had an excellent reputation as a Catholic reform theologian. At that time, dialogue with the Protestant and secular worlds was the magic formula triggered by the Council, and Hans Küng showed us how this works and what consequences this had for a Catholic understanding of a church that remains medieval and anti-Protestant. Under his leadership, theology once again became an incredibly exciting intellectual enterprise, a laboratory of the spirit in which one dared to think new things—as guardians not of the ashes of the past, but of the fire of the future. A church renewed in doctrine and life seemed to us to be quite differently credible in a secular-pluralistic society. Hans Küng convinced us of this. Were we too naïve? Would this society be impressed at all by reforms within the church? Or did the "crisis of faith" go deeper, the "crisis of God," as some call it?

Since that time, I have known him in many "roles": as a brilliant speaker, passionate researcher, hard worker at his desk, a resistance fighter unimpressed by hierarchs, warrior for a common Christianity with Protestants and Orthodox, but also as a charismatic priest at eucharistic celebrations, as a multilingual communicator at international conferences, a successful publicist, and a hands-on organizer. And also—despite his international standing—as a Swiss patriot who was proud of the democratic history of freedom in his home country. In recent years, I also saw a contrasting image: Hans Küng as a sick person who bravely endured the slow decline of his body as he became more and more dependent on the care of others.

A critic of the church and the papacy is dead, but reducing him to this cliché is a cheap shot. Others point to the fact that he remained in the church and kept many other people in the church. But there is so much more to it than that, a lifework that grew over a good sixty years and at the end of 2020 totaled twenty-four volumes in the complete German edition of his works. What it means for the history of theology in the twentieth century cannot yet be estimated. An overall appreciation of his accomplishments, let alone an evaluation of the individual writings, has not yet begun. Surprising discoveries could be made if one looks closely at how Küng receives, for example, Indian, Islamic, and European philosophy, analyzes paradigm shifts in Judaism, Islam, and Christianity, or interprets the music of Mozart, Bruckner, and Wagner and the works of Hermann Hesse or Thomas Mann.

Ecclesia semper reformanda: Küng never had inhibitions about orienting himself on this motto of the Reformation and working until the end for church renewal, until Parkinson's disease literally took the pen out of his hand. *Can We Save the Catholic Church?* he had asked in 2011, an ambiguous title in view of the abuse scandal that had become public by that time. And he had answered: Yes, in spite of everything, if the church lives according to the original message of Jesus, perhaps then it would again be taken seriously as the conscience of the nations, as a prophetic voice against moral decay, and thus as an instance of living by eternal values. Seen in this way, one understands the double thrust of Küng's oeuvre: it holds up a mirror to church and society in equal measure.

In this mirror, he believed, the Catholic Church would recognize that it could let go of traditions if they were neither evangelical

On the Death of Hans Küng on April 6, 2021

nor of value today. This double criterion is the key to Küng's theology and his far-reaching demands for reform. And they are not due to a decay in the *zeitgeist* with which despisers of his kind of theology tend to reproach him, but to the consistent emphasis on the "freedom of a Christian." For Küng, unlike so many others, Christianity is not identical to the historical form of present-day Protestantism and Catholicism. From him I learned to distinguish between Catholicism as a sociological category and Catholicity as a spiritual ideal and that—beyond the old confessionalist camps—there have long been new lived syntheses of Christianity: a catholicity lived by Protestants and an evangelical spirit lived by Catholics. In short: through basic theological research, Küng made a significant contribution to liberating the Catholic Church and theology from their anti-Protestantism.

Because this is the case, Küng found, for example, that the biblically well-founded Petrine ministry for the Catholic Church should not be attached to two papal dogmas (primacy and infallibility), because this makes the Catholic magisterium largely incapable of reform. His church has punished him for challenging these dogmas, deeming his teaching no longer "Catholic." Küng also concluded that mandatory celibacy for clerics is both unscriptural and responsible for the dramatic personnel crisis in Catholic parishes, that the Roman prohibition of ordination for women is theologically wrong and has alienated countless committed women (and men) from the church, and last but not least, that the ecumenism demanded by the Council is scandalously half-heartedly pursued by church leaders. The commemoration of the Reformation in 2017 was just lip service, and decisive deeds failed to materialize. There is still no recognition of Protestant ministries and their celebrations of Holy Communion, no training of theologians in ecumenical faculties, no introduction of ecumenical religious education in state schools. Having to witness delaying tactics and procrastination for years often drove Hans Küng to despair. As an insider, he was well aware that the decades-long ecumenical research and dialogue process had long since produced consensual results that no longer justified a schism. Did the church leaders not understand that many committed Christians had either quietly said goodbye or resorted to self-help?

But with his own charisma as a communicator and profound scientific work behind him, Küng also reached the largely secular, postchurch society. Already at the beginning of the 1970s he had understood that, despite all his commitment to ecumenism, Christianity questioned it all: by historical criticism of the sources, by criticism of religion and atheism, and by the pluralism of the great religions. In fact, these challenges could not be met with some reforms within the church, they went to the substance—keyword: God's crisis. Küng was aware of the explosive nature of this development for the survival of religious faith, without intending to play off the renewal within the church against the crisis of faith.

Taking up the results of the historical-critical research of New Testament sources, he described historically reliable basic features of Jesus's original message as an orientation for today's Christianity (*On Being a Christian*, 1974). In a self-critical reappraisal of the criticism of religion in modern times, he presented an argumentative draft that, with rationally tested "good reasons," makes trust in God responsible (*Does God Exist?*, 1978). In conversation, especially with the natural sciences, he faced recent research on microcosm and macrocosm in *such a way that* the biblical-Qur'anic belief in the Creator of all things remains a meaningful option (*The Beginning of Things: Science and Religion*, 2005). Challenged by the major world religions and their claim to truth, which competes with Christianity, Küng tried to understand the religions of Asian and Middle Eastern origin from within and at the same time to build bridges for interreligious dialogue (*Christianity and World Religions*, 1984). Groundbreaking above all his portrayal of a complex religion such as that of Islam in its genesis and development, unique for a Christian theologian in the recent history of theology (*Islam: Geschichte, Gegenwart, Zukunft*, 2004).

What's more, Küng took the "factor of religion" seriously in many parts of the world in the face of frequently held theses that religion would wither away or become completely privatized in the course of modernization processes. He had seen enough of the world to know that religions still play a formative role for large masses of people. Ambivalent, of course. Not in Western and Northern Europe, but in Middle Eastern, Asian, and African countries under the influence of Islam, Confucianism, and Buddhism. To underestimate the influence of religions politically would be a serious mistake. Küng did not do so, especially since he had to experience again the rise of the demons of religious extremism worldwide, legitimizing terror and wars in the name of God. Küng then intensified and motivated research on the potential for peace in religions and showed that the world religions have great similarities in ethics. He called this the contribution of the world religions to a world ethos and recognized in such a common ethos the indispensable prerequisite for world peace. He had understood that a global peace policy cannot succeed without and certainly not against the representatives of religions. And that these representatives have a heavy responsibility for world peace. In short: Just as Küng contributed to liberating Catholic theology and church from their anti-Protestantism, so also he sought to free secular, Western society from its blindness to religion and to religious influences in world society.

With his program word *Global Ethic*, Küng achieved a previously unknown international and interdisciplinary resonance with effects far beyond theology and religious studies not only into the realm of political, social, legal, and economic sciences, but also into that of operational politics. When the face of an unscrupulous "predatory capitalism" (H. Schmidt) arose that shakes the world financial system and with it the entire world economy, Küng called for common world ethical standards, especially in the area of global economic activity with its computer-controlled world stock exchanges and internationally networked capital markets. Together with specialist economists, he supported a "Manifesto Global Economic Ethic" (2010) and in the same year published his program *Anständig Wirtschaften: Why Economics Needs Morality*. Küng believed that international economic actors also have a conscience, that the global market needs a global ethic.

Having become president of the newly founded "Global Ethic Foundation" in 1995, Küng used his international reputation for regular small "coups." His invitation to a global ethic speech at the University of Tübingen was followed by, among others, a British Prime Minister (Tony Blair), a Secretary General of the United Nations (Kofi Anan), a current Federal President (Horst Köhler), a former German Chancellor (Helmut Schmidt), and a bishop, the racial reconciler Desmond Tutu from South Africa. In Tübingen people were amazed and came in droves. For people at the grassroots level, it was a motivational boost every time. And at a time when the Trumps, Putins, and Erdogans are in power, dividing the world and their nations again, the Global Ethic Agenda is far from finished. It will remain explosive in the future. A Global Ethic Institute in Tübingen and above all the Global Ethic Foundation will keep Küng's legacy alive and adapt it to new challenges.

Having lived more than ninety years, Hans Küng could look back on a rich life. As a Christian, he was aware of how much grace he had received in his life and did not exclude even the bitter conflict with Rome at the time. He received personal signs of appreciation from countless readers of his works at home and abroad and also from Pope Francis, but formal rehabilitation failed to materialize—a disappointment. There can be no talk of a "reconciliation" with the church in the Roman sense. But Hans Küng was able to complete his work, even the completion of his complete edition, which was professionally supervised by Stephan Schlensog. Increasingly disabled by his illness, he also lived to see his ninety-third birthday on March 19. He did not die alone. Until the end, he was cared for in his house by nurses as well as former and current employees. As his eyes failed, he enjoyed listening to his confidants read aloud to him. He never woke from a nap around noon on April 6, a gentle dying. For this, too, he will be grateful to his Creator. And posterity is grateful for the work of Hans Küng. His equal will not be seen again for a long time in Catholic theology.

2

TRUST THAT ENDURES

Hans Küng on Justification

Hermann Häring

Introduction: Beginnings

In 1948, Hans Küng, a critical republican spirit from Switzerland, entered the German-Hungarian College in Rome, whose students studied philosophy for three years and theology for four years at the Pontifical Gregorian University. The Germanicum was founded in 1552 by Pope Julius III and handed over to the Jesuits with the aim of creating an elite group of theologians to overturn the Reformation. A large number of the German bishops have gone through this training, which is about clarifying, profiling, and systematizing Roman Catholic doctrine. When, after 1945, intensive international encounters were again possible in Rome, the college became the focal point of a cosmopolitan theology that eagerly absorbed new trends. This included great interest in new philosophical movements, especially in existentialism, historical thinking, and ecumenism. It was time to leave behind rigid neo-Scholasticism and its strict "controversial theology."

Our young Swiss student took these trends seriously. With the will to explore new things, he concentrated during his student years on the justification of the sinner, the central point of contention of the Reformation, with the intent of understanding and reconciling the different positions. Having received the licentiate in philosophy (1951) and theology (1955), he followed it with two years of study at the Institut Catholique in Paris. In 1957 his dissertation entitled "Rechtfertigung [Justification]" was published.[1] As Karl Barth confirmed in his preface, Küng was able to claim that as a result of his work this central ecumenical controversy had lost its church-dividing character. He would hold on to this conviction for the rest of his life.

In the Protestant world, this conclusion was received with great interest, but on the Catholic side with some restraint. This is not surprising. Küng had broken an ecumenical taboo that has legitimized the Evangelical-Catholic difference for over four hundred years. In addition to the quarrels over Martin Luther and the Protestant confessional writings, the Council of Trent emphasized the Roman Catholic side with its detailed decree on justification (1547).[2] At first, the epochal extent of Küng's thesis could hardly be gauged; presumably the author himself was not yet aware of the possible consequences, although he declared that this could be "no more than a beginning."[3] It was clear from the start that his first theological work went beyond the previously standard positions of even the most progressive ecumenists.[4] The Holy Office, today the Dicastery for the Doctrine of the Faith, promptly registered it on the Index of Forbidden Books under the number 399/57/i. The suspect was to keep these numbers for life. The World Council of Churches, founded in 1948, also held off on judgment. It was not until 1999, forty-two years after Küng's initiative, that a very restrained consensus was reached between the Lutheran World Federation and the Roman Catholic Church, which will be discussed later.

An Explosive Memory

The subject matter dealt with under the term *justification* is complex and has changed over the centuries. Since the Reformation, the questions have been: Does God grant people salvation on the basis of human achievements, do they at least play a complementary role, or does God call sinners into his salvation completely undeservedly, that is, *out of pure goodness* and without human intervention? Can we be saved "independently of works [of the Torah]" (cf.

Rom 3:8), or is faith really dead without works (cf. James 2:15–17)? Does the Protestant slogan "by faith alone, by Christ alone, and by grace alone" apply, or does the Catholic slogan "faith and works" get it right? This confrontation was accorded such weight that it led to the separation between Catholic and Protestant churches.

Even this simplified question shows how much the topic is affected by different confessional presuppositions. In retrospect, the issue of justification points to a complex problem. First of all, it recalls the justification of Abram (Gen 15:1–6), which Paul brings into play in his dispute over the validity of the Torah. Abram trusts YHWH. In return, YHWH "justifies" him, and Abraham becomes the progenitor of the Jewish people (Rom 4:13–22). But in the Christian world, this narrative is integrated into specific contexts that primarily concern the salvation of individuals. Worth mentioning are Paul's criticism of the Torah (according to which all people sin), the Augustinian theory of original sin (which declares all people are born sinners), as well as the Reformation controversies about indulgences and ecclesiastical authority (which is supposed to guarantee the salvation of souls). In all probability, Christian theology in modern times knows of no other topic that has become so starkly representative of confessional disputes. With Küng, it remains to be asked in which modern and postmodern contexts justification plays a new, albeit undercover role.

But the original situation of the doubting Abram was hardly mentioned in these disputes. Instead, they led to anti-Jewish resentment, to a shadowy image of the human person and an abysmal distance from the world, to confessional polemics. In addition, there are later inner-theological questions that have become prominent, such as rejection and salvation, condemnation and acquittal, redemption, sanctification and vocation, merit and gratuitous grace, as well as the dialectic of justice and sin. These questions, as Küng writes, arise "uncannily frequently" in confessional disputes and develop— especially since the Reformation—the tendency to ever new variations. So how can one solve this complex knot of often incompatible questions without strictly separating them from one another and thus dissolving the inner unity of the questions? Küng makes it his goal to find the common and unifying ground for all these questions and thus to work out an overarching basis for solving the centuries-old aporia.

In this war of many fronts, Catholic theology, as already indicated, had created new conceptual distinctions. Karl Barth accused it of dealing too exclusively with human conditions and not with the *event* of salvation, which had to hold all questions together.[5] For some decades we have also been aware that formally speaking, the problem of justification as we have known it since Paul is almost absent from the message of Jesus, and it does not appear in the later writings of Hans Küng. However, this does not make the discussion of the matter unimportant. After all, the use of this language in modern times is more misleading than ever, almost incomprehensible to outsiders. The Jewish central concept of *zedakah*, which permeates the Hebrew Scriptures, means righteousness, justice, or simply that which belongs before God, what is okay, what makes a life worth living. It is the central concept of the Jewish faith par excellence. The one who is justified is the one who can be considered "righteous" before God. Therefore, this term can never be isolated. It always targets the whole of Jewish piety.[6]

Jewish righteousness includes at the same time the whole of the Torah, the visions of the prophets, the divine word, wisdom par excellence. This holistic dimension has mostly been overlooked in the tough ecumenical debates. Moreover, Catholic discourse was strongly determined by the juridical and apologetic secondary meaning of those who *have to justify* themselves in court or defend their position; a salvific, egoistic undertone crept in. The saving or condemning judge of the people, the fear of salvation, became the depressing measure of consideration.

It is not clear whether Küng sees through the highly complex character of the problems at the beginning, but intuitively he takes a goal-oriented path. He does not develop an abstract discourse on the doctrine of justification per se, but compares the then-current state of Catholic discussion (little changed since the Council of Trent) with the then-highly topical doctrine of justification of the Protestant Karl Barth.[7] As a Reformed theologian, Barth was not (like Luther) totally fixated on the problem of justification. More soberly, he perceived it as an elementary theological question, as the central *salvation event* of the Christian faith. This led to a great advantage in the ecumenical discussion at that time: like Barth, Küng does not want to get caught up in endlessly complicated questions of detail, nor does he want simply to ignore the multiplicity of specific questions.

Rather, Küng focuses on the *tension* between inner unity and the great number of questions of detail in order to get to the core of the problem. In the first part of the book, he creates space for his own reflections by first examining Barth's doctrine of justification "in the whole of the Dogmatics." In this way, he can—in indirect speech, so to speak—keep an eye on the overall background of the Christian message behind the individual analyses. Only toward the end of the first part (chapter 15) does he deal with the bundle of special questions. In the second part, guided by the Council of Trent, he presents the Catholic justification within the framework of the specifically Catholic tradition. Only at the end of this section does he draft a Catholic answer (chapter 32).

At the same time, it was already clear to the young theologian that further answers were not to be found where one would expect them to be, in the Roman lecture halls. Of course, he cannot and does not (yet) want to openly contradict the overpowering Roman magisterium of Pius XII, and this fact led to some restraint in his language. He also knows how difficult it is to translate complex contexts and their consequences into clear and sober language. Finally, Luther (from 1517) does not deal with the question neutrally, and the decree of justification of the Council of Trent (1547) does not simply take up Luther's concerns with objectivity. Paul had developed the doctrine of justification as a doctrine of struggle. Nevertheless, the will for an ecumenical breakthrough is palpable after 430 years of progressive hardening of positions. After all, Küng was not the only Catholic theologian who felt a new sense of ecumenical reconciliation.

The Agreement between Karl Barth and Hans Küng

The choice of Karl Barth as an ecumenical interlocutor proved to be a stroke of luck for Küng in several respects. In Barth, too, independence of judgment is important. Forty-two years older than Küng, Barth demonstrated it through his resolute resistance to National Socialism. Hans Küng himself had addressed this issue as a schoolboy.[8] Added to this was Barth's ability to confidently shape theological contexts. He was more familiar than many others with the philosophical idealism and Protestant theology of the nineteenth century and was one of the few Protestant theologians with a lengthy and well-informed concern for Catholic theological literature. Additionally, the Catholic theologian Hans Urs von Balthasar had made him more familiar to the Catholic public in a persuasive monograph.[9]

In the 1950s, Barth not only enjoyed a high moral reputation but was also regarded as one of the leading figures of European Protestantism in the study of theology. His *Church Dogmatics* immediately established itself as an undisputed standard work.[10] First, Küng presents Barth's complete system in a highly streamlined form and then offers a "Catholic response." In doing so, he sets himself a modest goal, but ambitious in its final effect. He is not interested in outlining the ecumenical doctrine of justification, but instead wants to show that the factual doctrinal differences and their discussions do not justify the separation of the different denominations.

The conditions for this conversation are favorable. In the end, there is an underlying relationship between Barth's style of thought and the Gregorian approach, marked by an encyclopedic style of thinking, the joy of logical consistency, the appreciation of the great theological traditions, and a transparent confrontation with contemporary discussions. In addition, Küng finds, following Balthasar, that "Barth's theology combines both the strongest development of Protestant thought and the best approach to the Catholic." Küng also brought with him a level of knowledge that was considerable, but he remained open to learning more, something he had learned to do during his studies.

Under these conditions, Küng wants to show that it is possible to reach an understanding in conversation with Karl Barth. He does not present his answers as definitive statements and does not propose himself as someone in total command of the problem. Rather, he develops a feeling for the situation of upheaval that manifests itself a few years later in the Second Vatican Council, and thus prepares himself for an open path to ecumenical rapprochement. Learning from Barth, he also does not present the doctrine of justification as a coherent statement of faith, which he only has to tinker with here and there. And like Barth, he too consistently places it in the wide-ranging discourse on God and Christ, creation and redemption.

Küng anchors his Catholic starting point in the aforementioned justification decree of the Council of Trent. It was adopted in 1547 and still has considerable authority in the Catholic world. Barth and Küng respected its qualities, appreciating it as a carefully crafted document that argued surprisingly openly in view of the tensions at the time. But Küng does not allow this document, which has hitherto determined Catholic doctrine, to become the unquestionable standard of Catholic identity, as happened with neo-Scholasticism and sometimes still happens today. Rather, Küng makes use of the new historical consciousness that the movement of *nouvelle théologie* had so emphatically proclaimed.[11] He reads the highly scholarly text of Paul as well as the thinking of the early church theologians, he makes his unhistorical, strictly ontological categories more flexible. Moreover, he can show that Barth's idea of justification is also much more flexible and less one-sided than first appearances suggest. But something else is even more important: Küng allows Barth to take him by the hand to demonstrate the complex idea of justification throughout his theological system. Küng's working hypothesis is that the full scope of the doctrine of justification can only be properly measured from the perspective of the comprehensive message of faith.

This is the reason why Küng first gives an overview of the major themes of Barth's dogmatics in the first part of his book. It is about the goodness of God, which outshines everything, about the unconditional yes of the Savior toward people, and about the covenant that God makes with humankind, as well as the reconciliation offered to people despite their failings. In sum, Karl Barth is emphatically concerned with "supremacy," the "sovereign act of the grace of God," with which God meets people. Against this backdrop, the event of salvation ("the fulfillment of justification") acquires its own decisiveness: in Christ, even in his death, it is God who confronts us and we, who ultimately want to be God, are rejected. *We* destroy ourselves because we cling to our freedom and responsibility.

The grace of a God who remains true to himself despite this catastrophe and takes humankind into his own justice and reconciliation seems all the more radiant: "The innermost part of God's righteousness is grace." However, Karl Barth takes this contrast to such extremes for Catholic ears that the question arises: Can it really also become human justice? For Barth it is clear: the Reformation understanding of human beings, who are both righteous and sinners (*simul iustus et peccator*), applies without any compromise. They are forgiven their sins, have the rights of God's children, and can hope for the divine inheritance.

Hans Küng's answers to Barth's positions do not need to be referred to in detail here. He presents consensual answers to the well-known basic questions: What does *justification* mean in the New Testament sense of a "declaration of righteousness"? What does God's creative grace mean? What victory really happens in Christ's death and resurrection? How is "righteous and sinner at the same time" also anchored in the Catholic image of the human person, in the liturgical and spiritual piety of Catholicism? Küng can show in each case how close Catholic and Protestant thought are to each other. He reveals countless testimonies of scripture, of the great theological tradition (still full of vigor from the theologians of the early church), and of present-day theological reflection. With concise quotations, he rescues many similarities from oblivion.

For the Catholic readership, these chapters were of enormous importance, because with these testimonies of Catholic origin, Küng could adopt Barth's theological concept and at the same time expand it. While Barth places all emphasis on *God's* actions, the Catholic testimonies stress *human* attitudes and actions. At the same time, they bridge the traditional confessional differences, because, like Karl Barth, they also accentuate the comprehensive anchoring of the doctrine of justification in the common faith in God, Christ, creation, and redemption. Basically, therefore, the confessional opposites are of secondary importance. At best, they point to imbalances, but they do not justify a sectarian exclusionary confrontation. As a preliminary result of his thorough consideration, Küng states: "As far as the foundations of the doctrine of justification are concerned, Barth, taken as a whole, is on the same ground as we Catholics."

Basic Trust in God

What does this mean for the doctrine of justification in the narrower sense? The holistic view of the foundations of Christian faith has brought the topic out of its controversial theological isolation and at the same time prepared the ground for a more relaxed method. With Küng, it also left behind the strict, logically calculating rationalism of neo-Scholasticism in the Catholic world. On the one hand, Küng formulates the questions so simply that clear, generally convincing answers become possible. Küng summarizes Barth's concerns in the question: "Does the Catholic doctrine of justification take justification seriously as the gracious act of the sovereignty of God?" Küng's Catholic-oriented counterquestion is: "Does Karl Barth take justification seriously as the justification of *the human person*?" On the other hand, this double question clears the undergrowth of exaggerated controversial theological considerations and overly detailed discourses in which one no longer sees the forest for the trees and easily confuses the zeal for God's action with church interests. The ecclesiastical models and institutions of salvation can also distract from trust in God.

In addition, Küng's recourse to the fundamentals of faith leads to a hermeneutically conversational approach without delving into Barthian hermeneutics. He repeatedly speaks of a mutual understanding or of the fact that every theology has its "gradient" with strengths and weaknesses. This applies to Barth as well as to Catholic theology. Moreover: "The implicit truth content, insofar as it is divine truth, always exceeds the explicit formulation, and there is where its mystery is encountered." Even Catholic theology must not pose as the dictator of Christian doctrine.

So we have to be clear that we always speak liminally. The doctrine of justification is closely interwoven with the doctrine of faith, and it is only in Christology that all this gets its sonorousness. This is a "melody" from which certain chords cannot be omitted with impunity. "So we always have to move away from the formula…to understand it *secundum spiritum*." This is how Küng deciphers basic attitudes and finally decodes the message of justification as a statement about human newly won freedom.

With this cautious perspective, always ready for interpretation, the two final chapters of the treatise are prepared. Its titles are "*Sola fide* [By faith alone]" and "*Soli Deo gloria* [Glory to God alone]." In the first concluding chapter on faith, Küng can show that the Reformation formula of faith *alone* can already be found in numerous theologians of the early church and in Thomas Aquinas, according to whom the "works" (as Paul understands them) cannot bring salvation. Nevertheless, within this consensus there is still room for different emphases. Thus, the later controversies that have divided the denominations since the Reformation were only a continuation of earlier controversies within the church that did not lead to a schism. Küng recalls the strong competition among the schools of Augustinianism, Thomism, and Scotism. They, too, belong to the heritage of the church as a whole, because according to the pre-Reformation understanding, they only illuminate different aspects of the one great event of salvation. A glance at the early church shows how much the modern conflict between the denominations has narrowed the room we have for language and understanding. For these reasons, Küng agrees with the "arch-Protestant" Barth in many aspects, without accusing him of holding Catholic positions. Rather, he can simply say that he is "seen as a whole, on the same ground with us Catholics." Thus, he speaks of a "fundamental agreement."

At the same time, the chapter culminates in a statement with unexpected emphasis: "Faith is indeed also *trust*." These are words that would profoundly shape Küng's basic attitude and thinking. As we shall see, Hans Küng is breaking new ground here. In the New Testament, faith and trust are almost synonymous; as a rule, they are interchangeable, because the Christian or biblical faith has a thoroughly personal character. Thus, Küng understands justifying faith not as a believing insight into an objective process, but primarily as the trusting recognition of God's saving action. This challenge arises with the inevitable question of how we humans deal with our insurmountable limits without finally failing. In this situation, everything comes down to the fact that we can not only rely entirely on God but can also really rely on ourselves, that nothing distracts us from this trust.

The second concluding chapter on the glory of God ("*Soli Deo gloria*") turns once again to the One in whom we trust. According to Küng, God's glory and human freedom are not mutually exclusive within the framework of justification. It is not about submissive obedience. Although the salvation of the human person begins with the recognition of one's own insurmountable limitations, this recognition can lead to the highest human activity. Therefore, for Küng it is true that "in his passive receptivity, man is highly active by God's grace." For the time being, for a Christian understanding of the world, the question remains whether the church's doctrine of faith and its practical implementation really take God's absolute primacy seriously and at the same time grant freedom its space.

With this test of human freedom, Küng's work raises an explosive question for the early years of the era of secularization. Initially, it remains oriented toward intra-ecumenism: Does the religious practice of the churches with their innermost intentions really give glory to God, God alone? From an anti-liberal standpoint and in view of his experiences with National Socialism, Barth demands that God's act of sovereignty be taken seriously without reservation; in return, his young Catholic interlocutor emphasizes, from a perspective that is critical of authoritarianism, that—assuming the sovereignty of God—the justification and recognition of the human person follows. Since Barth accepts Küng's explanations unreservedly (and hopes that they will also be heard by Küng's church), for him the main reason for the great Western schism is over. For the state of discussion at the time, this is an epochal result. How explosive this was to be for Küng would show in later developments.

Forms of Resistance

Küng's book on justification resulted in a brief but intensive period of research.[12] In addition to an initial and broad ecumenical agreement, a controversy ensued, but the prospects were good.[13] Karl Rahner vigorously defended Küng's core thesis,[14] and ten years later it was confirmed by Otto Hermann Pesch, the expert on Thomas Aquinas and Luther.[15] But facing a broad phalanx of irritated Catholic dogmatists and power-conscious bishops, the talks soon become more difficult. In the long term, the new impulses would recede into the background; for the ecclesial public in Europe, the justification of the sinner remains a Protestant issue and is soon pushed out of everyday theological life.

Nevertheless, Küng's continuing separation from traditional Catholic teaching led to polarization. On the one hand, his theological breakthrough earned the thirty-two-year-old a chair at the University of Tübingen as early as 1960; on the other hand, official concerns led to a growing distancing, which became increasingly obvious after the end of the Council (1965). His Institute for Ecumenical Research, founded in 1963, was increasingly cut off from official channels of communication, and Küng himself consistently kept away from the emerging ecumenical bodies and commissions. Uncritically conservative arguments gained the upper hand, as if there had been neither a Reformation nor a Second Vatican Council and the Roman Catholic Church had always followed a spotless scriptural path.

Küng's emphasis on God's sovereignty and on the primacy of the Christian message was simply perceived and condemned as banal criticism of the church. The points of contention focus on the exclusive truth and official claims of the Catholic Church. Over the years, theologians such as Henri de Lubac, Hans Urs von Balthasar, Joseph Ratzinger, and even Walter Kasper emerged as opponents. The strategy of their arguments is typical: instead of dealing with justification in the sense of Paul, Augustine, or Luther in a differentiated way, they sing the praises of a gifted church, its sacramental structure, and an ecclesiastical unity, effectively an act of submission to the official leadership.

Does this development still have anything to do with the discussions about justification? Initially, as already mentioned, this topic was sidelined. The disappearance of the topic was initially understandable because the announcement of the Second Vatican Council in January 1959 under the slogan of *aggiornamento* accentuated structural and pastoral, not theological themes. At the Council itself (1962–65), justification did not play an explicit role, despite the debates on ecumenism.[16] Even Hans Küng—and this may come as a surprise—did not bring this topic up for discussion in his publications at that time.[17]

Why the silence on justification? One could point out that Küng did not like repeating himself. Or perhaps he was too optimistic and assumed that his books had been read and, he hoped, understood. But in reality, he remained true to his intentions and his original democratic orientation. Also regarding Barth's image of the church, he had never forgotten the *practical* consequences for church structures. Once the idea was accepted in 1957 and an ecumenical consensus was announced, it was no longer worthwhile for him to continue to develop the subtleties of abstract theory. He was not concerned with the details, but with the big picture and its consequences for the practice of faith.

In addition, the doctrine of justification has always been oriented to crisis and praxis. It has had practical significance in polemics and in boundary issues. This applies to Paul, Augustine, and Martin Luther, for each of whom difficult disputes played a central role. The doctrine could only achieve its objective in concrete conclusions: in the possible renunciation of the Torah, in the recognition of its own weakness, and in the criticism of exaggerated promises of salvation on the part of the church. Küng probably understood this intuitively and therefore did not found a theoretical school of justification. No, first he developed a research program on various church images and understood the question of justification as a kind of critical detector. He intended this to reveal the stress points in church practice, in which an affirmation of offices and institutions overshadows the outstanding *Gloria Dei*, its truth and the message of salvation.[18] From this point on, Hans Küng would spend his life identifying neuralgic fields that would put people's faith to the test in order to tell them: trust in God's message more than in the self-appointed bringers of salvation.

Where Trust Is Undermined

Küng's most important achievement in terms of justification is that he has detached the promise of justification from its traditional contexts and focused on the modern question of unconditional trust. As early as 1974, the question of personal justification was confronted with the question of social justice.

As already mentioned, the decisive keyword of the Hebrew biblical tradition is *zedaka*, usually understood as a righteousness that already includes community-building care and solidarity in the Jewish Testament. Against this background, Genesis 15:1–6 could once again become the *primordial narrative* in which the question of justification must be anchored. Decisive is YHWH's liberating word: "Abram trusted the word of YHWH and God blessed his sincere faithfulness." It is enough to trust fully and energetically in God; then we are in divine favor. It is also well known that Jesus criticizes the self-righteous Pharisee who thanks YHWH for not being like the robbers, deceivers, and adulterers. But the tax collector, aware of his failure, goes home "justified" (Luke 18:9–14). Obviously, the pious are in danger of replacing their humble trust with pious achievements.

For this reason, and not because he despises the Torah, Paul denies that it brings it any guarantee of salvation. Three and a half centuries later, Augustine (d. 430) exaggerates this justified criticism of the pious guarantee of salvation by condemning the children of Adam as born sinners and humanity to the "damned heap" (*massa damnata*). Finally, Martin Luther rejects all ecclesiastical guarantees of salvation since they would be surrogates for divine action. Following this trail, Küng uncovers further modern and postmodern contexts that could also undermine this trust and must therefore be critically examined. These sensitive areas to be examined are: (1) ecclesiastical institutions, (2) church doctrine, (3) interreligious dialogue, and (4) the goal of a reconciled world.

Church Structure in Historical Criticism

Küng looks first at the official demands of his own church in matters of church leadership, truth claims, and the mediation of salvation. These demands have hardened since the time of the Reformation. From the nineteenth century onward, the Catholic Church has been praising itself — especially in progressive circles — as the "living Christ."[19] Is it not blasphemous to replace trust in God with trust in the church? Just look at the Council of Trent and the First Vatican Council (1870), which dogmatically cemented the de facto existing powers by promoting the pope in a frighteningly realistic way as the visible representative of the invisible head of the Church.[20]

Küng ventures into this area of conflict, before and after the Second Vatican Council, with the books *Structures of the Church* (see note 16), which the Council understood as representative of the church, and *The Church*,[21] which designs a synodally and charismatically anchored image of the church. *Truthfulness*[22] is dedicated to the virtue of openly arguing transparency, and one can read this book as a critique of the system of a veiled language of domination. In the summer of 1970 Küng produced *Infallible? An Inquiry*,[23] a general discussion of the papal claim to "extraordinary" infallibility, which had been officially defined one hundred years earlier.

All these initiatives resist any undermining of simple trust in

God because it comes to be replaced by unconditional trust in the church and her institutions. In doing this, Küng works in the idea of justification, which, like the Reformation, aims at a renewed church. But nowhere does he mention the doctrine of justification as a formal principle. On the other hand, Küng argues well in a modern fashion, employing the principles of secular science, above all the historical-critical method, as well as recent church history and the history of dogma. In doing so, he rejects any official ecclesiastical absolutes. Nothing can be considered true just because the church, the Holy Spirit, or an official representative claims it is. Therefore, he concentrates his discussion on the original challenges of the biblical or Christian message, which always leads to unconditional trust in God. Küng is passionately careful that ecclesiastical determinations do not patronize faith: "An absolutized church disenfranchises faith, that is the Catholic danger. It is crucial that God's saving action precedes both faith and the Church." The glorification of God must not lead to triumphalism but, rather, to the consistent limitation and relativization of church institutions.

This principle becomes most serious in the sharp criticism of the dogma of extraordinary papal infallibility in *Infallible?*. With this warning, Küng spent his life in the theologically sterile relations between Catholic and Lutheran churches. The Lutheran World Federation must have found it insulting when Benedict XVI declared in Erfurt on September 23, 2011, that he had no "gift" of hospitality to offer. Perhaps he and his Vatican authorities never really understood what justification is really about. In 1999, after lengthy preliminary talks, a *Joint Declaration on the Doctrine of Justification* had been adopted,[24] but the document produced a sterile, abstract definition. Thus, no clear but only a "differentiated" consensus was reached, that is, no agreement that could become a constitutive part of the creed, but only a "balance" that basically reproduced the confessional differences, albeit in milder words. The document distinguishes between the common "basic truths" and the "applications" but overlooks the fact that this acid test of the Christian faith was designed to clarify differences and can only become effective in concrete contexts. The balance sheet became so abstract that it still had no ecumenical effect. Once again, Küng, the ecumenical troublemaker, remained misunderstood.

HANS KÜNG

Overcoming the Hellenistic Doctrine

The growing uncertainty of many committed church members after 1965 introduces a second phase of critical questions for Hans Küng, because now not only does the right of the denominations to exist come into the discussion, but also the language and biblical justification of the Christian message. This is an epochal, highly momentous question, and he takes time to respond to it. Since 1957 he had gradually familiarized himself (with necessary interruptions) with the highly complex theological path of thought of G. W. F. Hegel and wrote a monograph of over seven hundred pages, which appeared in 1970.[25]

The complex research results cannot be reproduced here, but regarding the Christian message, they contain a disturbing result: Hegel's doctrine of Christ and God, according to Küng, once again understood concrete history under the banner of "historicity." Similarly, even Hegel did not overcome the Hellenistic form of thought of the classical ecclesiastical language of faith[26] and so offered no access to the exegetically newly discovered event of the "historical Jesus."

Because of all this, the venerable Creed of the year 451, which still has the highest validity in the great churches, comes into play, for historical-critical exegesis brought enormous uncertainty to the debate on faith. In the context of the demythologization debate, Rudolf Bultmann rightly emphasized the mythical or symbolic character of religious language, which no longer offers objective certainty.[27] Ernst Käsemann referred to the loss of certainty caused by the paradigm shift from the Hellenistic confessional formula to the narrative report.[28] With clear definitions that suggest objectivity, we no longer create certainty; we must therefore find new ways of understanding instead of fundamentalistically stabilizing tradition. Küng was one of the few Catholic theologians with the courage to address this challenge and to come to terms with the doubts that arose. He faced the task in two steps.

In *On Being a Christian*, Küng drafts a historically responsible and systematically reflective account of Jesus, that is, a "Christology from below." He relativizes the rationally calculated Hellenistic models of thought. Instead of representing a new, noble, and powerful model of Christ as *Pantocrator* or Lord of the World, he asks the all-important and most revealing question, the one at issue in Jesus's condemnation: was Jesus a teacher of truth or a false teacher, a prophet or liar, a heretic or the victim of his prophecy? There are "clues but no clear evidence" for an answer. The questions therefore do not demand obedient adherence but require individual judgment, a free decision that arises from an "unconditional and unshakable trust." Only following Jesus Christ can we "live, act, suffer, and die truly humanly...held by God and helpful to humanity."

In *Does God Exist?* Küng examines the tension between these "hints" and a firm trust. The book explores the concept of *inner rationality*, in which Blaise Pascal's "reasons of the heart" are reflected. The believers experience the power of this inner reason from a free consent that sets itself apart from a radical basic mistrust. From an epistemological and psychological perspective, this basic trust becomes a constitutive and indispensable condition for a free yes to the meaning of life. Christian faith thus grows—always embedded in everyday life experience—from the attempt to hear the story of Jesus concretely and to grasp it through a life of practical discipleship.

Thus, Küng inserts the question of God into a situation that (in a secular context) returns to the classical question of justification, with its doubt and hope: "If God existed, then the founding reality itself would no longer ultimately be unfounded." This proposition, which recognizes all doubts, cannot be refuted by any external rationality; only the reasoning of the heart can provide a fundamental certainty. Thus, faith in God ultimately shows itself not as an achievement, but as a gift. In *Does God Exist?*, Küng develops a *double strategy* that escapes the lure of objective assurance. He confronts the vividly designed Jesus narrative of the New Testament with a current discourse of meaning that demands universal validity. In this always open confrontation, a language and a conviction emerge that understand faith to be based on hope, even offering it to a secular audience, because it does not demand submission to formulas of faith.

Dialogue in a Globalized World

With a third step, Küng opened up a final dynamic with far-reaching consequences. Since the 1980s, religions and worldviews have inevitably been in dialogue with each other, and even in Western cultures Christianity has lost its monopoly position. Many churches find this a humiliation. But for Küng, the question now arises whether they are not too full of themselves to meet each other in trust. Now the trust in God of justification formulated in many contexts is revealed as readiness for worldwide reconciliation. *No peace among nations without peace between religions.* This motto, which from now on appears on the title page of his books, has a profound theological significance. The stories *of all* religions have their own dignity, which must be respected humanly and theologically. A present-day conversation presupposes unconditional mutual communication. Religious dialogues are therefore no longer limited to special religious studies programs to satisfy human curiosity or to confirm certain theses. Rather, they move into the center of an interreligious-theological work that grants every religion (and every worldview that is constructively supported by humane values) comparable trust. They can and should all set out on a search for truth.

The broadening of this horizon is dramatic, because in this dialogue religious, often universal experiences of meaning meet that complement each other and, if necessary, relativize each other. Conversely, there is no longer any morality, no religious or ideological system that can rise above others, claiming to guarantee the one truth for every situation. As early as 1978, Küng declared: "And we are not alone on the way, but with millions and millions of other people from all kinds of denominations and religions, who go their own way, but with whom we stand continually in dialogue. What matters is not mine and yours, my truth/your truth. On the contrary, always willing to learn, we should learn from the truth of others and speak without envy of our own vision of things."[29]

As a matter of fact, here Küng comes into conflict with the monopoly claims of his own Christian church (also with the monopoly claims of other religions). These claims fundamentally contradict the idea of justification, that truth itself is always greater than its human vessels. Küng thus stands in diametrical opposition to Joseph Ratzinger, later Benedict XVI, who declared in 2000 as Prefect of the Congregation for the Doctrine of the Faith: The non-Christian religions and those Christian communities that are not true churches are *"objectively"* in a severely deficient situation compared to those who possess the abundance of means of salvation in the Church."[30] This sentence makes a mockery of any worldwide universal trust in God.

Finally, in this universalized trust in God, the circle of an unconditional trust in the world can be completed in a fourth and final step because the scope of *all* (explicitly and implicitly) religious narratives, confessions, teachings, symbolic worlds, rituals, and promises of salvation is now up for debate. They exhibit the most diverse cultural, social, and historical characteristics. But where is their common core message to be found that creates decisive trust?

For Küng, it lies in a holistic (practical, spiritual, and intellectual) attitude of mutual trust, love, and affirmation. It is expressed in the Golden Rule as well as in the appeal to humanity. Küng formulated this core message in the Global Ethic project.[31] It becomes the guideline and the appeal and criterion of all religions and worldviews and—in the spirit of the doctrine of justification—reveals their ambivalences. Religions in particular must not degenerate into a form of identitarianism or become fanatical institutions, although they are exposed to precisely this temptation. Therefore, according to Küng, the Global Ethic project is "not an explicitly religious…project. It can be supported by both religious and non-religious people. Philosophical justifications are just as possible as theological and religious-scientific foundations."[32] More precisely: arguments from philosophy, theology, and religious studies are called to a fair and respectful cooperation ordered to global results in a global world.

Thus, the doctrine of justification has reached its culmination, which is inherent in the world religions. Not only will the Torah (Paul), moral achievement (Augustine), or ecclesiastical claims to authority (Luther) fail to guarantee salvation, but nor, either, will church confessions and teachings, individual religions or religions in their entirety, once they forget "the primacy of the ever greater." On all these levels, we remain dependent on a fundamental trust in God and reality, on respect for life. Unfortunately, the representatives of the Roman Catholic Church have not yet taken note of this work for a fundamental trust in God, humanity, and the world. All other religions and religious communities face the same challenge.

HANS KÜNG

Conclusion: Trust That Endures

Paul, Augustine, and Martin Luther made the doctrine of justification the *negative*, so to speak salvation-egoistic focus of their warning against sin, the impending judgment and final condemnation. Küng demonstrates an epochal paradigm shift. He makes them the *positive* focal point of a fundamental trust in God and the meaning of life and the world. From a biblical perspective, this is an elementary perspective that recalls the blessing of Abraham and opens up a future for all humanity. For Küng, this impulse became an elementary driving force of his thinking, faith, and life. A biographical reference illustrates this clearly.

In 1953, a discussion with a skeptic plunged the young theology student into inner doubt. He recognized that his neo-Scholastic proofs of God could not convince the critic. And so he set out on a passionate search until one day during a spiritual conversation light dawned. Küng puts it this way: "Dare to say yes! Instead of an unfathomable mistrust, dare a fundamental trust in this unfathomable reality! Instead of a basic mistrust, a basic trust: in yourself, in other people, in the world, in life, in the questionable reality above all! And then meaning appears and light shines."[33]

The importance of this testimony can hardly be overestimated. It demonstrates the central motif of Küng's spirituality, his theological and religious-scientific thinking. In his writings, this theme appears again and again. Already in the justification book, as we saw, the question of trust was addressed and in *Does God Exist?* analyzed in detail. The motif of trusting hope runs through his writings on church reform,[34] and on the last pages of his memoirs there appears this verse of the Psalms: "In you, Lord, I have trusted, in eternity I will not perish" (Ps 71:1).[35] Finally, at the age of eighty-five, he wrote: "When I rely on God, I keep myself free from all finite powers and instances that are not God....My unconditional yes...I cannot give to any earthly authority or power, state or church, superior, guru, leader, or pope." Once again, as a Catholic Christian, he quotes this psalm verse, which forms the conclusion of the ancient Catholic proclamation, "Mighty God, we praise you."

Of course, for Küng, justification remains a controversial doctrine that only unfolds its effects in concrete texts. As in a magnetic force field, it makes neuralgic test questions visible to him and polarizes his own church in conflict with its particular, often small-minded interests. It is often overlooked that Küng attaches great importance to religious institutions, structures, and systems, because they—properly understood—arise from trusting righteousness, often lead to justice, open up and protect corresponding spaces of praxis. This applies within Christianity, for example, to doctrine, sacraments, and ecclesiastical offices, as well as to the guiding models of non-Christian religions, of religions as a whole. But that is precisely why he makes sure that they do not become independent or degenerate into substitutes for basic trust. They have to serve.

No religion or ideology, no strong institution or conviction can escape this critical question, for they all develop particular interests. The question of credibility is therefore: where are the limits beyond which these institutions take the place of God, of people or human communities, obscuring and ultimately destroying their truth, destroying freedom and the meaning of life? It is these questions and concerns that have made Küng a perceptive critic of ecclesiastical arrogance. From this point of view, it is a scandal and a sign of blindness that his own church has not yet properly perceived this warning call, not even discussed it self-critically in interdenominational dialogue. But it would not be in the spirit of Hans Küng to end with these bitter words, because until the end of his life he was convinced that even in his church the necessary humility would triumph one day.

Notes

1. *The Doctrine of Karl Barth and a Catholic Reflection* (London: Nelson, 1964).

2. *Decree on Justification*, Denziger-Hünermann (1991, 1520–1583).

3. [Ed. The author has provided frequent references within the text, accompanying many short quotations, to the complete edition of Küng's works that Karl-Josef Kuschel mentioned in the opening chapter. These references make little sense to someone without access to the German text, and so I have removed most of them, or

in some cases substituted a more accessible reference in an English translation.]

4. This can be exemplified by the well-known work of Yves Congar, *Vraie et fausse réforme dans l'Église* (Paris: Cerf, 1950), translated as *True and False Reform in the Church* (Collegeville, MN: Liturgical Press, 2010), which still insists on the strict validity of the official Roman Catholic doctrine.

5. For K. Barth, see note 7. Küng adopts from Barth no less than eight pairs of opposites of grace, with which traditional Catholic theology deals: (1) *gratia increate–creata*, (2) *externa–interna*, (3) *gratum faciens–gratis data*, (4) *actualis–habitualis*, (5) *medicinalis–elevans*, (6) *praeveniens–concomitans*, (7) *operans–cooperans*, (8) *sufficiens–efficax*, (9) *Dei–Christi*, (10) *supernaturalis–naturalis*.

6. The Egyptologist Jan Assmann speaks of a central concept under which "the whole of the social context" was conceived in ancient Near Eastern cultures. It reads "'Justice,' Egyptian *Ma'at*, Vedic *rta*, Postvedic *Mesharu*, Hebrew *ṣedeq/ṣedaqa*, Greek *dike* and *themis*. All these terms, but above all the first five, have in common that they also mean world order, that is, they mean a natural law conception of justice. Just action is acting in accordance with the meaning inherent in the world" (*Herrschaft und Heil* [Munich: Hanser, 2000], 202).

7. See also n9. The central reference text by K. Barth can be §61 "Des Menschen Rechtfertigung," in *Die Kirchliche Dogmatik*, Part IV, 1: *Die Lehre von der Versöhnung* (Zurich: Theologischer Verlag, 1953), 573–718.

8. Hans Küng, *Erkämpfte Freiheit. Erinnerungen I* (Munich: Piper, 2002), 20–24; SW 21, 19–22.

9. Hans Urs von Balthasar, *Karl Barth, Darstellung und Deutung seiner Theologie* (Cologne: Hegner, 1951).

10. Of Barth's thirteen-volume monumental work *Church Dogmatics*, ten volumes from I/1 to IV/2 were available at the time. The first volume of this life project appeared in 1932, the tenth (IV/2) in 1955. Later, another fully elaborated volume (1959), a fragment (1967), and, after Barth's death, a collection of further fragments (1976) appeared. Karl Barth died in 1968 at the age of eighty-two. The full set of volumes are published in English by T. & T. Clark.

11. The most important representatives of *nouvelle théologie* are Marie-Dominique Chenu, Yves Congar, Henri Bouillard, Henri de

Lubac, and Jean Daniélou. Also included are Hans Urs von Balthasar and (with reservations) Teilhard de Chardin, who developed his own theological profile as a paleontologist.

12. Johannes Brosseder, "Konsens im Rechtfertigungsglauben ohne Konsensus im Kirchenverständnis? Zur Bedeutung des Rechtfertigungsstreits heute," in *Neue Horizonte des Glaubens und Denkens. Ein Arbeitsbuch,* ed. H. Häring and K. J. Kuschel (Munich: Piper, 1993), 344–54.

13. Christa Hempel, *Rechtfertigung als Wirklichkeit. Ein katholisches Gespräch; Karl Barth, Hans Küng, Rudolf Bultmann und seine Schule* (Frankfurt: P. Lang, 1976), 8–20.

14. Karl Rahner, "Zur Theologie der Gnade. Bemerkungen zu dem Buch von Hans Küng: Rechtfertigung. Die Lehre Karl Barths und eine katholische Besinnung," *Theologische Quartalschrift* 138 (1958): 40–77.

15. Otto Hermann Pesch, *Die Theologie der Rechtfertigung bei Martin Luther und Thomas von Aquin. Versuch eines systematisch-theologischen Dialogs* (Mainz: Matthias-Grünewald-Verlag, 1967).

16. Justification is only briefly mentioned in the Apostolic Constitution *Lumen Gentium*, nos. 9 and 40, and in the Decree on Ecumenism *Unitatis Redintegratio*, no. 3.

17. *Konzil und Wiedervereinigung. Erneuerung als Ruf in die Einheit* (Vienna: Herder, 1960), trans. Cecily Hastings as *The Council, Reform and Reunion* (London: Sheed & Ward, 1961); *Strukturen der Kirche* (Freiburg: Herder, 1962), trans. Salvator Attanasio as *Structures of the Church* (London: Nelson, 1964); and *Kirche im Konzil* (Freiburg: Herder, 1963).

18. Further texts on the doctrine of justification can be found in SW1, 389–532.

19. Walter Kasper, *Katholische Kirche. Wesen—Wirklichkeit—Sendung* (Freiburg: Herder, 2011), 191 and 194n59.

20. This theory is elaborated in the encyclical of Pius XII of June 1943, *Mystici Corporis*, https://www.vatican.va/content/pius-xii/en/encyclicals/documents/hf_p-xii_enc_29061943_mystici-corporis-christi.html.

21. *Die Kirche* (Freiburg: Herder), 1967. Trans. Ray Ockenden as *The Church* (London: Sheed & Ward, 1968).

22. *Wahrhaftigkeit. Zur Zukunft der Kirche* (Freiburg: Herder 1968). Trans. as *Truthfulness: The Future of the Church* (London: Sheed & Ward, 1968).

23. *Unfehlbar? Eine Anfrage* (Zurich: Benziger, 1970). Trans. as *Infallible? An Inquiry* (London: Collins, 1971).

24. *The Joint Declaration on the Doctrine of Justification.* All official documents of Lutheran World Federation and Vatican (= texts from the VELKD; No. 87, June 1999). Lutherisches Kirchenamt der VELKD, Hanover 1999, ISSN 1617-0733. https://www.velkd.de/publikationen/texte-aus-der-velkd.php?publikation=386&kategorie=22. This declaration was solemnly signed on October 31, 1999, in Augsburg on behalf of the Lutheran World Federation and the Roman Catholic Church. Eberhard Jüngel draws attention to the main problem of this declaration. In the sense of Hans Küng, he misses the critical function of this declaration: *The Gospel of the Justification of the Godless as the Center of the Christian Faith. Eine Theologische Studie in Ökumenischer Absicht* (Tübingen[3]1999).

25. *Menschwerdung Gottes. Eine Einführung in Hegels theologisches Denken als Prolegomena zu einer Zukunft Christologie* (Freiburg: Herder, 1970). Trans. by J. R. Stephenson as *The Incarnation of God* (New York: Bloomsbury, 2001).

26. Important for Küng are the principal considerations of Ernst Käsemann, "Das Problem des historischen Jesus," in Käsemann, *Exegetische Versuche und Besinnungen* I (Göttingen: Vandenhoeck & Ruprecht, 1960), 167–214.

27. "There is no difference between security based on good works and security based on objectifying knowledge" (Rudolf Bultmann, "Jesus Christ and Mythology," in *Glauben und Verstehen* IV (Tübingen: Mohr, 1965), 141–89; cit. 188). This essay was originally published in English as *Jesus Christ on Mythology* (New York: Scribner, 1958).

28. "The question of the historical Jesus is legitimately the question of discontinuity[!] of the Gospel in the discontinuity of times and in the variation of the kerygma" (Käsemann, "Das Problem des historischen Jesus," 213).

29. *Theologie im Aufbruch. Eine ökumenische Grundlegung* (Munich: Piper, 1987), 305. Trans. by Peter Heinegg as *Theology for the Third Millennium: An Ecumenical View* (New York: Doubleday, 1988).

30. Congregation for the Doctrine of the Faith, *Dominus Iesus*, Declaration on the Uniqueness and the Salvation Universality of Jesus Christ and of the Church (August 6, 2000), 22. http://www.vatican.va/roman_curia/congregations/cfaith/documents/rc_con_cfaith_doc_20000806_dominus-iesus_ge.html.

31. The best access to the (content-wise and structurally) complex project *Global Ethic* is at www.weltethos.org.

32. *Handbuch Weltethos* (with Günther Gebhardt and Stephan Schlensog) (Munich: Piper, 2012), 29.

33. *Erlebte Menschlichkeit. Erinnerungen* III (Munich: Piper, 2013), 702. No English translation.

34. Cf. *Die Hoffnung bewahren. Schriften zur Reform der Kirche* (Munich: Piper, 1994), 9–36, 201–6.

35. *Erlebte Menschlichkeit*, 702.

3

GOD, THE FOUNDATION OF LIFE

Anthony J. Godzieba

Looking for Meaning in the Midst of Uncertainty

To plunge directly into an analysis of Hans Küng's reflections on the existence of God would do a disservice both to Küng's memory and to his work. For that would bypass the crucial reflections on *experience* that are at the heart of Küng's argument, and indeed the critical role that his own experience—full of questions and doubts—played in his search for what he terms the "foundation of life."

Küng relates that during his student years in Rome, he came to realize that the "crystal clear" intellectual arguments of Greek and Thomistic metaphysics and the traditional neo-Scholastic manuals that he had studied offered scarce help in dealing with his deep-seated existential questions. He arrived at this point despite his love of philosophy and his commitment to intellectual rigor. Instead, there remained "a suppressed uncertainty" that "kept forcing itself on me even during my first semester of theology and made me doubt that everything was ultimately illuminating, calculable, and provable. Is it really so clear, so obvious, that my life has a meaning?"[1]

God, the Foundation of Life

The beginnings of an answer came, rather like an epiphany, during his discussions with his Jesuit spiritual director: he must *believe* rather than merely desiring to *know*. And that meant expanding the traditional religious definition of "belief." Küng came to realize that any search by believers or nonbelievers for the "deliberately rational grounding of human existence" is necessarily preceded by questions about life, meaning, and freedom that seek something more fundamental.

> What suddenly happened to me? In this existential question an elementary wager was required of me, a wager of trust! What a challenge to venture a *Yes*! Instead of a bottomless mistrust in the garb of nihilism or cynicism, risk a fundamental trust in this life, in this reality. Instead of mistrusting life, venture to trust life, a fundamental trust in yourself, in others, in the world, in the whole of questionable reality.[2]

These questions and crises were not only Küng's—they saturate our human experience. They are even more acute now as we try to recover from the shocks of the early 2020s: the staggering loss of lives due to the COVID-19 pandemic; the stunning negative effects of climate change; the ongoing failures of political will that have encouraged a return to autocratic oppression. We are certainly experiencing the full force of the fragmentary character of modern life, along with (as Terry Eagleton puts it) "a crisis of narration, as the world ceases to be story-shaped. History is no longer informed by the plot once known as progress."[3] None of this should be mistaken for an abstract philosophical or theological problem: this pervasive sense of fragmentation, of not being able to find one's footing in life, of the failure of past expectations to solve present-day problems all generate a deeply felt sense of disorientation and loss. That disorientation is only intensified in contemporary life lived under technology-driven "social acceleration" and a "now-ism" that experiences only narrow time-slices of the present that are disconnected from past memory and future expectation.[4]

It is ironic that at the moment in the late twentieth century when thinkers of all types began to take as self-evident the inadequacy of foundationalism and the critique of the cogency of metaphysical foundations, Küng insisted on the importance of discovering for oneself and for our times the foundation that transcends all fragmentary, time-bound experiences, that grounds our lives despite the uncertainties that confront us. For him, the effort to find a reason to trust in life leads to the search for God.

> In short, those who in a reasonable trust say *Yes* to a primal foundation and primal meaning, to God, know not only what but why they can ultimately trust in life....It must have become clear that fundamental trust and trust in God show a similar basic structure; they are a matter not only of human reason, but of the whole human being with spirit and body, reason and drives. Trust in God is beyond reason, but is not irrational.[5]

This emphasis on the human search for meaning in the midst of uncertainty and an insistence on the reasonable character of fundamental trust both form the pivot on which Küng's argument for God turns.

A Contemporary Catholic Natural Theology

TERMINOLOGY AND TYPOLOGY[6]

Before we take up Küng's reflections on God, we first need a clarification of terminology and a helpful typology.

Terminology: What Küng offers can be characterized as a very Catholic natural theology. This has little to do with what one might consider the standard contemporary philosophical definition of "natural theology," one that assumes a strictly held difference between reason and faith:

> Natural theology [is] the study of God solely through the use of human reason. Typically, theology relies upon God's revelation for knowledge about God....Natural theology, however, works independently of the content of revela-

tion. Processes observable by any human person, along with human reason, provide the sources for the knowledge of God gained by natural theology.[7]

"Typical" natural theology arguments have used the tools of human empirical observation and reason without recourse to supernatural revelation in order to prove the existence of a unipersonal God reduced to a set of divine attributes. With their emphasis on "reason independent of revelation," these arguments assume modernity's "extrinsic view" of God that overemphasizes God's transcendence and otherness. They basically restate the modern rationalist distinction or even rigid opposition between nature and human reason on the one hand and supernatural revelation and faith on the other, thereby betraying their indebtedness to Enlightenment (and particularly Deist) discussions of rational religion.[8] Küng disassociates himself completely from this kind of natural theology. At the conclusion of his argument in *Does God Exist? An Answer for Today*, he says bluntly that "there is…no continuous, gradual, rational ascent of man to God" and no *praeambula fidei* "established by the rational arguments of pure reason." Rather, the contemporary person "should start his [sic] quest from the point at which he is actually living, in order to relate what he knows of God to things that move him."[9]

Natural theology in a more Catholic key considers the roles of faith and human reason in a more cooperative, mutually supportive, and mutually implicating light. Walter Kasper's short description is helpful: natural theology is the search for "the natural 'access-point' of faith," and its major task is to demonstrate "the internal reasonableness of a faith which has its substantiation in and from itself."[10] This more expansive vision of natural theology demonstrates "how belief in God is rationally plausible and how the natural knowledge of God can serve as a 'clearing' wherein human experience is already in touch with the mystery of God and already open to the possibility of a more intimate relationship with God that revelation brings about."[11] The key is *access*: access to transcendence from within immanence, access to what exceeds our finite experience despite its historically situated constraints. Every natural theology argument is thus a transcendental limit argument. In a contemporary context where "buffered selves" and an "exclusive humanism" concede nothing beyond those constraints,[12] the task of the Christian theologian is to show that this intentionality-toward-transcendence is not only plausible but actual. In other words, natural theology's task is to show how human experience is inherently open to transcendence and participates in a dynamic movement toward God that can be more fully articulated through a faith commitment to God's further self-revelation.

Typology:[13] Natural theology arguments for God's existence fall into two general types. Those that look to the natural world as a source of evidence for our natural knowledge of God are *cosmological arguments*. Their point is to trace the contingency of the world to the necessary divine cause of its existence. *Anthropological arguments* take their evidence from the human experience of self and the structure of human subjectivity. They attempt to argue for a similar necessary connection between the contingent self and its divine ground.[14] Some commentators have sorted these types out chronologically, arguing that ancient and medieval arguments are fundamentally cosmological while modern and contemporary ones are necessarily anthropological. The theologian Wolfhart Pannenberg offers some reasons for this typical division:

> Plato stands at the beginning, and Kant at the significant turning point for modern man, of a process which can be described as one of the continuous anthropologizing of the idea of God....But for Plato the soul was still embedded in the world of nature, and rooted, together with this world, in a divine origin. The philosophical theology of the modern age, on the other hand, has been guided by the apprehension that there is no assured way leading from nature to God, and that therefore the whole burden of proof of the truth of faith in God falls upon the understanding of man, upon anthropology.[15]

The "turning point" refers to a principle developed in early modern science: bodies at rest or in motion persist in that rest or motion without any particular cause, thus eliminating any need for an explanatory first cause or prime impulse. Modern science thus seemed to make nature's relationship to God ambiguous at best or to eliminate God as a factor altogether, and the Platonic links among nature, soul, and God became impossible to maintain. If a way to the knowledge of God is to be found anywhere today, Pannenberg argued, it would be only within human experience itself. And even this is made more difficult by the effects of the rise of atheism during the nineteenth century. Similar to the challenges posed by modern science, atheism challenges any assertion of the necessary connection of the human person to God. "If it cannot be shown that the issues with which religion is concerned, the elevation of man above the finite content of human experience to the idea of an infinite reality which sustains everything finite, including man himself, are an essential [element] of man's being...then every other viewpoint with which one may concern oneself in this field is an empty intellectual game, and what is said about God loses every claim to intellectual veracity."[16] While "no anthropological argument can prove God's existence in the strict sense," theology is obliged to demonstrate, as far as it is able, "that we are referred to an unfathomable reality that transcends us and the world, so that the God of religious tradition is given a secure place in the reality of human self-experience."[17]

This is precisely the task of a Catholic natural theology: to offer not a rational demonstration apart from faith, but rather the clarification of the reasonable presuppositions of faith in God, the portrayal of the human encounter with divine revelation as a real possibility for human experience to act as a "clearing" for the appearance of revelation and thus provide an opportunity for the free assent of faith.

While the cosmological-anthropological grid is a useful tool for evaluating the presuppositions of God arguments, the division of the types into periods of dominance before and after modernity is less useful. In fact, much contemporary evidence refutes it, as we shall see with Küng's clever and convincing argument.[18]

Küng's Argument from "Fundamental Trust"[19]

A diagnostic prelude: Küng's arguments in *Does God Exist?* have much in common with the classical Christian natural theology tradition.[20] However, that does not render his constructive argument any less contemporary. With the advent of those key nineteenth-century and early twentieth-century atheists whom Paul Ricœur deemed the "masters of suspicion"—Ludwig Feuerbach, Karl Marx, Friedrich Nietzsche, and also Sigmund Freud—and their wholesale critique of religion and God, the terrain of Western thought and belief changed.[21] It is clear that we no longer comfortably inhabit the thought-world of the premodern tradition. Küng mentions his fascination as a philosophy student with these "great atheists" and wanted to discover "what provoked them and their quite personal motives. Why did they in particular come to deny God?"[22] His overall argument replies directly to their critique of religion and seeks to counteract the broader post-Enlightenment attempt to argue religion away as superfluous.

In his diagnosis of the contemporary context for the discussion about God, Küng notes that while the nineteenth-century critique of religion had promised the eventual withering away or even destruction of religion, clearly this has not happened. Rather, complex affirmations of the value of religion have developed, new signs of openness to religion and religious experience that by no means unambiguously support traditional religious institutions but that nevertheless indicate a growing appreciation of the function of religion in human life. For example, there has developed a more positive relationship between science and religion, despite the mistrust that has often existed between them. From the side of the natural and social sciences there has been an increased openness to religion, particularly among physicists and those who have argued for the necessity of a framework of ethical responsibility to guide scientific and technical activity.[23] There also has been the growth of what Küng terms "secular quasi-religiousness," the tendency for secular groups or movements to resemble and take on the functions of religious groups, a sign of "the recognition of the permanence of man's religious needs, needs of course that might be satisfied in a 'secular' way" (555).

Most importantly, Küng wants to emphasize what he sees as the widespread desire for a sense of an overarching value within contemporary culture, something that transcends and reconnects the fragmented meanings strewn throughout everyday life today. Psychologists and sociologists have shown that faith in the general order of existence plays a crucial constitutive role in the development of all aspects of human consciousness.[24] Küng calls attention to Peter Berger's notion that various "signals of transcendence" are disclosed within everyday life, signs of a reality that transcends the immanent empirical world and to which human beings are open by nature. One crucial signal is a "faith in order," a "fundamental trust" in reality that is apparent in as ordinary a scene as a mother comforting her frightened child and assuring the child that everything is all right. "Man's propensity for order is grounded in a faith or trust that, ultimately, reality is 'in order,' 'all right,' 'as it should be.' Needless to say, there is no empirical method by which this faith can be tested. To assert it is itself an act of faith."[25] A developed description of the workings of fundamental trust is key to Küng's argument.

From these and similar desires for meaning, for religious experience, or for something close to it, Küng discerns a common recognition, by believers and nonbelievers alike, that our world is "not in order." This widespread discomfort keeps alive a common yearning for some value system or set of norms by which all is put back into order, for the ultimate ground of meaning that makes sense out of the whole of reality—a common yearning for something that approximates or is identical to religion. "Genuine religion...is found only where this ground of meaning, this absolutely final concern, that with which I am unconditionally involved, is not something merely of this world (secular) but something that is in the broadest sense 'divine' ('absolute,' 'holy')" (561). Behind this diagnosis, however, lurks a crucial and unavoidable question: does this common yearning for the ultimate reality point us toward an *actually existing* ultimate, absolute reality? Or is that yearning a projection of our own desires? In response to the assumption that projection is the norm and desire for an ultimate reality has no referent, Küng flips the assumption around. "This in particular was the false conclusion of the projection argument of Feuerbach and his countless followers: they think that God does not exist because I only want him to exist. I ask in return: why should something that I wish, hope for, long for, a priori not exist? Why should what has been proclaimed, venerated, worshipped for thousands of years in thousands of temples, synagogues, churches and mosques be sheer illusion?" Even after the critique of metaphysics and various psychological analyses of religious experience, "that does not prove the slightest thing in respect of an absolute reality independent of my psyche. That means that my wish for God can perhaps correspond to a real God."[26] Theology cannot avoid the fact that "signals of transcendence" can be ambiguous and arise from some other impulse. Nonetheless, the question "does God exist?" remains a genuine question, demanding "an absolutely unequivocal answer" (561).

The argument: Küng's answer has two parts. First he considers how the anxieties of existence and the desires for meaning might be fulfilled if God were assumed to exist—a hypothesis proposed as a response to Fyodor Dostoevsky's chilling statement "if there is no God, everything is permitted" and a positive counterproposal that is "more difficult" to develop (562).

He develops this hypothesis first by considering reality as a whole. In the face of "the *thoroughgoing uncertainty of reality* in the ontic, noetic, and ethical senses" (565), human beings exhibit a fundamental trust in the cohesion of reality and in its ultimate meaningfulness. Reality is precarious precisely because of its contingency; it appears groundless, evolving without any aim, "its unity repeatedly threatened by disunion, its meaningfulness by meaninglessness, its value by worthlessness" (567). Despite this state of affairs, human beings expect reality to be coherent and search for the universal meaning that will "make sense" out of everything. In our experience of reality, there is something that engenders our trust, but our expectations alone do not alter the precarious character of reality. "Trust in uncertain reality does not eliminate its radical uncertainty. Reality, which can justify a fundamental trust, appears itself to be mysteriously *unjustified*....Reality is there as a fact, but enigmatically, utterly lacking in any manifest ground, support, or purpose" (565). If reality is truly this precarious, what is our trust ultimately based upon? "What, then, is the *condition of the possibility of this uncertain reality*" (565) and of our trust in its cohesion and persistence?

If God exists, then we would have a reason why reality, despite its radical uncertainty, holds together, why it supports our trust: because God would be the ground, support, and primal goal of reality. "If God exists, then reality suspended between being and nonbeing is not ultimately under suspicion of being a void. Why? Because God is then the being itself of all reality" (566). If this hypothesis is true, then our fundamental trust in reality would be supported not by reality itself but rather by reality's ultimate ground, God. We would also have a reason why reality itself *is* radically uncertain: "Because uncertain reality is itself *not God*. Because the self, society, the world, cannot be identified with their primal ground, primal support and primal goal...with being itself" (567).

If we were to formulate the hypothesis from the point of view of individual human existence, the formulations would be similar. Why is it that, despite "the riddle of my persistently uncertain human existence"—despite the menacing factors of emptiness, meaninglessness, sin, and death—we have a fundamental trust in the coherence and meaningfulness of our own existence? Again, if God exists, we would have an answer: because God would be "the primal source...ultimate meaning...all-embracing hope of my life" (567). We would also have a reason why human existence itself appears so precarious: "Because man is *not* God. Because my human self can *not* be identified with its primal source, primal meaning, primal value, with being itself" (568).

Does the hypothesis about God, from the point of view of either reality as a whole or individual human existence, indeed point to the reality of God? In the second part of his argument, Küng considers the alternatives.

The complete denial of God is possible. Indeed, "atheism cannot be eliminated rationally. It is irrefutable" (568). The assertion of God's unreality presupposes an emphasis on reality's radical uncertainty. It relies on what the atheist would interpret as empirical or "realistic" evidence, which definitively points away from any primal ground or support or goal. The atheist alternative is a choice, a *personal decision* based on a reasonable evaluation of the evidence of experience, an evaluation of reality as a whole that accounts for the evidence in a certain way. That evaluation in turn is guided by a presupposition, a judgment whose truth has been assumed in advance, namely, that reality's radical uncertainty is the fully adequate framework for understanding the conflicting evidence that reality provides. The ultimate decision, then, is that reality gives no indication whatsoever of any covert divine support; there is no God. "Neither a strict proof or an indication of God can prevail against such an assertion. For this negative statement rests on a *decision*, a decision that is connected with the fundamental decision for reality as a whole" (569).

On the other hand, the affirmation of God is just as possible and cannot be rationally refuted. The theist's assertion of God's reality is based on the experience of reality as well, but one that emphasizes fundamental trust and thus a confidence in reality's fundamental coherence. The theist alternative, too, is a *personal decision* based on a reasonable evaluation of the evidence of experience, an evaluation of reality as a whole that accounts for the evidence in a certain way. And that evaluation in turn is guided by a presupposition, a judgment whose truth has been assumed in advance, namely, the consistency and meaningfulness of reality that are also evident. The assertion of God's existence is grounded in a confidence in reality as a whole and points to the condition that renders this confidence and meaningfulness possible, namely, the primal ground, support, or goal of reality. "Atheism...cannot prevail against such confidence imposed on us in the light of reality itself. The affirmation of God also rests, in the last resort, on a *decision*, which, again, is connected with the fundamental decision for reality as a whole. This, too, is rationally irrefutable" (596).

Which alternative is true? Is this a stalemate? After all, each appears to explain reality with equal cogency. Each also represents a *personal decision* to interpret ambiguous reality in a particular direction, a decision grounded upon an assumption that is not strictly provable.

Since reality and its primal ground, primal support, and primal goal are not imposed on us with conclusive evidence, there remains scope for human freedom. The human person must decide without intellectual constraint but also without rational proof. Both atheism and belief in God are therefore ventures, they are also risks. The critique of the proofs of God itself shows that belief in God has the character of a decision, and—conversely—a decision for God has the character of belief (570).

What helps break any apparent stalemate is the correct understanding of the roles played by faith and reason in these decisions. Küng emphasizes that a reasonable trust or belief, rather than absolute rational certainty, is involved in both steps of each argument. The evaluation of the status of reality (first step) provides a basis for the decision for either belief or unbelief in God (second step). Belief in God is rooted in "a trusting commitment to an ultimate ground, support, and meaning of reality" (570), a trust that is reasonable without being exclusively rational. Unbelief, on the other hand, is the refusal of trust in an ultimate ground and is instead a belief that uncertainty and contingency together form the sole overarching truth. Each position interprets the evidence of reality as a whole and of one's individual life as well from a critical rational perspective. But this rational interpretation itself depends on a prior act of trust in an overarching presupposition that itself escapes the certainty of rational proof.

This resolution of the question of reality's fundamental character, however, is only the first step. The judgment regarding the ultimate meaning and telos of the evidence of reality is the final step and results from a person's free decision to trust in the guiding presupposition and to make sense of reality with the hypothesis that is the most adequate to the evidence. In other words, this final step goes beyond the decision "for or against reality as such" to the deeper and unavoidable decision concerning the reality of God (570). And a decision regarding God is ultimately a risk based on the interpreted evidence of reality, taken, in the end, without absolute certainty or the Cartesian clarity that would have marked an older natural theology.

But this does not mean that atheism and theism offer equally valid construals of reality. Although one cannot rationally refute a "personal decision" to construe the evidence of reality as either leading toward or away from God, one can judge each decision's relative adequacy to the evidence and evaluate its existential consequences—the choice does matter. Thus, atheism's denial of God can be judged irrational. "Denial of God implies an *ultimately unjustified* fundamental trust in reality. Atheism cannot suggest any condition for the possibility of uncertain reality. If someone denies God, he does not know why he ultimately trusts in reality" (571). The atheist, along with everyone else, acknowledges the day-to-day "workings" of reality with a fundamental trust and experiences reality's order and positivity amid its uncertainty. But the atheist either will not or cannot account for these factors, leading to an unjustified assent to reality and "a freewheeling, nowhere-anchored and therefore paradoxical fundamental trust....For this reason [atheism] lacks not perhaps all rationality but certainly a radical rationality" (571). It can thus give no satisfactory answers to the perennial questions regarding the truth of our knowledge, the efficacy of our actions, and the object of our hope.[27] The ultimate price of the denial of God is to leave oneself open to the experience of the "hollowness of reality" (571) and the danger of existential meaninglessness and despair.

Theism, on the other hand, can be judged as rationally justified. "Affirmation of God implies an *ultimately justified* fundamental trust in reality. A radical fundamental trust, belief in God can suggest the condition of the possibility of uncertain reality. If someone affirms reality, he knows why he can trust reality" (572). By means of the affirmation of God as primal ground, support, or goal, the theist can indicate where one's trust in reality is ultimately anchored. One's fundamental trust, while directed to reality, is not grounded in uncertain reality itself but rather in the condition that makes reality possible. And the theist can show why this decision in favor of God's existence is rationally justified, having been led in that direction by the evidence provided by reality that supports one's fundamental trust. While taking seriously reality's multiple and even contradictory aspects (negative and positive, ordered yet precarious, "hollow" yet meaningful [567]), the theist's affirmation of God as the primal ground is a construal of reality that is at once more reasonable, more encompassing, even more "realistic" than the atheist's denial of God.

Küng's strong advocacy of theism in the face of the hermeneutics of suspicion falls within our definition of natural theology (the search for the natural access point of faith), despite the fact that, as we saw, he explicitly denies that he is doing "natural theology," since for him the term refers to any reflection on God that presupposes a radical discontinuity between the natural and the supernatural (as in neo-Scholastic natural theology) or that assumes "an autonomous reason capable of demonstrating a foundation of faith but having nothing to do with faith itself" (577). But what Küng in fact rejects is what we rejected as well at the outset of this section: the truncated, modern rationalist version of natural theology.[28] He argues instead for a belief in God that is both rationally justified and yet also dependent upon God's revelatory initiative. This is a strongly Catholic position that mirrors the teachings of both Vatican I and Vatican II regarding the validity and the limitations of the natural knowledge of God as well as the human need for divinely given faith. For Küng, both reality as a whole and the course of an individual human life mediate the presence of God as primal ground, support, or goal. Rationality is active throughout the process of interpreting uncertain reality, particularly as human beings probe for reality's authentic depths. Reason cannot prove the existence of God with absolute certainty, since reason is too limited and reality is too enigmatic for that.[29] But the act of rational probing opens the mind to the possibilities of truth beyond the empirical, thereby preparing the way for an act of trust in God as the ground of reality. Within this openness, belief is accomplished at the convergence of two movements, the human decision to trust and God's revelation of God's own presence through reality: "For what cannot be proved *in advance* I experience *in the accomplishment, in the very act of acknowledging what I perceive*" (573). This act of faith in God, supported by reality, confirms both the reasonable nature of our fundamental trust and the validity of our reason itself, while also pointing up the gratuitous character of God's act of mediated self-disclosure. "Belief in God is a *gift*. Reality exists before me. If I do not cut myself off, but open myself entirely to reality as it opens out to me, then I can accept in faith its primary ground, its deepest support, its ultimate goal: God, who *reveals* himself as primal source, primal meaning and primal value" (576).

I opened this section by claiming that Küng offers us an argument that is strongly reminiscent of the classical arguments. This is due to the resolutely metaphysical categories he uses to characterize the reality of God and the relationship between God and reality. By defining religion as "a particular social realization of a relationship to an absolute ground of meaning" (560–61) and by describing God as the absolute ground, support, and goal of reality and of human existence, Küng places his argument squarely in what has been called (after the influence of Martin Heidegger) the ontotheological tradition—that is, the tradition that speaks of God as the *archê* of reality or the "highest/deepest" being who grounds all other beings. There are also strong echoes of Thomas Aquinas's famous "five ways in which one can prove there is a God."[30] These are heard in Küng's claim that our knowledge of God is mediated by our experience of the world, in the "foundational" language with which he characterizes God, and especially in the way that both the structure and the basic goal of his argument recall the underlying four-stage pattern of Thomas Aquinas's "Five Ways": (1) one begins with an observation of ordinary experience, noting that things are changing, temporally limited and contingent, and so forth; (2) which leads to the question of what else is implied that makes sense out of our experience—the necessary precondition, as it were, for our experience to be this way; (3) which turns out to be itself unchanging, unlimited and absolute; (4) and this we call "God."[31]

This does not mean, though, that Küng simply replays the classical arguments in a more contemporary idiom. Two major differences make this obvious. First, in Küng's reading of the contemporary situation, reality is not as easily interpretable in the direction of God's presence as it was for the scholastics. According to Thomas, for example, once one had an insight into being and how participation-in-being formed the backbone of the metaphysical structure of reality, one could trace the "effects" of creation back to their necessary cause without much difficulty. For Küng, however, reality is polyvalent and hence ambiguous, "utterly lacking in any manifest ground, support, or purpose. That is why the question of reality, of being or not-being, of fundamental trust or nihilism, can emerge again at any time" (565). On its surface, our experience can support either belief or unbelief. Only when one reflects more closely on both reality and our situated experience of it do their fundamental structures and presuppositions appear.

The other difference involves the estimation of the power of reason. Although earlier thinkers like Anselm (in the so-called ontological argument) and Thomas were clearly aware of the limits of rationality, they were optimistic about reason's ability to demonstrate God's existence with certainty and thereby give support to one's faith. Küng is less optimistic; for him, rationality plays a more ambivalent role. On the one hand, reason at first plays an evaluative role in dealing with the evidence of reality. But it does not and cannot fully determine a person's stance toward God since, as Küng repeatedly emphasizes, this is the result of a personal decision to construe the evidence along the lines of a presupposition whose validity is plausible yet rationally unprovable. Reason therefore contributes to one's decision but is not the sole determinant of the content of that decision. Rational certainty has been scaled back; neither atheist nor theist arguments per se can be rationally refuted. On the other hand, rationality returns at the conclusion of the argument as a criterion and the final arbiter of the overall *results* (rather than the *content*) of one's personal decision and judges its relative value vis-à-vis all other construals of reality based on the amount of evidence for which it can account. In this light, atheism is the irrational choice, theism the rational and hence better choice.

In short, those who in reasonable trust say yes to a primal foundation and primal meaning, to God, know not only what but why they can ultimately trust in life. The yes to God means a trust in life that is consistent and has an ultimate ground. It is a primal trust rooted in the ultimate depth, the ground of grounds, and directed toward the goal of goals, God as the name for the supportive ground of meaning of the whole. Despite all the uncertainty of life, a radical knowledge and security is given to me.[32]

Finally, when we ask how Küng's argument fits into the anthropological/cosmological typology for classifying natural theology arguments, we find that it is not a perfect fit since it is both types at once. The cosmological argument, employing our experience of reality with its positive and negative elements, is the apparent starting point. But *only* apparently, for Küng clearly shows that an anthropological argument is simultaneously at work that describes how the structure of human subjectivity—seen here as the act of fundamental trust that supports all other human acts—functions as a clue pointing toward God's existence while mediating the cosmological element's own value as a clue. Küng's natural theology demonstrates that the cosmological argument is not simply a remnant of a premodern worldview but can still be effective after the hermeneutics of suspicion and after the collapse of the hegemony of modern rationality. But it also demonstrates the point that, after the modern turn to the subject, the way to the knowledge of God in the contemporary situation must take the structure of human experience as a primary piece of evidence. The rehabilitation of the cosmological argument does not take place without a strong link to an anthropological argument. By combining the two, Küng's argument respects the insights of the older Christian tradition while also responding to the problems and possibilities of a new situation.

For These Distracted Times

Finally, we need to ask, "So what?": Does Küng's "contemporary" argument truly address *our* contemporary context, the problems and possibilities of *our* situation?

Allow me to start from an oblique angle. While writing this chapter, I attended a harpsichord recital that opened with the elegiac *Sad Pavan: For These Distracted Times* by the composer Thomas Tomkins (1572–1656). The recitalist prefaced her performance with some necessary historical context, pointing to the political upheavals of the English Civil War (the "Puritan Revolt") of 1642–1648, the trial and beheading of King Charles I for treason in January 1649, and the tremendous sense of loss and disorientation that gripped the country in the aftermath. Tomkins's slow lament, meandering through dissonances and consonances, was written shortly after these horrible events and "bears witness to his loyalty and his sorrow at his former patron's fate."[33]

"Distracted times" is a description of our context as well. No one can deny that it is a time of widely experienced loss and disorientation—loss of the old certainties and a fitful scramble for direction. Recall Eagleton's comment cited earlier: "The world ceases to be story-shaped. History is no longer informed by the plot once known as progress." In a real sense we have lost the plot and meander through what seem to be more dissonances than consonances. We live in a time of "multiple overwhelmings," as the theologian David Ford puts it.[34] Amid social acceleration, digital information and image storms, political upheavals and demagoguery, sexual abuse crises that have undermined the credibility of churches, and a host of other occurrences, we no longer easily discern an underlying thread that might tie together our disparate experiences and allow us to easily make sense of the world and our lives in it. But doesn't this automatically lead to the obsolescence of religion as another of the "old certainties"? Not really. As Ford sagely notes, all major religions, from their premodern origins until now, have experienced "overwhelmings" throughout their histories and have reacted in different ways to maintain continuity and community. Even more, "being overwhelmed" is of the essence of religion itself. "Most of them are themselves about being overwhelmed—by God (or however we name the transcendent present to humanity); by revelations and imperatives from beyond ourselves which invite us into radical transformation; by worship, prayer, meditation, service, and other activities which call for all we have and are."[35]

Küng's argument for God fits in right here. Although first published in the 1970s, a time of both upheaval and optimism in the West and seemingly very different from the third decade of the twenty-first century, his search for God as the foundation of life speaks directly to the contemporary search for meaning and direction amid loss and disorientation. Küng's narration of his own deeply existential questions and doubts as the starting point for his search is a confession of his own experience of being overwhelmed. "How can I affirm meaning in my life despite all the meaninglessness? How can I say *Yes* to the reality of the world and humankind as it is in its enigmatic and contradictory nature?" And then a more positive and orienting overwhelming occurred after a session with his seminary spiritual director, when Küng had "a spiritual experience" in the midst of his interior wrestling match between his desire to know and the admonition to believe, an insight that any attempt to know and make rational sense of the world presupposes something "more elementary, more fundamental," that a "wager of trust" was being asked of him, a fundamental trust in the meaningfulness of his own life, a fundamental trust in uncertain and precarious reality.[36] From that wager for fundamental trust, Küng is able to make another wager: that a reasonable and persuasive account can be given of God as the ultimate ground of that fundamental trust, using the clues of our everyday experience of ourselves and the world.

In our own "distracted times" of loss and disorientation, the basic human desire for sense, meaning, and goodness often clashes with those experiences that *almost* convince us that our world is becoming a dystopian hellhole beyond all redemption. But the unquenchable fundamental desire for meaning, that everyday faith that everything will eventually be all right, and the experience of "signals of transcendence" must be accounted for in some way. Küng's reflections on God provide that reasonable accounting, while at the same time making room for faith at the very beginning: "The eternal God bestows ground and meaning on all that is temporal, and today no one need make excuses for an enlightened faith in God."[37]

Notes

1. Hans Küng, *What I Believe*, trans. John Bowden (New York: Bloomsbury, 2009), 4.

2. Küng, *What I Believe*, 10.

3. Terry Eagleton, "The Marxist and the Messiah" (review of F. Jameson, *The Benjamin Files*), *London Review of Books* 43, no. 17 (September 9, 2021): 27–28.

4. See Hartmut Rosa, *Social Acceleration: A New Theory of Modernity*, trans. Jonathan Trejo-Mathys (New York: Columbia University Press, 2013), as well as the summary discussion in Anthony J. Godzieba, *A Theology of the Presence and Absence of God* (Collegeville, MN: Liturgical Press, 2018), 285–90.

5. Küng, *What I Believe*, 93.

6. Material in this section is taken (with revisions) from my *A Theology of the Presence and Absence of God*, chapter 3.

7. *The HarperCollins Encyclopedia of Catholicism*, ed. Richard P. McBrien (San Francisco: HarperCollins, 1995), 908 (s.v. "natural theology"). For a more detailed philosophical discussion, see Andrew Chignell and Derk Pereboom, "Natural Theology and Natural Religion," *The Stanford Encyclopedia of Philosophy* (Fall 2020 ed.), ed. Edward N. Zalta, https://plato.stanford.edu/archives/fall2020/entries/natural-theology/.

8. For the difference between the biblical "dialectical view" of God and the modern "extrinsic view," see Godzieba, *Presence and Absence of God*, chapter 2.

9. Hans Küng, *Does God Exist? An Answer for Today*, trans. Edward Quinn (Garden City, NY: Doubleday, 1980 [German orig. 1978]), 577–78. Subsequent page references to this edition appear in the text (in parentheses).

10. Walter Kasper, *An Introduction to Christian Faith*, trans. V. Green (New York: Paulist, 1980), 20 (natural access-point); Kasper, *The God of Jesus Christ*, new ed., trans. [Matthew O'Connell and] Dinah Livingstone (New York: Continuum, 2012), 145 (internal reasonableness).

11. Godzieba, *Presence and Absence of God*, 104.

12. These terms come from the philosopher Charles Taylor, *A Secular Age* (Cambridge, MA: Belknap Press/ Harvard University Press, 2007), 38–41.

13. This section takes material (with revisions) from my *Presence and Absence of God*, 108–10.

14. In the late eighteenth century, Immanuel Kant had classified what he considered "the only three possible ways of proving the existence of God by means of speculative reason" as the physicotheological (arguing to the reality of God as supremely perfect being from the contingent structure of the sensible world), the cosmological (arguing from the existence of the sensible world), and the ontological

(arguing from concept of being itself). See *Critique of Pure Reason*, trans. Norman Kemp Smith (New York: St. Martin's Press, 1965), 499–500 (A 590–91/B 618–19).

15. Wolfhart Pannenberg, "Anthropology and the Question of God," in *The Idea of God and Human Freedom*, trans. R. A. Wilson (Philadelphia: Westminster, 1973), 80–98, at 82.

16. "Anthropology and the Question of God," 88–89.

17. Wolfhart Pannenberg, *Systematic Theology*, 3 vols., trans. Geoffrey W. Bromiley (Grand Rapids: Eerdmans, 1991–98), 1:93.

18. Pannenberg eventually moved away from a strict periodization, saying that even though cosmological arguments have an anthropological basis, "there can be no strict [anthropological] proof because the existence of God would have to be proved in relation not only to us but above all to the reality of the world" (*Systematic Theology*, 1:93–94).

19. This section takes material (with revisions) from my *Presence and Absence of God*, 128–38.

20. Küng, *Does God Exist?*, 552–83. His argument appears in a shorter form earlier in Küng, *On Being a Christian*, trans. Edward Quinn (Garden City, NY: Doubleday, 1976 [Ger. orig. 1974]), 69–79.

21. See Paul Ricœur, "The Critique of Religion" and "The Language of Faith," trans. R. Bradley DeFord, in *The Philosophy of Paul Ricœur*, ed. Charles E. Reagan and David Stewart (Boston: Beacon Press, 1978), 213–22; 223–38; *Freud and Philosophy: An Essay on Interpretation*, trans. Denis Savage (New Haven: Yale University Press, 1970), esp. 32–36. See also Richard Kearney, "Religion and Ideology: Paul Ricœur's Hermeneutic Conflict," *Irish Theological Quarterly* 52 (1986): 109–26.

22. Küng, *What I Believe*, 75–76.

23. Küng's optimistic (and almost prophetic) assessment has been affirmed by a flood of work over the past few decades seeking to develop a positive relationship between science and religion.

24. In *What I Believe*, Küng mentions the influence of Erik Ericson (13–14) and Peter Berger (71), as well as the theologians Karl Rahner and Gustavo Gutiérrez (71), on his argument regarding "fundamental trust."

25. Peter L. Berger, *A Rumor of Angels: Modern Society and the Rediscovery of the Supernatural* (Garden City, NY: Doubleday, 1969), 71–72, cited by Küng, *Does God Exist?*, 557.

26. Küng, *What I Believe*, 76–77.

27. Echoing throughout Küng's chapter are Kant's famous three questions from the *Critique of Pure Reason*: "All the interests of my reason, speculative as well as practical, combine in the three following questions: 1. What can I know? 2. What ought I to do? 3. What may I hope?" (635 [A 804–05/B 832–33]). For Küng's citation, see pp. 563–64.

28. For Küng's detailed analysis of natural theology, see *Does God Exist?*, 509–28, 577–78.

29. "But also like fundamental trust, trust in God cannot simply be decided on, willed, extorted or produced. I cannot simply create or produce ultimate certainty, security, stability, for myself. God…is not an object of immediate experience….It is just because of this that belief in God is seen as a *gift*" (575).

30. Thomas Aquinas, *Summa theologiae* Ia, q. 2, a. 3, resp., in *Summa theologiae*, vol. 2 (1a. 2–11): *Existence and Nature of God*, trans. Timothy McDermott (London: Eyre & Spottiswoode; New York: McGraw-Hill, 1964), 12–17.

31. See Thomas Gilby, "Appendix 5: The Five Ways," in *Summa theologiae*, 2:189.

32. Küng, *What I Believe*, 93.

33. Richard Taruskin, *The Oxford History of Western Music*, vol. 2: *The Seventeenth and Eighteenth Centuries* (New York: Oxford University Press, 2005), 124.

34. David Ford, *Theology: A Very Short Introduction*, 2nd ed. (Oxford: Oxford University Press, 2013), 7–10.

35. Ford, *Theology*, 9.

36. Küng, *What I Believe*, 18–19.

37. Küng, *What I Believe*, 93.

4

REVISITING KÜNG'S CHRISTOLOGY

Roger Haight, SJ

Every person is unique. So too is every writer and theologian. But calling the theology of Hans Küng unique recalls some of the distinct reasons why he merits a reappraisal of his work in our time. For one thing, he was exceptionally brilliant and outspoken when he finished his theological education just prior to the Second Vatican Council and when the church was ripe for change. Pope John XXIII intended the council in part to open up the Catholic Church to ecumenical dialogue, and Küng had just finished doctoral work with an ecumenical study of the doctrine of justification. The subject matter of Vatican II fitted under the large umbrella of understanding the church, and Küng contributed a study of the genesis and historicity of church structures. Küng was still a relatively young man during the council. The final session left the Catholic Church with a universal enthusiasm for and expectation of change, however those hopes may have been defined. It also marked the beginning of Küng's most creative period in Christian theology.

This chapter examines Küng's work in Christology. In Catholic theology prior to the Council, it was customary for dogmatic theologians to specialize in topical areas of expertise such as God, Christ, sacraments, or church. Küng did not study to fill a systematic niche; he was not a specialist in Christology. But his work *On*

Being a Christian had its centering focus on the person and work of Jesus Christ and remains the signal example of his Christology.[1] The thesis of this chapter proposes that Küng's main contribution to Christology consisted of his bringing his historicist imagination to the understanding of Jesus Christ.

After a brief situating of Küng's *On Being a Christian*, I examine the structure of Küng's Christology because therein lies the marked significance of that work. This crucial section shows how revolutionary his Christology appeared in contrast to the theology textbooks used universally prior to the council. This shift in an imaginary framework for understanding governs all the content. The third part fills out the christological "structure" with content, with brief considerations of five essential subtopics to complete a portrait of Küng's Christology. The final section offers commentary, a reflection on key elements of Küng's contribution to this field of theology.

Situating Küng's Christology

One could situate Küng's Christology in different ways. We will be able to make some judgments about the relevance of his work to our present situation at the end of this chapter. At this point it seems appropriate to locate his Christology against the background of pre–Vatican II theology and then within his conception of Christian faith as a whole way of life as that appears in *On Being a Christian*.

Catholic theology found little or no public interest prior to the Second Vatican Council. Why should there have been? After the centering of authority in the papacy at Vatican I and the condemnation of efforts to "modernize" Catholic theology in 1907, theology in the seminaries was centrally controlled. It was a clerical and male discipline. The textbooks for doctrinal theology were either written in Rome or their content was surveilled by authority that reflected the center. The universal teaching of the church minimized distinctive regional theologies. American Catholic theology did not exist; the sources of its theologians were European. A tight control of the discipline can be read in the condemnations of the encyclical *Humani Generis* in 1950 that feared the inroads of evolutionary thinking.

Vatican II changed things quite suddenly. One can make a list of contrasting theological positions before and after the council. But three sweeping changes in the atmosphere shed light on Küng's theology. First, theology after the council became a public discipline, beginning at the council when the press covered it and discovered debate and even controversy within the leadership of the Catholic Church. Second, Catholic theology became self-consciously ecumenical. One realized that if it were not ecumenical, it would be anti-ecumenical, because no movement toward unity could go forward if denominations retained nonporous boundaries and talked only to themselves. And third, Catholic theology became creative, not in terms of new doctrines, but in finding new methods or partnerships of analysis and forms of expression to meet the signs of the times.

The years following Vatican II were a very creative period for Hans Küng. He wrote *The Church*, *On Being a Christian*, and *Does God Exist?* after the end of the council in 1965 and during the 1970s. These three major works together cover the essence of Christian doctrine. Küng was nothing but ecumenical as a Catholic theologian. Especially in *On Being a Christian*, Küng also tried to communicate with a wider public audience than theologians and their students. He drew the subject matter from current scholarship, but the mode of presentation attempts to break out of the narrow halls of a theological academy to reach a wider public. He worked with a team to make this work accessible to an expansive audience.

One can situate Küng's Christology more pointedly in relation to the subject matter of *On Being a Christian*. The work describes the nature of Christianity. Its title partly shows the distinctiveness of its approach, especially in contrast to theology before the council, on two counts. First, "being a Christian" refers to the Christian life. It could be said that he moves away from abstract analysis of the church as an objective religion toward fixing before the imagination what it means to live the Christian life. Second, as already mentioned, the existential approach leaves the objective scholasticism of the Catholic theological tradition behind.

Where does Küng's Christology fit in this large work that synopsizes an understanding of being a Christian in our world today? Küng radically simplifies that delicate question in this work: understanding Jesus Christ itself entails an understanding of Christian life. Encountering Jesus as mediator of God contains a call to travel with him. In terms of the table of contents this work logically consists of three parts as distinct from its actual four. The first sets up the context for understanding Christology/Christianity today. The second presents Küng's Christology. And the third describes the church and its practice as a following of Jesus Christ. In other words, understanding who Jesus Christ was and is and what he did and does contain within themselves the substance of being a Christian today.

The Logic of Küng's Christology

This and the following sections present Küng's Christology in two stages that correspond to the logic or structure of his way of approaching Jesus Christ and then a fuller account of the content of his understanding. The distinction is important, and in some ways it bears the most important contribution of Küng to the subdiscipline of Catholic Christology.

The term *logic* carries a meaning that some analogous terms might clarify. The term *structure* may often be substituted for *logic* when it refers to the way an argument unfolds, the relations between premises, reasons, and inferences in reaching a conclusion. *Paradigm* offers another more holistic term that bears associations with *logic*. A paradigm usually refers to the bundle of assumptions, definitions, and methods of reasoning about a given subject matter that are shared within a discipline by all or distinct groups within it. The description of paradigm shifts by Thomas Kuhn relative to science is sometimes transposed to theology, and one might make a case that Küng's Christology represents something like a paradigm shift in relation to the textbook Christology before the council.[2] Finally, *types* and *models*, when referring to similar constellations of qualities that bind schools or families of theological positions to one another, can be associated with the formal character of a Christology as distinct but not separated from its content.

The logic of Küng's Christology has to be set in contrast to theology before the Council. The predominant method of Catholic theology had been to explain church doctrine. Authority governed the procedure. The form of theology was "neo-Scholastic," of the schools, referring to the synthesis achieved in the Middle Ages by adopting the language of Aristotelian philosophy and producing a comprehensive body of teachings. Catholic theology structurally was a didactic discipline, based on church authority,[3] using an objective scholastic language, which teachers explained to students and researchers refined by commentary on historical documents. In many respects, the textbooks of theology offered highly technical catechetics.

What follows describes the logic of Küng's Christology as implicitly contrastive to the scholastic Christology prior to the council. This has to be done briefly, but the schematic laying out of two premises flowing from historical consciousness and three foci of attention will demonstrate a logic, or paradigm, or model different from its scholastic predecessor.

Two premises underlie Küng's Christology, both stemming from the historical embeddedness of human understanding. To understand anything in history requires inquiry into its historical precedents and surroundings. Everything that exists is historical, and one cannot understand anything adequately apart from its historical genesis or origins. This imposes a certain narrative (in contrast to exclusively analytic and systematic) form of analysis. Küng's being a historical theologian allowed him from the beginning to think in a historical way about Jesus's appearance and significance.

The other premise applies historicity to existential understanding. All understanding bears the influence of the social vectors that influence an age, a culture, society and subculture, and each person in it. Küng explicitly takes into account the contemporary context for thinking, for looking back and bringing Jesus forward from the past. He highlights secularization, the present problematic character of knowledge of God, and the fact of other world religions now experienced as suggesting relativism. Theology today has to address a distinctively new and challenging context.

The next three points turn to strategic foci of attention in the story of the development of a Christian understanding of Jesus of Nazareth as Messiah/Christ. The narrative recounts how Jesus appeared and how Christianity's interpretation of Jesus developed. The premises and the key points in the narrative provide the basic logic of Christology.

First, the defining center of Christianity is the historical figure, Jesus of Nazareth. To be more specific, the character of Jesus resides in two aspects of his teaching: his message about God and his message about human existence. One can distinguish these two aspects of

Jesus's teaching, but they remain inseparable. One cannot uncouple the God whom Jesus preached and the self-knowledge gained by standing before God so revealed. Likewise, one can distinguish between Jesus teaching verbally and teaching by his actions. He used different genres of communication such as scriptural reference, parable, saying, moral precept, or prayer. Jesus also taught by his actions and his associations. But these distinctions collapse into the historical person. Thus the concrete human being, Jesus of Nazareth, becomes the focal center of Christian faith and the referent of Christology.

Second, after a consideration of Jesus through his teaching and action, Küng's Christology turns to two foci of Jesus's life and destiny that are essential to Christian faith's appropriation of him: his death and his resurrection. These are two different kinds of events, the first historical, the second beyond history and experienced through faith. But the two events correlate with each other, and neither can be adequately understood separately from the other. Together they define two essential elements of his significance.

Third, after Jesus's followers witnessed Jesus's death and then experienced a common faith that he was alive with God, Christian interpretation of Jesus as the Christ took off. The books of the New Testament are the primary witness to the development of faith's interpretation of the person and work of Jesus as the Christ. That development extended well beyond the chronological limits of the New Testament's composition into patristic speculation and debate and conciliar church teaching. All of this adds to the ongoing narrative of interpretation that constitutes church tradition.

These five elements define the logic of Küng's Christology. They rest on historicist premises about reality and epistemology conditioned by time. Applying them to the understanding of Jesus of Nazareth yields the following formal characterization of the discipline: Christology seeks to understand the historical person Jesus of Nazareth in the light of the narrative of his ministry, death, and the disciples' faith experience of his resurrection and to interpret his significance for human life in our time. This section marks Küng's departure from the scholastic pattern of Catholic teaching in place since the Middle Ages. It still has not been fully appropriated into Catholic teaching.

The Content of Küng's Christology

We turn now to the content of Küng's Christology. Küng offers a wide-ranging discussion that can be digested around five salient topics. The first, the rule of God, represents a holistic view of Jesus's public ministry. Exegetes generally agree that it points to a unifying center of Jesus's activity. The remaining four also represent standard elements of any Christology. Jesus's death and his resurrection culminate his life and are supercharged with meaning. Then, after the disciples recognized Jesus's resurrection, he became the subject of intense reflection and interpretation. The questions focused pointedly on what he did for human salvation and how he stood in relation to God and other human beings. These five issues schematize Küng's Christology, but they also implicitly enable a comparison with other especially pre–Vatican II theologians.

The Rule of God. This phrase, *the rule of God*, encapsulates the deepest intention of Jesus's teaching and activity. Küng defines the kingdom of God subjectively, "God ruling" rather than the objective or local effect of God ruling, a "kingdom": "It means God's reign, the activity of ruling which God will take over" (215).[4] This more readily allows us to understand how Jesus could understand himself as an agent who participated in a movement of God ruling. What kind of kingdom would this be? "It will be a kingdom where…God's name is truly hallowed, his will is done on earth, men will have everything in abundance, all sin will be forgiven and all evil overcome" (215).[5]

Küng, relying on the literature of his time, feels that Jesus had an apocalyptic horizon. "May his kingdom come: like that whole apocalyptic generation, Jesus expected the kingdom of God…*in the immediate future,*" that is, "the future rule at the consummation of the world" (216). Küng concedes that this feeling of his age was chronologically mistaken (218). But "what is involved in this immediate expectation is not so much an error as a time-conditioned, time-bound world view which Jesus shared with his contemporaries" (220).

But this loses significance in the light of the religious dimension of this teaching. In the presence of God there is no past, present and future: "God's name is already sanctified, God's will is already done on earth…the kingdom of God has itself dawned—'in your midst.'" (221). Küng stresses the point that the religious meaning and truth of the kingdom transcend time. "As God is the beginning, so too he is the end. God's cause prevails in any case. The future belongs to God. It is with this future, God's future, that we have to reckon: we do not have to calculate days and hours" (223). In the end, this talk refers to a different dimension of reality. "The consummation comes by *God's action*, which cannot be foreseen or extrapolated. It is an action of course which does not exclude but includes man's action here and now, in the individual and the social sphere" (224).

Küng neatly folds a short treatise on Jesus's "miracles" into action promoting the rule of God. With these stories, the Gospels intend to show "that in these deeds God's power itself was breaking through. Jesus's charismatic cures and expulsions of devils were not an end in themselves. They were *at the service of the proclamation of God's kingdom*. They interpret or confirm the words of Jesus" (234–35).

Küng offers no general theory of Jesus's miracles. He diffuses interest in what actually happened in each of these stories. We cannot know this exactly; the accounts should be seen as testimonies of faith about the person Jesus rather than reports. "The Gospels were not interested in a breach of nature's laws" (234). Today many of these stories are incredible, sometimes an embarrassment, always in need of explanation. They function on a religious level as testimonies to the person of Jesus in the terms of his own age. They recount not medical but religious acts that bore witness to the power of God directing Jesus's ministry.

The phrase *the rule of God* takes on different dimensions in various contexts. It points to future reality and the present; it can be within me, or among us, but always a power greater and different from us. But, in all, it encompasses the most basic truth or interpretation of reality itself and should govern the basic human attitude toward our very existence. It is not natural law (238–40); it is not even revealed law (240–41); more simply, it refers to God's will. Küng reads this most directly in the Lord's Prayer: "There cannot then be any doubt—and it is confirmed throughout the whole of the New Testament—that the supreme norm *is the will of God*" (242).

Küng also turns to the Sermon on the Mount to find the rule of God underlying not a new law but a new disposition toward life. "This is the common denominator of the Sermon on the Mount: God's will be done" (246)! But here the rule of God becomes radical.

God "demands not only external acts which can be observed and controlled, but also internal responses which cannot be controlled or checked. He demands man's heart. He wants not only good fruits, but the good tree: not only action, but being; not something, but myself—and myself wholly and entirely" (246).

The Cross. The second major topic that factors into Küng's Christology consists of his treatment of Jesus's crucifixion. He first approaches Jesus's death historically. He notes that early on Jesus's ministry created conflict with various factions within his Jewish community. On a historical level, his ministry raised a host of questions whose answers are not really clear but still elicit opinions. For example, did Jesus think of himself as Messiah? One cannot reach into Jesus's consciousness for an answer. Küng submits that Jesus did not make any claim to an office or title. All clearly messianic titles were post-Easter interpretations added to the gospel stories. Jesus did not make his own self the center or the main issue of his teaching and actions.

But the question of his person and identity remained implicit in his ministry (286–91). Küng believed that the various facets of Jesus's ministry as a whole contained a messianic character and thus implicit messianic claims could be read into his actions. He sums up the way Jesus represented himself to his fellow Jews with the phrase "God's advocate." Jesus, in criticizing certain Jewish institutions and practices and their representatives, implicitly exhibited a certain religious authority (291–94).

Was Jesus's idea of God offensive or challenging to his community? Jesus's God is Jewish, but Küng calls his portrait of God revolutionary. God transcends ritualism and legalism and is absolutely personal and forgiving. Jesus represents a God of pure grace, although not to the exclusion of judgment. Küng appeals to the parables, for example, to the father of the prodigal son, that Jesus's God broke all the rules of proportionality and human reckoning (312).

Was Jesus conscious of the possibility of his death? Küng thinks that he undoubtedly reckoned on the possibility or probability of his death (319–22).

Küng closes in on the final events of Jesus's life with the question of what was going on at the last meal Jesus had with his followers. One should not imagine that Jesus was inventing a rite. The story of the Last Supper may have reflected an actual paschal meal of Jesus with his disciples, or possibly the meals Jesus had during his ministry, whose meaning was transformed into later practices that became a ritual (322–25). Küng does not presuppose the historicity of the last meal. The gathering of disciples for meals in memory of Jesus figure deeply in the postpaschal assemblies and formation of a Jesus movement (323).

Nevertheless, in the season of Passover, Jesus was condemned to death as a result of collaboration between religious (Jewish) and political (Jewish and Roman) authorities (332). From the Roman perspective, Jesus represented messianic possibilities, and with them came a risk of uprising (333). Küng calls Jesus's execution a historical necessity. The historical motives were not an accident, nor a misunderstanding, but were historically inevitable. The "necessity" combined an indecipherable mix of political and religious motivations. He died because of his ministry and message. It was the logical outcome of his proclamation and his behavior (335). The charges were straightforward: heretical teacher, false prophet, blasphemer, seducer of the people (336). The conflict that gradually arose around his public ministry led to the paroxysm of crucifixion.

How are we to understand the gospel witness to the cry that Jesus uttered from the cross: "My God, my God, why hast thou forsaken me?" (Mark 15:34)? Küng states that this saying cannot be construed as a cry of despair because it is addressed to God. Rather, it expressed an experience of abandonment or isolation in the moment. It reflected the situation: all he had said of God seemed to be denied. No rule of God, no presence, no intimacy, no miracle (241). It seemed to be the end of the movement because it was in fact so centered in him. God's cause announced by Jesus seemed to die with him (342).

The Resurrection. Küng offers a clear, nuanced, and accessible discussion of Jesus's resurrection in a relatively short space. He begins by clarifying basic ideas needed to begin reflection because the Gospel stories readily leave the imagination with anthropomorphic impressions. He affirms the resurrection of Jesus as a matter of faith and not something that could be witnessed. But Küng the historian knows that he has to give some account of how this faith conviction came about, because at first Jesus's disciples were depressed at his death and then were actively preaching him as alive.

To begin, then, the nature of Jesus being raised should not be conceived as a supernatural intervention into history, not an externally perceived miracle proving the identity of Jesus; it can only be a datum for faith. One should not think of Jesus's resurrection as either in fact or principle an observable event (346–48). These negative assessments clear the way to make the resurrection credible in the sense of a reasonable object of faith (348–56).

To be more specific, the resurrection of Jesus "can *not be a historical* event in the strict sense; it is not an event which can be verified by historical science with the aid of historical methods" (349). The resurrection of Jesus's body cannot refer to his reanimated corpse; it means Jesus's continuous existing self and his history (351). In Semitic and biblical thought body is equivalent to self, to person and personal continuity; the subject matter does not lie within the confining sphere of biology or physics (351). Resurrection involves a completely new form of existence in God's wholly other mode of being. Jesus risen is unimaginable in the completely different sphere of God's transcendence. There can be no direct knowledge of Jesus risen (350).

These negatives open up a positive way or mode of thinking about Jesus's resurrection. Although resurrection can be perceived and affirmed only through faith, faith grasps it as reality prior to faith and not created by faith (352). Different terms express the same transcendent truth. For example, *exaltation* and *resurrection* point to the same thing. Luke's division of resurrection, ascension, and Pentecost are literary divisions. Faith's affirmation of Jesus's resurrection also carries attendant impulses and valences. Encountering Jesus risen makes those who encounter it into Jesus's agents in history. Call to mission is intrinsic to Easter faith.[6]

One can sum up Küng's insistence on the transcendent character of the resurrection by recognizing the character of the various versions of the discovery of an empty tomb. With many exegetes Küng views these empty tomb stories as legends, not as historical reports but as stories that illustrate or dramatize the message (364). Resurrection is not a miracle justifying faith in resurrection. Some exegetes hold out for the historicity of these stories; but for Küng they emphasize the reality of resurrection by presenting it in physical spatial form (366).

As a historically conscious theologian, Küng still has to consider the many attempts to reconstruct historically how resurrection faith first arose. This he does by considering the pros and cons of a series of theological reconstructions (370–81). For example, it may seem plausible to think that extended reflection and discussion led to a discovery that Jesus was risen prior to their coming to this faith conviction (370–71). But this theory makes consciousness of the resurrection seem like a deduction rather than an active revelation of a new reality; something that came *to* the disciples. Other theologians postulate that Jesus's disciples had some new experience that became the basis of their new faith. The New Testament emphasizes that this is a new experience of faith. But this should not be confused with a supernatural event of intervention or an objective miracle. Küng supports new experiences but not external interventions.

Ultimately Küng relativizes the form of the new experience to the content of the Easter faith. The form of the experience is subordinate to the message: recognition that Jesus is alive and that the mission must continue his ministry to the rule of God. The structure of the apparitions bears analogy to the calling narratives of certain prophets where God as Spirit works within a person (377). The callings involve faith, but they are also prior to and elicit faith; the calling overcomes unbelief.

Two points, at once historical and theological, shape Küng's account of resurrection faith. First, the inner core of faith in the resurrection does not consist of belief in apparitions but of making Jesus the criterion of one's mortal life. The deciding factor is existential: the blending of one's own life with the person and cause of Jesus vindicated by God. The second point notes how the relation between Jesus and his message change in the light of his resurrection. During his public ministry, the two can be distinguished but are mutually related. With the resurrection of Jesus, the two become identified: Jesus risen becomes merged with the message of God whose cause is human existence. The resurrection confirms by actuating God's character in the person of Jesus. Jesus becomes his own message of God loving human existence through death to eternal life (383–84).

Salvation. The last two of five essential elements of Küng's Christology focus on postbiblical doctrinal interpretation of Jesus Christ. The question of salvation is cast in objective terms in response to the question "What did Jesus do to accomplish human salvation?" Before considering Küng's direct answer to that question, however, he offers two considerations that serve as an introduction to it.

Revisiting Küng's Christology

One concerns the role of the apostle Paul in Christianity and later interpretation of Jesus. According to Paul, "the ultimate distinctive feature of Christianity is quite literally...'Jesus Christ crucified'" (410). But the cross means something more than a particular event; it signifies living in history with all its personal and social suffering that prevents any sense of escape from history (400). Paul also played a significant role in Christian faith as a whole. "He opened the way theologically and practically for non-Jews to approach the Christian message in absolute freedom. They did not have to become Jews.... Only through him did the small Jewish sect finally develop into a world religion" (402).

The other premise of salvation theory concerns interpretation itself. Küng prefaces his soteriology with a short statement about hermeneutics because Jesus Christ as savior requires new interpretation today. The main criticisms of doctrines about how Jesus saves charge them with being mythological. Myths minimally refer to stories that cannot be taken literally as reports. But religious truths too cannot be reduced to matters of fact; they represent a deeper level of perception and a higher dimension of reality. It follows that myths as myths should not be taken at face value, a definite tendency in Roman Catholic teaching. Rather, myths should be retained as myths or legends and their truth be interpreted realistically as symbolic language.[7] Thus does Küng move between rationalist reductionism and literal traditionalism (412–16). He recognizes that Jesus has been presented in mythic narrative forms, and his interpretation employs critical historical interpretation: "narrative presentation and critical reflection" (416).

On those premises, Küng notes that Christianity possesses no single uniform redemption theory. Using the scriptures as basis and starting point, Küng summarizes the salvation theories of Greek Christianity around two scenarios: (a) Jesus's death was a ransom to Satan purchasing release of humanity from evil power; (b) Jesus's death was a sacrifice, a cultic offering to God to atone for sin. In the West, Augustine took up the second conception of Jesus being offered to God as a satisfaction for sin, and this was worked out by Anselm in a classic fashion that was widely accepted (420–22).

It is generally conceded today that Anselm's construction of Jesus being offered to God as a satisfaction for human sin encounters strong negative reaction today. Küng reduces the rejection to three basic criticisms. First, the suppositions of an original fall have disappeared. Second, the idea of satisfaction does not work because the restoration of God's honor and justice remains purely extrinsic and sin continues. Third, the whole theory depends on the social-cultural imagination of a particular age, and it has lost its symbolic power (422–24).

Küng's understanding of how Jesus saves turns to an interpretation of Jesus's life and ministry. Fixing the imagination on the narrative of Jesus shows his obedience to his calling to serve the cause of God and humanity. Küng locates God's saving power in Jesus's commitment to God's cause, God's will, for human flourishing. Jesus's saving action basically consists of representing a faithful life in action (426). If one were to classify Küng's theory of salvation, it could be called revelational or representative: Jesus saves by dramatizing in a normative way the power of God working in human beings for salvation. As was said, the savior is Jesus Christ crucified. But the death of Jesus has to be seen in the light of his historical activity. That very historical engagement then reappears in the light of resurrection, as one who is still living and present. The saving narrative of Jesus Christ includes his ministry, his death, his resurrection, and his presence within the community.

The challenge to notions of salvation lies in continual human suffering. Küng invokes a distinction between emancipation as self-liberation and redemption as liberation by a power beyond the human. Neither one can be reduced to the other; and neither one can be adequate to the human situation without the other (430). Emancipation always falls short of the penetrating depth of God's love, and suffering still strikes at basic trust in God and in reality as a whole. In Küng's view, whereas Job found some relief and comfort in God's incomprehensibility, Jesus as representative offers trust in God as the power of resurrection. Jesus represents God being silently present in the senseless death of Jesus as a fulfilled promise of resurrection (341ff).

True God and True Man. The heading cites the classic christological formula for expressing the origin and status of Jesus Christ in relation to God and other human beings. Küng situates this doctrine in the transition from Jewish origins to Greek culture where biblical imagery took on speculative ontological meaning. The meaning of metaphors changed, and discussion shifted from centering on the life, death, and resurrection of Jesus of Nazareth to considerations of preexistence, the character of Jesus's unity with God, and then incarnation. The change of framework and approach can be described as from an "ascent Christology" beginning with Jesus, one could say "from below," to a "descent Christology," where the Word of God becomes incarnate, "from above." The accent turns from historicist thinking to ontological thinking about Jesus's "original" union with God. Küng considers this as a process of hellenization in a negative sense of distortion of scriptural meaning (436–40).

For example, "Son of God" was moved from its Jewish context, where it meant election, empowerment, and status as representative, to a Greek context, where it "meant an *ontological generation* of a higher kind. It is now a question less of the legal and authoritative status of Jesus Christ in the Old Testament sense than of his *descent* in a Hellenistic sense. It is a question less of function than of essence. Terms like essence, nature, substance, hypostasis, person, union, were to acquire increasing importance" (439).

Gradually, defending Jesus's human status became a problem. As Christianity moved into the Greek world, the idea of the incarnation of God was readily believable, but it complicated relationships with Jews and undermined Jesus's being a human being and a revelation of the human before God. In terms of Greek *paideia*: God as Son and Logos enters history, assumes human nature, and educates the human race according to a preconceived plan of salvation (441). This differs greatly from Jesus preaching God's rule and dying for it in a painful human execution. The problem became how to defend Jesus's authority against Docetism, that is, Jesus merely appearing to be, without really being, a human person (440–44).

The response to this issue is contained in the formula that Jesus Christ is true God and true human. Can this formula be translated into meaningful theological terms today? "If neither a simple duality nor a simple identity is possible, how can Jesus's relationship to God be positively expressed? We might put it in this way: the *true man* Jesus of Nazareth is for faith the real *revelation* of the one *true God*" (444). Küng explains this constructive response first by explaining the idea of "preexistence" found in the New Testament and then the meaning of the so-called two-nature doctrine.

A number of characterizations of Jesus in the New Testament seem to indicate his preexistence, that is, before his appearance on earth. They are meant to justify the unique position and claim about Jesus of Nazareth (446). Whether in the Philippians hymn (Phil 2:6–11), or Colossians (Col 1:15–20), or the Prologue to John's Gospel (John 1:1–14), these statements possessed credibility in the cultures that created them (445–46). They are mean to communicate that Jesus Christ can only be explained finally on the basis of his relation to God and that he has universal relevance. He is authorized by God and for all (446–47).

Turning then to the meaning of "true God," Küng notes that the New Testament expresses the relation of Jesus to God functionally, not physically or metaphysically, but in dynamic terms.[8] Jesus's divinity is expressed in terms of the salvation he mediates. As noted, the formal ontological way of thinking was later. Therefore, Küng concludes, "truly God" means God at work in Jesus; no Jesus without God animating him. He is God's representative. "God himself as man's friend was present, at work, speaking, acting, and definitively revealing himself in this Jesus who came among men as God's advocate and deputy, representative and delegate, and was confirmed by God as the Crucified raised to life" (449). All statements about Jesus's divinity come down to this: what is revealed in Jesus is "of divine origin and therefore absolutely reliable, requiring men's unconditional involvement" (449).

"True man" means that Jesus is not to be deified; he was wholly and entirely a human being with all the consequences. "As true man, by his proclamation, behavior and fate, he was a model of what it is to be human, enabling each and every one who commits himself to him to discover and to realize the meaning of being man and his freedom to exist for his fellow men" (449–50).

Küng's Christological Legacy

This appreciation of Hans Küng's Christology concludes by underlining aspects of his interpretation that were deep, groundbreaking for Catholic theology, and lasting. How his Christology was received at the time of its publication remains too complex and ambivalent to represent briefly and adequately. Küng published *Infallibility? An Inquiry* in 1970 (English 1971),[9] and it caused so much controversy that, from that time forward, discussion of his work became mixed with critical and uncritical loyalty to the church. The same year that Küng published *On Being a Christian* in German in 1974, Edward Schillebeeckx published the original Dutch version of *Jesus: An Experiment in Christology* (English 1979).[10] Almost simultaneously two of the foremost Catholic theologians turned to historical Jesus research for the starting point and foundation of their Christologies. Nothing in Catholic Christology could have been more important than that overt turn to critical scripture study. As a "paradigm shift," it needed time and reflection to be absorbed by the discipline at large, let alone by representatives of the Congregation for the Doctrine of the Faith.

In the background of the appearance of Küng's Christology lay the textbooks of Catholic theology from before Vatican II. The form and character of the seminary theology that dominated the field has largely faded from memory.[11] For those schooled in the Catholic Christology of the manuals, Küng's work could have appeared shocking rather than liberating. By contrast, many today may find his work commonsensical. This appraisal of Küng's Christology presupposes this tension and enumerates distinctive moves that he made that precipitated radical changes in the method and content of Catholic Christology in 1974.

Küng communicated with a wide audience. He did not write exclusively for fellow theologians or students of theology who knew the jargon. He exemplified a democratization of theological reflection. This was possible in the wake of Vatican II, when interest prevailed among an educated laity. People at large asked good questions that catechisms did not answer. But rather than writing popular theology, Küng used academic sources and painstakingly worked at addressing people in a less technical and more accessible language. But in doing this Küng raised as many questions as he answered because he abandoned the cover of theological mystification. His theology was exposed, as theology should be.

One of Küng's unique contributions, although he shared this with Schillebeeckx, lay in his historicist imagination. Küng's theology, and his Christology in particular, raise the question of how a theological imagination is tied to history, that is, concrete events, and yet is able find a dimension of transcendence in them and make statements that bear general if not universal relevance. Küng's

Christology carries an implicit theory of the historical mediation of revelation. Epistemologically, God can only be found in the world and history, never detached from historical mediation, but also never limited to the temporal event because of God's transcendent character. Such a theory is implied in Küng's discussion of how Jesus of Nazareth, who was experienced empirically as a preacher of God's rule, was also experienced more deeply and existentially as a mediator of God's presence and power.[12] Küng sensed early that a turn to history in constructing theological understanding today requires critical reflection on the basic ideas of faith and revelation.

Along with the epistemology involved in history and theology, Küng's historical approach to Christology shows that contemporary context explicitly influences the process of interpreting Jesus Christ at any given time. Küng attended to the cultural situation of his day as a preface to his Christology. He knew that he was introducing changes in the framework for interpreting traditional Catholic teaching. He exemplified a theological method of correlation that he would later formally embrace. Theology always has to be responsive to the questions of the culture in place. He was not a process theologian, but he was historically conscious and stood for ongoing development in the discipline of theology in order accurately to represent the continuity of the faith in history.

A comparison between Küng's Christology and its counterpart today shows the speed with which theological interpretation keeps moving forward. Küng recognized early that religious pluralism was a fact and a challenge to Christian self-understanding. But over the past fifty years much more work has been done in the theology of religions and comparative theology, and today Catholic theologians are more open to a nonsupremacist interpretation of Jesus Christ. Küng was also aware of the beginnings of liberation theologies and noticed the social implications of salvation. But he did not appreciate the thoroughgoing and comprehensive character of a liberationist theological imagination and its deep influence, particularly on a historicist sensibility. The idea of *liberation* translates today the meaning of *salvation*. These developments moved beyond Küng's Christology, even though his thinking is far from hostile to them and still has remarkable traction today.

Two last points illustrate lasting contributions of Küng relative to an understanding of salvation and the formal christological question of the status of Jesus Christ. In his soteriology Küng proposed a historical existential view of salvation rather than an objective theory of salvation. Many draw the distinction between "objective" salvation, indicating a formal theory of what Jesus did to accomplish human salvation, and "subjective" salvation, referring to people's conscious existential participation in the effects of God's saving through Jesus. Anselm's theological theory of satisfaction exemplifies well an objective view of salvation. By contrast, Küng's pervasive attention to history always keeps salvation tied to human encounter and reception. Projecting a metaphysical story above history on the basis of scripture's providing objective information about God makes little critical sense. Küng's work consistently describes Jesus's work for human salvation in terms of his ministry, and human appropriation of Jesus's ministry provides the proper domain for the language of salvation. Today salvation should be conceived in the terms of multiple levels of the experience of liberation that Jesus mediates.

Turning to the discussion of the formal question of the meaning of Jesus Christ being truly human and truly divine, Küng has shown that one can give a relatively adequate response to this question to a broad audience in functional and descriptive terms.[13] Such a work can bypass speculative theological language. But it is hard to think of God in less than metaphysical terms. The relationship between these languages can fruitfully be conceived in terms of a tension. On the one hand, no talk about God in terms of truth, as distinct from meaning, without some kind of human experience that reflects the infinite mystery of *God*. Talk about God should resonate with transcendence. On the other hand, experience of God mediated through Jesus invites, if not demands, some form of critical examination and descriptive account of the status of the medium in relation to what it offers. The medium shares in the transcendence it mediates. In short, Küng's presentation of Jesus as divine on the basis of Jesus's representation of God corresponds with church teaching, even though he does not employ the traditional objective metaphysical languages of the churches.

In the end, reading Küng's *On Being a Christian* today demonstrates that it remains a remarkable work in Christian theology that can help many to find new depth to their being a Christian.

Notes

1. Hans Küng, *On Being a Christian* (Garden City, NY: Doubleday, 1976).

2. Thomas S. Kuhn, *The Structure of Scientific Revolutions* (Chicago: University of Chicago Press, 2012).

3. Thomas Aquinas held that the articles of the Creed functioned in theology like first principles for deductive reasoning. While ordinarily arguments based on authority are the weakest, "the argument from authority based on divine revelation is the strongest." *Summa Theologica*, I, 1, 8 and ad 2.

4. The numbers in parentheses refer to the pages of *On Being a Christian* cited earlier in footnote 1.

5. Küng frequently uses italics for emphasis; whole paragraphs may be italicized. This text is italicized in OBC, but when cited out of context italics lose their particular contextual force and thus are not always reproduced here or in other places, nor are they added to Küng's texts.

6. Küng notes how this new faith in Jesus risen has background in Jewish tradition. One finds testimony to faith in resurrection in scripture in the middle of the second century BCE. But Jesus's resurrection is particular and becomes for a Christian's faith the promise of a general resurrection. Also, on a thematic level, faith in resurrection relates to creation faith in God who, as source and ground of creation, is also creation's end and finisher: faith in resurrection is deeper faith in God Creator (360).

7. One can have this discussion without using the term *myth*, which in common understanding is fraught with unreality. Küng uses it as a technical term rather than something that can be dismissed as an untrue story.

8. Küng probably means "merely metaphysically" here because the idea of God as Spirit active in Jesus is surely metaphysical.

9. Hans Küng, *Infallibility? An Enquiry* (Garden City, NY: Doubleday, 1971).

10. Edward Schillebeeckx, *Jesus: An Experiment in Christology* (New York: Seabury, 1979).

11. See, for example, Ludwig Ott, *Fundamentals of Catholic Dogma*, 6th ed. (St. Louis: Herder, 1964), 125–95. There is a long his-

tory of the character and form of Catholic theology from the founding of the universities in the high Middle Ages to the present, and developments in the nineteenth century are of particular importance. But recent twentieth-century history is enough to illustrate the leap forward represented by Küng's initiative.

12. Küng describes how Jesus Christ as "representative" entails more deeply his being a person who communicates or mediates God's power to those who encounter him. OBC, 389–92. This epistemological analysis applies across the board as a supposition governing how revelation works in the tension between empirical historical events and their relation to theological affirmations. Note that the term *historical events* includes *linguistic events*.

13. The supposition here is that transcendent reality cannot be fully represented by finite names or conceptions. The term *relatively adequate* thus operates within a framework of "absolute mystery."

5

INFALLIBILITY AND THE VATICAN

Mary McAleese

By the time Hans Küng died, he had spent half a century engaged in a relentless, scholarly critique of Catholic Church teaching on infallibility. Küng had made quite a name for himself as a prominent and progressive contributor to the Second Vatican Council, but in 1967 the publication of his book *The Church*[1] stirred disquiet in Rome in the Sacred Congregation for the Doctrine of the Faith. Those rumblings of discontent were subsequently eclipsed by the curial reaction to the publication in 1970 of Küng's book *Infallible? An Unresolved Enquiry*.[2] It landed like a guided missile on a flustered Curia already dealing with the "shock caused by the encyclical *Humanae Vitae*[3] on birth control...and the authority and unity threatened by the outburst of experimentation and the explosion of debate which followed the Council."[4] Fueling that debate was not just Küng's earlier book with its forensic commentary on the church but the publication by "one of the giants of the second Vatican Council,"[5] Cardinal Suenens of Belgium, of a book in late 1968 on *Coresponsibility in the Church* and a subsequent interview he gave in the summer of 1969.[6] Suenens was undoubtedly a conciliar heavyweight for he had been one of the four Moderators at the Council. His radical views on church governance and its power structure were seen by some as inspiring, by others as incendiary. Küng's views on infallibility added

74

fuel to a raging fire. Published in the centenary year of the declaration of papal infallibility at the First Vatican Council in 1870, it triggered what he described as a "virulent conflict," especially with many of his fellow Catholic theologians, though he argued that his intent was not to be provocative but to constructively express his deep concern.[7] The theological argument raged, often bitterly, between Küng and his theologian contemporaries among whom was his Tübingen colleague, Joseph Ratzinger, who went on to head the Congregation for the Doctrine of the Faith, a body that regarded Küng as persona non grata, and who would later become Pope Benedict XVI. Despite an apparent cordiality between the two men, including meetings while Benedict was pope, there is no doubting they were poles apart on the issue of infallibility, church governance, and a host of other matters. Küng did not hold back in his trenchant criticisms of Pope Benedict and Pope John Paul II, both of whom, in his view, did nothing to address the problem he had first articulated in 1970 apart from making it worse: "In spite of the impetus of the Council, it has hitherto not been possible to decisively change the institutional-personal, power-structure of the Church leadership in the spirit of the Christian message: pope, Curia and many bishops…continue to carry on in a largely preconciliar way; they seem to have learnt little from the Council."[8] For Küng the link between infallibility and that power structure was toxic and was inflicting "the worst damage on the unity and credibility of the Catholic Church."[9] That view had not changed at the time of his death.

"The traditional doctrine of ecclesiastical infallibility," he argued, "rests on foundations which for a modern theology…could not be described as secure and unassailable."[10] In fact, he challenged the very idea that the doctrine of infallibility had any credentials rooted in the Bible or tradition, writing that "upon close inspection the historian must judge infallibility to be an innovation of the second millennium and really only of the nineteenth century."[11] An ardent supporter of ecumenical and interfaith dialogue, Küng noted that the Catholic Church's assertion of "an infallibility of the teaching office has always been unacceptable to non-Christians and to Christians outside that Church"[12] and was "the most serious stumbling block on the road to ecumenical understanding."[13] As a strong advocate for the church renewal promised but not delivered by the Second Vatican

Council, Küng declared that after the Council the infallibility issue remained "the biggest obstacle to renewal within the Church."[14]

Along with his insistence that his work should not be seen as "an attack from outside but as help from within,"[15] Küng stood firmly on his right to academic freedom and freedom of conscience. He challenged the authorities in Rome to embrace "a spirit both critical and self-critical" instead of the culture of obliging dissenting voices "to keep silent, which would go against their conscience, against the freedom of scholarly research and against the true interests of the Church and its leadership."[16]

Küng's pleas for academic freedom as well as freedom of conscience and opinion fell on deaf ears. His questioning of the pope's infallible magisterium provoked the Sacred Congregation for the Doctrine of the Faith in 1979 to remove his ecclesiastical teaching privileges so that he could no longer be considered as nor work as a Catholic teacher. His license to teach as a Catholic theologian was never restored, but he remained both a priest and teaching theologian until his death. If silencing Küng was the Curia's aim, and if silencing dissent on infallibility was the objective, then both failed dismally. Küng merely moved from his teaching post in the Catholic Faculty of Theology within Tübingen University to a powerful academic platform specially created for him within the secular part of the same university. There he spent the rest of his professional life. Instead of being muzzled by the Curia he was unchained, becoming a much-lauded celebrity theologian and ecumenist on a global stage. A forthright and confident man, nonetheless his treatment at the hands of the Holy See and Curia distressed him greatly. He described it as his "personal experience of the Inquisition."[17] He did not go quietly.

Küng's "brilliantly disputatious, lucidly expressed thoughts"[18] over his lifetime were brought to bear on many contentious aspects of postconciliar church teaching besides infallibility, through some fifty books and hundreds of learned articles, lectures, interviews, speeches, and letters. His persistent voice from the ecclesial wilderness found an audience among those faithful who had been inspired by the reforming spirit of the Second Vatican Council. Küng acknowledged that the Council "was a magnificent success" and "offered a splendid program for a renewed Church of the future."[19] However, many like Küng were disappointed at the speed with which the gravitational pull of ecclesial imperial conservatism reasserted itself.

Within five years of the Second Vatican Council, Küng was lamenting that "the renewal of the Catholic Church sought by the second Vatican Council...has come to a standstill."[20] He argued that "for the sake of the Church and of the human beings for whom the theologian does his work, the reasons for this stagnation must be exposed"[21] since "the people of God are being deprived of the fruits of the Council."[22] For Küng, the culprit was insufficient conciliar and ecclesial reflection on infallibility that had led the church "into a dangerous tight corner"[23] and a Roman "relapse into pre-conciliar absolutism, juridicism and centralism."[24] This began with Paul VI's 1968 encyclical *Humanae Vitae*,[25] which, against the clear advice of the Pontifical Commission on Birth Control, banned the use of artificial contraception. It was not accompanied by a formal declaration of papally defined infallibility but was presented to a baffled church as nonetheless an infallible teaching. The encyclical was met with a wall of lay and clerical resistance. *Humanae Vitae* was a circuit breaker.

When Herbert Haag wrote that Küng's 1970 book "sparked off an international and interconfessional debate without precedent in more recent theology,"[26] that was something of an exaggeration, for the book landed into a vortex already characterized, thanks to *Humanae Vitae*, by the beginnings of mass disobedience of the faithful and condemnation by many clerics and theologians. It was a far cry from the words of Pope John XXIII, who, in calling the Council, had expressed the hope that it would "assert once again the magisterium which is unfailing and perdures until the end of time,...a magisterium which is predominantly pastoral in character...[and] prefers to make use of the medicine of mercy rather than severity."[27]

Skepticism among the faithful around contested teachings and widespread distrust generated by abuse scandals have today interrupted the passivity-tailored culture of deference. Individual intellectual autonomy informed by a dynamic human rights consciousness that has developed rapidly from the Universal Declaration of Human Rights[28] onward has challenged the legitimacy of the obligatory obedience of church members to the magisterium and the legitimacy of church laws that purport to impose both compulsory membership and the compulsory obligations of membership as a direct consequence of baptism. These challenges present a new and even more radical set of internal church questions that have put the legitimacy of infallibility somewhat in the shade. Küng certainly raised weighty questions concerning the rights of the faithful to freedom of conscience, belief, opinion, and religion, including the right to change religion, but, like most theologians and canon lawyers, he did not directly advocate the disaggregation of the theological from the juridic consequences of baptism, logical though that would have been given his views. That disaggregation drives a coach and four through the heart of the presumption of automatic church membership, of mandatory magisterial authority, right through infallibility and through the universal communion of the baptized. Whether it can be seen as a fruit of the Council is debatable; more likely it is a fruit of massified education and the internationalization of human rights discourse, both of which generated debates in which Küng was at the forefront.

Ladislas Orsy, veteran theologian, canon lawyer, and Küng contemporary, asserts that "creative thinkers are one of the greatest assets of the Church; they let the internal riches of the evangelical message unfold."[29] There can be no doubt that Küng was before, during, and after the Council one of the foremost of the church's creative and influential thinkers, and also one of its most critical. Impatience is a strong leitmotif in Küng's work. By contrast Orsy has long taken the view that councils are a slow burn: "Because Vatican Council II was so unusual in its convocation, operation and achievement, its reception in the universal church cannot be but slow. It calls for the conversion of the entire Roman Catholic communion."[30] Orsy sees the Council as having shifted the balance in the church from a strongly centrist institution where "there was a current that originated some nine hundred years ago":

> People were given little responsibility and were directed toward seeking their salvation through blind obedience. Then Vatican Council II generated another current....It recognized God's gifts dispersed in the community and asked each person to accept shared responsibility and exercise creativity for the benefit of the whole. After the Council the two currents met and clashed. The result was, and still is, turbulence among God's people.[31]

Küng pitched himself into that turbulence, offering leadership often at odds with the magisterium on a plethora of issues including clerical celibacy, female ordination, gay marriage, *Humanae Vitae*, abortion, euthanasia, church governance, ecumenical and interfaith relations, intellectual human rights within the church, the right to dissent, academic freedom, lay inclusion in decision-making, clerical child abuse and episcopal cover-ups, and more.

The infallibility debate Küng initiated did not disappear as the Curia intended, but rather leached down from the ivory tower of theologians into the bedrock of the faithful so that the disciplining of Küng marked not only the beginning of the end of passive acceptance of the doctrine of infallibility by the people of God, but the germination of a more skeptical, individual rights—based view of the notion of obedience to the magisterium and the basis upon which church membership is constructed. How far that view has developed, and in a direction set by Küng, is now particularly evident in the documents that have emerged from discussions at diocesan level during the synodal process initiated by Pope Francis in 2021.[32] Regrettably, Küng did not live to hear the words of Cardinal Ouellet, Prefect of the Dicastery for Bishops, complaining about the German synodal process during the German bishops' *ad limina* visit to Rome in November 2022. "It is striking," said Ouellet, "that the agenda of a limited group of theologians from a few decades ago has suddenly become the majority proposal of the German episcopate."[33] In fact, there was nothing sudden about it. The faithful had long since been debating among themselves about issues on which the magisterium offered fixed views and firmly opposed dissent. Guided by rare courageous clerical voices such as Küng's and informed by greater access to secular education, the faithful were increasingly persuaded by the integrity of their intellectual human rights and were exercising those rights to freedom of conscience and opinion. However, with no official church forum in which to have such debates until the synod opened an unexpected floodgate, the faithful had, over time since the Council, become dissociated from certain magisterial teachings and even from church membership itself. Ouellet's use of the word *suddenly* is telling of a Rome, a Curia, and a magisterium markedly still out of touch in 2022 and still of the view that a crack of the magisterial whip would bring people scurrying back into line. Ouellet (to no avail) scolded the ongoing German synodal debate on contentious issues, saying: "this hurts the communion of the Church because it sows doubt and confusion among the people of God."[34]

Küng could legitimately have replied, and with some satisfaction, that in fact the synodal process has revealed that there is a marked consensus rather than doubt and confusion among the people of God and that his is indeed an "agenda" whose time has come. Would it have come without Küng's persistent advocacy, simply by the passage of time? Hardly, though the evident developments in thinking among many of the faithful and the challenge they present to the magisterium, including on infallible doctrines, also vindicate Orsy's belief that "it always has taken more than 50 years for a council's teachings and reforms to take root in the Christian community."[35]

Küng would be the first to point out, however, that while dissent has grown loud and insistent, defying every attempt to subdue it, church teaching on these controversial issues remains largely intact. In fact, his overarching inquiry regarding infallibility remains utterly untouched at magisterial level and finds precisely no mention whatever in the ongoing synodal process.[36] What are we to make of that? Fifty years ago Küng was sure that infallibility had "become to a surprising extent at least questionable even within the Catholic Church."[37] Is it possible that the people of God have already moved beyond one of the titles of Küng's first book on the subject, *Infallible? An Unresolved Enquiry*? Has the issue of infallibility already been resolved by the faithful, leaving it marooned in that "dangerous tight corner"[38] as Küng described it? Does the tide of dissent and insistence on reform of so many contentious issues already spell the death knell of infallibility or at least faith in infallibility? And if it does, what does that mean for communion, for obedience to the magisterium, for the authority of the magisterium, and for the future of the church?

Orsy uses an intriguing expression when he writes of "the universal communio of the baptized believers."[39] There was a time when "the baptized" would not have needed the qualification "believers," for profession of belief was presumed and obligatory as a consequence of baptism. That the ever-insightful Orsy uses that qualification now indicates the ecclesial current that is drifting from a catechesis of obligation to a catechesis of invitation and that is at the core of the synodal responses today. It was the doctrine of infallibility which firmly embedded obligation and crushed invitation, insisting one must believe rather than that one has freedom to believe. It still does, and so we return to what Küng did, to examine the doctrine, its history, and its contemporary context.

According to James Coriden, "[t]he doctrine of infallibility has long roots in the history of the Church, but its solemn articulation took place in the final session of the First Vatican Council (1870)" and "should be viewed in the context of the more recent restatement of the teaching *in Lumen Gentium* 25."[40] The doctrine can be found today set out in Canon 749 of the 1983 Code of Canon Law.[41]

Canon 749§1 says the pope possesses infallibility in teaching when he "proclaims by definitive act that a doctrine of faith or morals is to be held." The college of bishops also possesses infallibility when in an ecumenical council they declare a doctrine of faith or morals is to be held definitively or, when dispersed throughout the world, in communion with the Pope they agree that a particular proposition on a matter of faith or morals is to be held definitively (canon 749§2). No teaching is to be regarded as infallible unless "this is manifestly evident" (canon 749§3). On the face of it the doctrine is circumscribed. It must deal with faith or morals, it must be proclaimed by definitive act, it must be manifestly evident that it is to be regarded as infallible (canon 749§3), and it must be proclaimed by either the pope or the college of bishops in communion with the pope. Curial departments and individual bishops cannot act infallibly, and much magisterial teaching (including all the documents of the Second Vatican Council) are not infallible.

It is often pointed out that in the almost century and a half since the declaration of papal infallibility at the First Vatican Council, it has been employed by definitive act only once, and that was in 1950 when Pope Pius XII declared the infallible dogma of the Assumption of the Blessed Virgin Mary.[42] However, in recent years it is not this rare exercise of papal infallibility (known as the extraordinary magisterium) which has caused controversy but the increasingly common exercise by successive popes of the so-called ordinary and universal infallible magisterium, which does not require a solemn form of definition like the Assumption dogma. It was employed in relation to *Humanae Vitae*. It comes into play often with ambiguity and absent the fanfare of the extraordinary magisterium. It is said to apply where the subject matter concerns confirmation or affirmation of a revealed truth or a teaching historically or logically related to it. According to the Congregation for the Doctrine of the Faith[43] in its commentary on Pope John Paul's apostolic letter *Ad Tuendam Fidem*,[44] "such a doctrine is to be understood as having been set forth infallibly."[45] What is more, "whoever denies these truths would be in the position of rejecting a truth of Catholic doctrine and would therefore no longer be in full communion with the Catholic Church."[46]

Pope John Paul introduced *Ad Tuendam Fidem* in 1998: "To protect the faith of the Catholic Church against errors arising from certain members of the Christian faithful, especially from among those dedicated to the various disciplines of sacred theology" and "to add new norms which expressly impose the obligation of upholding truths proposed in a definitive way by the Magisterium of the Church."[47] Almost twenty years on from the "silencing" of Küng, the debate on infallibility had clearly become more heated than ever and the response of the Holy See more hardline, still more oriented toward discipline rather than debate. Yet there was an air of desperation as much as exasperation.

In 1980, Pope John Paul II had previously attempted to close the infallibility debate once and for all when he wrote to the German bishops asserting that the doctrine of infallibility "is in a certain sense the key to the certainty with which the faith is confessed and proclaimed as well as to the life and conduct of the faithful."[48] The fact that the pope felt the need two decades later to further corral teachers of Catholic theology into conformity is evidence of the fact that the debate on infallibility was still very much alive and so, too, was uncertainty.

The Holy See itself can take credit for that. From the time of *Humanae Vitae* onward successive popes and the Congregation for the Doctrine of the Faith without any solemn form of definition—in other words, without using the extraordinary magisterium—had artfully asserted claims of infallibility for a raft of controversial teachings such as the ban on artificial contraception, church teaching on homosexuality and marriage, its refusal to bless same-sex marriages between Catholic couples, euthanasia, and the exclusion of women from ordination to the priesthood. Some have referred to this as "creeping infallibility."[49] But this "creeping infallibility," if it was designed to cement magisterial authority and promote obedience of the faithful, has instead provoked a level of disbelief and defiance that may in fact have almost soundlessly already dealt infallibility a fatal blow.

Looking to the foundational history of the doctrine of infallibility, Küng, Hasler, and Kertzer, among others, scrutinized in detail the circumstances in which Pius IX successfully pushed the doctrine of papal infallibility through the First Vatican Council. Each for somewhat different reasons concludes that the context is so problematic as to raise fundamental doubts about its legitimacy. Küng believed that the First Vatican Council was "trapped in its own time,"[50] that it was a beleaguered Pius IX's way of building an impregnable imperial bulwark against those (and there were many) who would challenge not only his temporal and spiritual empire but also his personal divine mandate. Küng states, "As painful as it may be to admit, this Council resembled a well-organized and manipulated totalitarian party congress rather than a free gathering of free Christian people."[51]

Hasler believed there was evidence that Pius IX was mentally unhinged, was engaged in "a desperate attempt to recover a lost sense of security,"[52] and "brought moral coercion to bear on the council fathers while offering no evidence of support for the dogma of infallibility from the Bible and tradition"[53] of the church. He saw "the dogma of papal infallibility...as an ideology...with no substrate in reality, something which arises out of the needs of interest groups and is spread and protected by them."[54]

Kertzer, an eminent Jewish scholar writing in 1996 and having had access to extensive Vatican archives, takes a fresh political and historical perspective much less dominated by Catholic theological considerations. He links Pius IX's determined push for a conciliar declaration on papal infallibility, among other pressures, to a hubristic search for personal vindication following the widespread international indignation and loss of papal esteem that greeted the pope's involvement in the kidnapping of the six-year-old Jewish boy Edgardo Mortara in 1858.[55] Kertzer's meticulous analysis of how the Mortara affair contributed to a weakening of the international political alliances that had kept the pope in power as emperor of the Papal States is persuasive. Regrettably, the Mortara affair is rather glossed over by Küng and Hasler just as it has been erased from church history in general.

The final loss of the Papal States after a millennium of the Pope as spiritual head of the church and as temporal emperor occurred in

October 1870 within weeks of *Pastor Aeternus,* the "First Dogmatic Constitution on the Church of Christ," which promulgated papal infallibility, and which was issued by the First Vatican Council on July 18, 1870. It was not just a convulsive year for the church but a major watershed in church history. It comprehensively ended a millennium of papal rule as emperor of the Papal States, as power broker across Europe, as a key influencer of governments, and as a temporal force to be reckoned with. As old empires began to give way to new republics on the way to becoming democracies, the Papal States disappeared despite Pius IX's strenuous efforts to hold on to them. He died still believing that God desired the entire world to be governed both spiritually and temporally by the pope; that there was no such thing as individual human rights especially in terms of freedom of conscience, and that no Jewish parents had the right to raise their own child who had been secretly baptized in the Catholic Church without parental knowledge or consent.[56] This, then, was the author of the doctrine of papal infallibility.

Küng was of the view that there was nothing infallible about the First Vatican Council's declaration on infallibility and that much in its context was troubling enough to justify internal investigation and debate at the least. He was among a number of scholars who had hoped the circumstances in which the doctrine of infallibility was theologically concretized in 1870 would be examined afresh at the Second Vatican Council. Instead, the First Vatican Council doctrine was not only not reexamined but speedily affirmed and increased in potency by the Council's Constitution on the Church, *Lumen Gentium*. Küng was caustic. The Second Vatican Council was, he said, "surprisingly uninterested in infallible definitions,"[57] and "for all its solemn and pious talk and decision on collegiality, Vatican II did not succeed in making headway against this papal absolutism."[58]

The following extract from the Synod of Bishops Working Document for the continental phase (2022) suggests the possibility that while Vatican II left the doctrine of infallibility intact, its failure to underpin the doctrine with substantial evidence-based scholarship has left it without much in the way of deep persuasive power beyond superficial polemic.

> The mission of the church is realized through the lives of all the baptized. The reports express a deep desire to

recognize and reaffirm this common dignity as the basis for the renewal of life and ministries in the Church. They affirm the value of all vocations in the Church, and above all, invite us to follow Jesus, returning to his style and way of exercising power and authority as a means of offering healing, reconciliation, and liberation. It is important to build a synodal institutional model as an ecclesial paradigm of deconstructing pyramidal power that privileges unipersonal managements. The only legitimate authority in the Church must be that of love and service, following the example of the Lord.[59]

These words are the views of the contemporary global faithful, gathered and expertly synthesized by the church's synodal office from the contributions of 112 out of 114 episcopal conferences and from all the fifteen Eastern Catholic Churches, plus reflections from seventeen out of twenty-three dicasteries of the Roman Curia besides those from religious superiors, from institutes of consecrated life and societies of apostolic life, and from associations and lay movements of the faithful. In addition, over one thousand contributions arrived from individuals and groups as well as insights gathered through social media thanks to the initiative of the "Digital Synod."[60]

The reference to "the only legitimate authority in the Church" goes right to the heart of Küng's fundamental problem with church teaching on infallibility, which he feared "has bequeathed a long winter on our Catholic church."[61] In his 2016 open letter to Pope Francis, Küng stated that "without a constructive 're-vision' of the infallibility dogma, real renewal will hardly be possible."[62] If he is right, that has quite strong implications also for the synodal process. Cardinal Mario Grech, Secretary General of the Synod of Bishops, has said that synodality promises an "ecclesial springtime."[63] But can it deliver that springtime if church teaching on infallibility remains officially unreviewed?

There is a startling new reality, namely, that with or without official review the doctrine of ecclesial infallibility has already been substantially weakened by these decades of unofficial review in the theological critiques led by Küng, Haag, Hasler, Curran, and others, and more recent broader historical analysis by scholars such as David Kertzer from outside the Catholic tradition. The question I want to pose here is whether in fact the issue of infallibility is now more resolved than even Küng believed, for, in many ways, although the doctrine remains fully intact at the magisterial level, in fact Küng successfully held the infallibility doctrine below the waterline, provoking not a catastrophic and rapid Titanic-style sinking but, rather, a hairline crack through which credibility has slowly but inexorably leached into the questioning thinking of the people of God. In fact, among the people of God it has to all intents and purposes already sunk despite strong defense from orthodox theologians and possibly because of "creeping infallibility" and the old weapons of forced obedience, forced acceptance, forced faith. Those weapons are long past their sell-by date, for the world has changed and attitudes toward church membership and the so-called obligations of membership have been changing also. It is these changes which present the most powerful fundamental existential threat to the church, a threat that even radical change to the doctrine of infallibility may not be in time to reverse.

Magisterial teachings backed by infallibility are being widely challenged, contradicted, and even ignored. The once normative bulwark of unchallenged deference, conformity, and obedience of the 1.3 billion faithful is no longer a given. The very legitimacy of the magisterium's claim to the obedience of church members is now disputed on legal, including fundamental human rights, grounds. Indeed, the legitimacy of the very concept of church membership as currently operated is itself disputed.

At the start of the 2019 film *Mary Queen of Scots* there is the legend: "Mary Queen of Scots was born a Catholic." It is factually wrong. No one is born Catholic. One becomes a Catholic by baptism. According to church teaching, that brief ceremony not only incorporates us into the body of Christ, absolves us from original sin, and thus opens up the pathway to salvation, consequences which are mystical-gratuitous divine gifts, it also makes us church members for life (a human-made canon law imposition). Church teaching insists that the baptismal promises we made create compulsory lifelong obligations of membership that we have a duty to honor and cannot resign from. The obligations include obedience to the magisterium, accepting magisterial teachings we find unpalatable, and refraining from dissent in order to maintain communion. In other words, by our baptismal promises we are deemed to have accepted the right of the magisterium to impose limitations on our freedom of expression, opinion, conscience, belief, religion, and right to change religion. Yet these are all fundamental human rights set out in the U.N. Universal Declaration of Human Rights (1948) and said to be the inalienable natural birthright of every human being.

The Second Vatican Council made no attempt to examine how its teaching was impacted by the Universal Declaration of Human Rights. In fact, it dissembled on this issue in its declaration on Religious Freedom, *Dignitatis Humanae*, which recognized only that those outside the church had the right not to be coerced into embracing the faith while insisting that those already baptized were obliged to profess the faith because of their baptismal promises. But consider this. Eighty-four percent of all church members were baptized as babies. How credible is it to regard them as obligatory members for life of a faith system on the basis of a ceremony conducted when they were nonsentient? How credible are the claims that as babies they made promises of such a profound nature that they oblige obedience to and acceptance of the teaching of the magisterium for life? How legitimate is such an insistence on obedience from anyone, whether baptized as an infant or adult, in the light of the Universal Declaration of Human Rights (1948), which insists that each human being is endowed by nature (God to believers) with inalienable intellectual human rights to freedom of conscience, belief, opinion, religion, and freedom to change religion. Küng's position could not have been clearer: "in the contemporary world the free expression of opinion is a basic human right that cannot be denied even to a Catholic theologian."[64]

This understanding of magisterial control over church members, which is so basic a given that its flawed nature has been long overlooked, is no longer sustainable. The synodal voices of the faithful indicate a need for reform of these ignored foundational presumptions that dare to limit our fundamental God-given faculties and freedoms to make up our own minds, speak with our own voices, and inform our own consciences. What God has given, the church has no right to take away. Yet the magisterium does just that.

Infant baptism, although normative in the church, in itself is not the problem. What is problematic here is the failure of the magisterium to separate the divine from the juridic human-made consequences of baptism and to integrate into church law the fundamental human rights that are integral to human dignity and are the divine birthright of all. The spell that has held generations of Catholics to the notion of binding baptismal promises and consequent obedience to the magisterium has been ruptured. Intellectual freedom to dissent (severely compromised by canon law) is a human right being exercised freely by many in the synodal process, just as many others have exercised their human right to freely leave the church (not recognized in canon law) or change religion (also not recognized in canon law) despite canon law's assertion that such behavior by baptized Catholics constitutes the canonical offenses of heresy, schism, or apostasy and as such is subject to canonical penalties.

The Holy See has never confronted the fiction of baptismal promises, nor the reality that the basic intellectual human rights of church members are incompatible with and contradicted by canon law's insistence on obedience to the magisterium. As a consequence, it is vulnerable to these contemporary juridico-legal disputes. As they play out in the hearts and minds and actions of the educated people of God,[65] it is these disputes, and not theological debates on infallibility, that are demolishing the legitimacy of obligatory submission to the magisterium. In fact, they are rendering obsolete the notion of automatic church membership itself. The baptismal promises so utterly central to the claims of magisterial control over church members and to membership itself are fictions, leaving the church of "obligations" and magisterial control on sinking sands. The contemporary crisis in church governance and membership leave the theological debate on infallibility in a place of increasing irrelevance. If church members are free to form their own consciences and opinions, free to dissent from magisterial teaching, not bound by fictitious baptismal promises, then magisterial teaching loses the controlling power of infallibility and its essential facilitator, obligatory obedience. For the teaching on infallibility to work, it needs the teaching on membership, baptismal promises, obedience, the unacceptability of dissent, the crack of the whip of the magisterium. It needs the faithful to jump when the magisterium shouts. It needs baptized conscripts, not baptized believers. But that day is passing into history.

The debate among the people of God has not just veered from infallibility, it has outmaneuvered it. Küng's assertion that "the only way to solve the problem of contraception is to solve the problem of infallibility" is the fallible assertion of a theologian who had not yet felt the cancelling power of mass disobedience, mass education, mass exercise of autonomous individual human rights. Yet Küng can take more than a little of the credit for how the people of God have quietly deactivated the doctrine of infallibility. Can they believe in Christ without believing in infallibility? Can they be members of the church without accepting infallibility? Can the synod offer answers?

Although it is still not achieved, Küng argued for a humble, fallible magisterium that learns from its errors, and this is surely the essential message to be gleaned so far from the synodal process. "The truth of the Church," Küng argues, "is not dependent on any fixed infallible propositions but on her remaining in the truth throughout all propositions including erroneous ones."[66] With notable prescience, in remarking on *Humanae Vitae* in 1967, Tübingen canon lawyer Johannes Neumann accused the magisterium in its use of infallibility "of going beyond its brief and [it] can claim neither obedience nor credibility."[67] It is a near-perfect description of where the magisterium's creeping infallibility has brought it today.

A sour and wounded but well-warned Curia thought they had found in Küng and his absence of meekness, his celebrity and his unmanageability, the perfect scapegoat through whom to quell dissent by making an example of him, forcing him into the obedience the magisterium believes it is entitled to demand. Instead, by silencing him they amplified his voice, sent it viral, connecting him to a universal audience through which his views were tested and found convincing. A Christ-centered authenticity ran through Küng alongside a belief, despite his many disappointments, in the church's potential for good as a fallible Christ-centered institution. Despite his painful experience of official sanction but buoyed by widespread support from around the world, he could still, in his eighties, humbly write to Pope Francis, asking him to open "a free and serious discussion of infallibility, *non in destructionem, sed in aedificationem ecclesiae*, 'not in order to destroy but to build up the church.' For me personally, this would be the fulfillment of a hope I have never given up."[68]

For Küng, that hope had begun half a century earlier with the Second Vatican Council. But as he watched the hope evaporate, a frustrated Küng turned to the questions the Council had, in his view, failed to probe convincingly: is the magisterium, the pope, the church, really infallible? Kung's answer is a studied no. Today the voice of the faithful seems to say a resounding "no," which indicates that the doctrine of infallibility "has not been received" by the faithful and is not seen as necessary to their faith.

On his installation as bishop of Galway in April 2022 in that once most Catholic conformist of countries, Ireland, Bishop Michael Duignan remarked,

> It feels like we have been out all night without a single catch. We can no longer ignore the fact that much of what the Church has built up in Ireland over the last two centuries is crumbling before our eyes. The more and more I see, the more and more I am convinced that much of our infrastructure, our systems, our pastoral practices that were beneficial in the past, now hinder rather than help the life of faith. Here too we stand at a "threshold moment….Perhaps the Lord is asking us to throw out our nets in a different direction.[69]

If ever a statement vindicated Küng's concerns Bishop Duignan's raw, unadorned judgment does, and it applies far beyond Ireland. Hans Küng claimed that "in the wake of the Second Vatican Council it is simply impossible for the Church to bury the issue of infallibility."[70] In fact the people of God may have already killed infallibility. It just awaits a certified official burial, possibly somewhere along the synodal journey. Then perhaps the embers of the spirit of the Second Vatican Council may yet fan to a flame and Hans Küng can rest in peace.

Notes

1. Hans Küng, *The Church*, translated from German by Ray and Rosaleen Ockenden (London and New York: Sheed & Ward, 1967).

2. Hans Küng, *Infallible: An Unresolved Enquiry*, trans. Eric Mosbacher (London: Collins, 1970). (In the American edition it is entitled *Infallible? An Inquiry*. See n9 below.).

3. Pope Paul VI, *Humanae Vitae*, July 25, 1968, *AAS* 60 (1968), 481–503 (Latin text). For English text see: https://www.vatican.va/

Infallibility and the Vatican

content/paul-vi/en/encyclicals/documents/hf_p-vi_enc_25071968_humanae-vitae.html.

4. José De Brouker, *The Suenens Dossier: The Case for Collegiality*, translated from the French (Dublin: Gill and Macmillan, 1970), v.

5. Gordon Wheeler, "Coresponsibility," *Ampleforth Journal* 74 (Summer 1969): 212.

6. Léon Joseph Cardinal Suenens, *Coresponsibility in the Church* (New York: Herder & Herder, 1968). The interview appeared simultaneously in *Informations Catholiques Internationales* (May 15, 1969) and in *The Tablet* (May 17, 1969).

7. Cf. Hans Küng, *Infallible? An Unresolved Enquiry*, new exp. ed. with preface by Herbert Hagg (New York: Continuum, 1994).

8. Hans Küng, *Infallible? An Inquiry*, trans. Edward Quinn (New York: Doubleday, 1971), 12.

9. Küng, *Infallible?* (New York: Doubleday, 1971), 15.

10. Küng, *Infallible?* 124.

11. August Hasler, *How the Pope Became Infallible*, Introduction by Hans Küng (New York: Doubleday, 1981), 2.

12. Küng, *Infallible?*, 31.

13. Hasler, *How the Pope Became Infallible*, 3.

14. Hasler, *How the Pope Became Infallible*, 3.

15. Hasler, *How the Pope Became Infallible*, 4.

16. Hasler, *How the Pope Became Infallible*, 3.

17. Hans Küng, *The Catholic Church, A Short History*, trans. John Bowden, repr. ed. (New York: Modern Library, 2003), xviii.

18. D. Martin, "Hans Küng, Catholic Theologian Critical of the Church, Dies at 93," *New York Times*, April 6, 2021.

19. Küng, *Infallible? An Inquiry* (Doubleday, 1971), 17–18.

20. Küng, *Infallible?*, 11.

21. Küng, *Infallible?*, 11.

22. Küng, *Infallible?*, 26.

23. Küng, *Infallible?*, 28.

24. Küng, *Infallible?*, 19.

25. Paul VI, *Humanae Vitae*.

26. Küng, *Infallible? An Unresolved Enquiry*.

27. John XXIII, speech on opening of the Second Vatican Council, October 11, 1962: https://jakomonchak.files.wordpress.com/2012/10/john-xxiii-opening-speech.pdf.

28. UNGA, *Universal Declaration of Human Rights* (UDHR), resolution 217A (III), adopted December 10, 1948. The UDHR is nonbinding. Article 18 says: "Everyone has the right to freedom of thought, conscience and religion; this right includes freedom to change his religion or belief."

29. Ladislas Orsy, *Receiving the Council* (Collegeville, MN: Liturgical Press, 2009), 103.

30. Orsy, *Receiving the Council*, 85.

31. Orsy, *Receiving the Council*, 86–87.

32. Sometimes dubbed "The Synod on Synodality," Pope Francis initiated a two-year (now extended to three years) synodal process on October 9–10, 2021, in Rome themed "For a Synodal Church: Communion, Participation and Mission." The diocesan consultation phase showed remarkable consistency throughout the universal church among participants in their willingness to challenge a range of magisterial teachings and practices. Cf. Synod of Bishops, *Working Document for the Continental Phase*: https://www.synod.va/content/dam/synod/common/phases/continental-stage/dcs/Documento-Tappa-Continentale-EN.pdf, para. 57.

33. Report of *ad limina* meeting on November 24, 2022, as published in *L'Osservatore Romano*, November 25, 2022.

34. Report of *ad limina* meeting on November 24, 2022, as published in *L'Osservatore Romano*, November 25, 2022.

35. Ladislaus Orsy, Speech during Week of Prayer for Christian Unity at Centro Pro Unione, Rome, January 25, 2013; https://www.ncronline.org/news/vatican/jesuit-says-confusion-over-vatican-ii-normal-even-50-years-later.

36. Cf. Synod of Bishops, *Working Document for the Continental Phase*; https://www.synod.va/content/dam/synod/common/phases/continental-stage/dcs/Documento-Tappa-Continentale-EN.pdf.

37. Küng, *Infallible?*, 31.

38. Küng, *Infallible?*, 28.

39. Orsy, *Receiving the Council*, 6.

40. J. A. Coriden, "Infallibility of the Pope and of the College of Bishops," in *New Commentary on the Code of Canon Law*, ed. J. P. Beal, J. A. Coriden, and T. J. Green (Mahwah, NJ: Paulist Press, 2000), 913–14.

41. Strangely there is no specific canonical norm on papal infallibility in the 1917 Code of Canon Law.

42. Pius XII, Apostolic Constitution *Munificentissimus Deus*, November 1, 1950, *AAS* 32 (1950), 757. https://www.vatican.va/content/pius-xii/en/apost_constitutions/documents/hf_p-xii_apc_19501101_munificentissimus-deus.html.

43. Since June 5, 2022, known as the Dicastery for the Doctrine of the Faith. Note that the Congregation/Dicastery has no authority to definitively declare infallible any teaching of the magisterium.

44. John Paul II, Apostolic Letter issued Motu Proprio *Ad Tuendam Fidem*, May 18, 1998, *AAS* 90 (1998), 457–61; https://www.vatican.va/content/john-paul-ii/en/motu_proprio/documents/hf_jp-ii_motu-proprio_30061998_ad-tuendam-fidem.html.

45. Congregation for the Doctrine of the Faith, Doctrinal Commentary on *Ad Tuendam Fidem*, June 29, 1998. This document does not appear on the website of the Dicastery (formerly the Congregation) for the Doctrine of the Faith.

46. Doctrinal Commentary on *Ad Tuendam Fidem*.

47. John Paul II, *Ad Tuendam Fidem*.

48. John Paul II, Letter to the German Episcopal Conference, May 18, 1980; https://www.vatican.va/content/john-paul-ii/de/letters/1980/documents/hf_jp-ii_let_19800515_conferenza-episcopale-tedesca.html.

49. A term said to have been coined by Bishop Basil Christopher Butler, OSB, in an article on *Humanae Vitae* in *The Tablet* in 1971. An Anglican convert, Bishop Butler was a significant contributor to the Second Vatican Council.

50. Hasler, *How the Pope Became Infallible*, 24.

51. Hasler, *How the Pope Became Infallible*, 12.

52. Hasler, *How the Pope Became Infallible*, 37.

53. Hasler, *How the Pope Became Infallible*, 314.

54. Hasler, *How the Pope Became Infallible*, 275.

55. Cf. D. I. Kertzer, *The Kidnapping of Edgardo Mortara* (New York: Vintage, 1997); Kertzer, *The Pope Who Would Be King* (New York: Random House, 2018).

56. Pius IX, Encyclical *Quanta Cura* (with appendix *Syllabus of Errors*), December 8, 1864; https://www.vatican.va/content/pius-ix/la/documents/encyclica-quanta-cura-8-decembris-1864.html.

57. Küng, *Infallible?*, 71.

58. Küng, *Infallible?*, 85.
59. Cf. Synod of Bishops, Working Document, 57.
60. Synod of Bishops, Working Document, 5.
61. Open letter from Fr. Hans Küng to Pope Francis, dated March 9, 2016, and published in *National Catholic Reporter*, March 9, 2016.
62. Küng to Pope Francis, March 9, 2016.
63. Cf. Address of Cardinal Grech to the Irish Catholic Bishops' Conference, March 4, 2021.
64. Küng, *Infallible?*, 24.
65. Cf. M. McAleese, *Children's Rights and Obligations in Canon Law* (Leiden: Brill, 2019), 10–11; 69–108; 147–172; 465–466.
66. Küng, *Infallible?*, 150.
67. J. Neumann, interview published in *Die Enzyklika in der Diskussion. Eine orientierende Dokumentation zu 'Humanae Vitae'* (Zurich 1967), 47.
68. Küng to Pope Francis, March 9, 2016.
69. Homily of Bishop Michael Duignan at his Installation as Bishop of Galway and Kilmacduagh and Apostolic Administrator of Kilfenora, May 1, 2022; https://www.catholicbishops.ie/2022/05/01/homily-of-bishop-michael-duignan-at-his-installation-as-bishop-of-galway-and-kilmacduagh-and-apostolic-administrator-of-kilfenora/.
70. Hasler, *How the Pope Became Infallible*, 1.

6

PRIESTHOOD

Susan A. Ross

If one were to read what Hans Küng wrote about priesthood without knowing when he wrote it, it would not be a surprise if one were to think that his ideas had been written in the recent past—perhaps to underscore Pope Francis's call for a more synodal church,[1] perhaps to criticize clericalism or what James Keenan has recently called "hierarchalism,"[2] perhaps to strengthen ties with other Christian churches, such as the Lutheran Church, on the universal priesthood of all believers. Yet the greater part of Küng's work on the priesthood, written in the years during and just after Vatican II at which he had served as a *peritus*, or theological expert, is fifty or more years old. His understanding of church offices, including the papacy, episcopacy, and the priesthood were, for the most part, based on extensive and thorough historical research and grounded in his conviction that the early church's conception of ministry was normative. Like many of his contemporaries, Küng stressed a return to the early sources of the Christian tradition as the church sought to understand itself anew in the twentieth century. And despite the fact that he largely turned from intra- and inter-church concerns to wider issues in his later years, Küng's early work on the priesthood in the immediate wake of Vatican II still sounds strikingly relevant for the present—that is, if one has a progressive view of the church.

Yet there is also much about the priesthood that Küng does not discuss. Clergy sex abuse, while undoubtedly occurring at that time around the world, was nowhere on Küng's radar. Küng does not discuss seminary formation or the psychosexual development and maturity of those who aspire to ministry. The culture of clericalism, which he fiercely condemns, was protecting priests while children and vulnerable people were being abused. Nor did he have any way of knowing in the early 1970s that there would be a considerable conservative backlash to the changes following the Council, and that the very accoutrements of clerical life he so strongly criticized (privilege, being set apart, ornate vestments, sacramental character) would be seen as highly attractive to younger generations who were born after Vatican II. In the wake of the clergy sex abuse crisis, reading Küng on the priesthood recalls the enthusiasm and hope for radical change held by so many in the years immediately following Vatican II, but in retrospect it seems somewhat naïve.

Küng's experience as a *peritus* at Vatican II gave him an insider's perspective on the workings of the Catholic Church (he was only thirty-four at the start of the Council!). In this essay, I will draw largely on *Structures of the Church* (1964) and two subsequent works: *The Church*, published in 1967, a dense and scholarly study of the institution, and *Why Priests?* (1971), a much slimmer volume that ends with "The Image of the Church Leader Today"—that is, one who models himself after Jesus.[3] These three books offer a theology of the priesthood that is in many ways well ahead of its time, with its focus on the ministry of Jesus as its model, its grounding in the priesthood of the baptized, and its critique of clericalism. After reviewing these three books, I will comment on some more recent work on the priesthood. But while Küng's is a compelling vision, at least for some, it is also reflective of an optimism that would eventually be disappointed. No doubt there are some who would see Küng's theology as emblematic of the worst of Vatican II. It does, however, represent a vision of the priesthood that tries to get to the roots of what Christian ministry was and is intended to be. And while this is an essay on Küng's understanding of the priesthood, it cannot be separated from his theology of the laity, since for him the ordained priesthood emerges from the shared common and universal priesthood of the baptized, a point he emphasizes repeatedly in all three books.

Priesthood

Structures of the Church (1964)

Structures was written in the midst of the Second Vatican Council, an event that promised *aggiornamento*: literally, bringing the church "up to date" with a greater openness to what was happening in the world at large and how the church would adapt to these changes, a sense that the church was moving into uncharted territory with dialogue with other Christian churches and even non-Christian religions, and with the guidance of the Spirit. And while the calling of the Council by Pope John XXIII may have come as a surprise to many Catholics, a number of Catholic scholars and lay experts had been laying the groundwork for the Council for some time. Küng was certainly among those who were setting the stage for a new vision of the church. His doctoral dissertation concerned the theology of Karl Barth, a Swiss Reformed theologian, on the doctrine of justification, which exemplified Küng's openness to other Christian traditions, and he had published a 1960 book on councils that became an international best-seller.[4]

Structures of the Church opens with a preface by Richard Cardinal Cushing, the Archbishop of Boston, who praises Küng's book, dedicated to Karl Rahner, SJ, one of the most significant theologians of the twentieth century. In the first chapter, Küng states that "whoever reflects on ecumenical councils reflects, expressly or not, on the Church herself."[5] And that is what Küng accomplishes in this book. In presenting a history and theology of ecumenical councils, Küng argues the point that "the Church [is] an Ecumenical Council by Divine Convocation"—the title of the second chapter. Thus, the history and theology of ecumenical councils, which may not seem immediately relevant to the question of the priesthood, is the starting point for his ecclesiology and his theology of ministry. His overall aim is to establish the fact that the church (and therefore the Council) is composed of laity *and* clergy and that the laity have a right to participate in councils. He considers the ecumenical implications of the history of councils and the laity's participation, or lack of same, in them. So, while this book does not contain a fully developed theology of the ordained priesthood—that will come in a later book—the repeated emphasis on the importance of the universal priesthood of the laity indicates the basis for such a theology.

One of the most striking things about this book is the immense amount of scholarship that Küng evidences: his knowledge of ancient languages, his close study of the earliest theologians, his detailing of the complex history of ecumenical councils, his intimate knowledge of Protestant theology. It is through these lenses that Küng develops his understanding of the priesthood of all believers and its relationship to church structures. Küng grounds the priesthood in two connected realities: the first is that Christ is the one and only High Priest, and the second is that the universal priesthood of all believers is shared by all the baptized. It is only in the light of these two prior and fundamental points that one can speak of *priesthood* (although Küng prefers the term *ministry*) as referring to the clerical position of the ordained person we think of today. His emphasis in *Structures* is largely on the universal priesthood of the baptized and what this entails.

Küng argues that the privileged position of the clergy, particularly regarding conciliar participation, is neither a theological nor a historical inevitability. He points out that the Second Council of Nicea was actually opened by a woman, the Empress Irene, who co-presided over it in 787. The laity, largely in the persons of the nobility, the kings, and emperors, were not only among those attending the councils, but a member of the laity had actually preached a sermon at the Council of Trent (1545–1563). It was only at the First Vatican Council (1869–70) that laity were actually barred from attending and participating. Küng's point is that clerical domination of councils is a relatively recent historical phenomenon, and he cautions against using that as a norm. He argues that development is not a one-way street:

> One should take care not to start out from the status quo, tacitly regarded as the optimal peak of development up to now, in order to demonstrate, if possible, that even this status quo is of divine law.[6]

A few lines after this, he argues that "*the universal priesthood of all believers* is the foundation that makes it possible for the laity to participate in an ecumenical council." He then states: "The doctrine of the universal priesthood is part of the fundamental truths of Catholic ecclesiology." In an interesting footnote, Küng criticizes the position of Josef Ratzinger in an article on the theology of councils as limiting the concept of collegiality to that of bishops and not of the entire church.[7] Küng also refers to the work of Yves Congar, in his groundbreaking *Lay People in the Church*,[8] in arguing that the "hierarchical principle" and the "community principle" came into existence at the same time, are mutually dependent, and that hierarchy does not precede community.

Küng could not be clearer on the basis for his understanding of the priesthood. Priesthood is for him, fundamentally, a participation in the priesthood of Christ and at the same time a shared responsibility of all believers. Throughout the book, he draws on Luther's understanding of the priesthood of all believers, and this remains a touchstone throughout his writings on the clergy and the clerical state. He recognizes that the practical dimensions of this theology raise a number of complicated questions. For instance, the question of the specific role of the ordained pastor, as Luther understood it, raises the issue of the distinction between the one ordained to office and the baptized, which Luther never clearly describes. To clarify this point, Küng asks to what extent the office of the priest matches the conception of leadership in the New Testament. Quoting Luther, Küng observes, "Since although we are all priests, to be sure, nevertheless we all cannot and should not preach or teach and govern." Küng identifies the development of various offices in the church as human, not divine, law.[9]

Küng reserves some of his most withering comments for the church of the Counter-Reformation: "Hence it is not strange that the theology of the Counter Reformation offered no theological appreciation of an active participation of the laity in the Church and the councils." But he notes approvingly how, in *Mystici Corporis*, Pope Pius XII said that "all members...are called to cooperate in the edification and perfection of the Mystical Body of Christ."[10]

After extensive reviews of the history of church offices ("Council and Ecclesiastical Offices," "The Petrine Office in the Church and in Council"), Küng concludes *Structures* with a chapter on infallibility ("What Does Infallibility Mean?"). In sum, his efforts throughout this book are to ground theology in scriptural and historical context, to consider the arguments made by Protestant Reformers, and to establish that the church is the community of *all* believers, not just the hierarchy.

Responses to *Structures* were largely positive, especially those coming from Protestant reviewers. In *Church History*, Robert McAfee Brown writes that "[Küng] manages to raise, and to discuss with ample documentation, almost every significant issue that needs clarification in the Protestant-Catholic dialogue."[11] Charles Lee Mitton, in *Expository Times*, notes Küng's "sensitive appreciation of some of the basic aims of the Reformation."[12] *Structures* firmly established Küng as a force to be reckoned with among Catholic theologians. The ecumenical implications of Küng's ideas about church structures would eventually be further developed. But it is important to note here that even at this early point, Küng was very skeptical of the power of the hierarchy, a position that would be much more fully developed in subsequent years.

The Church (1967)

In 1967, Küng published *The Church*, an even lengthier and equally dense study of the institution. The Council had ended in 1965, and the changes in life and teaching (liturgy, ecumenical relations) had more or less settled into the life of the church. In his introductory words to the book, he notes that "one can only know what the Church should be now if one also knows what the Church was originally." He acknowledges the mixed reactions to the Council ("whatever disappointment we might feel in retrospect"), but defends such innovations as the vernacular liturgy, ecumenical efforts, and theological renewal as showing how the church has been "awakened to new life."[13] As he did in *Structures*, Küng turns to church offices and the priesthood only after giving extensive scriptural and historical background to the ways in which the church has developed over time.

Reiterating his emphasis on the priesthood of all believers, which is the title of the first chapter in Section E ("The Offices of the Church"), Küng immediately notes the "fundamental error of ecclesiologies" that they turn out to be no more than "hierarchologies" by failing to realize that the church is primarily a community of believers, not of dignitaries. As in *Structures*, he argues for the mutually equal relationship of community and office as they both arise simultaneously in the New Testament, which constitutes the main criterion for evaluating church offices. Küng points out early in this chapter that the word *priest* (Greek *hiereus*) is not used in the New Testament to refer to the ministers of the community, nor did Jesus ever use the term to refer to himself. And it was only after his death that the term *sacrifice* came to be used in reference to his life and death, particularly in the Letter to the Hebrews. This understanding is also significant because it shows that human priesthood "has been fulfilled and finished by the unique, final, unrepeatable and hence unlimited sacrifice of the one continuing and eternal high priest."[14] Christ is thus unique; there is no other priest. Sacrifice is no longer the offering of an animal to God; rather, it is the offering of oneself, as Christ offered himself on behalf of all humanity.

After establishing that the priesthood of Christ is not a continuation of the priesthood of the Old Testament, and that Christ is the one and only high priest, Küng goes on to speak of the priesthood of all believers, before any mention of those who hold the title of priest:

> The abolition of a special priestly caste and its replacement by the priesthood of the *one* new and eternal high priest has as its strange and logical consequence the fact that *all* believers share in a universal priesthood.[15]

Küng's repeated emphasis on the priesthood of all believers as constitutive of the church, and therefore as members of an ecumenical council, reflects the renewed understanding of the church as community that was developed in *Lumen Gentium*, the Vatican II Constitution on the Church. The order of the chapters of *Lumen Gentium*—the Mystery of the Church (I), the People of God (II), and the Hierarchical Structure of the Church (III)—was a deliberate statement by the bishops of the Council on the church's self-understanding, in that the priesthood, and thus the hierarchy, only emerges from the entire church.[16] As Avery Dulles's commentary on *Lumen Gentium* observes, "Among all the documents of Vatican II, probably none underwent more drastic revision between the first schema and the final approved text."[17] Where the original schema gave priority to the primacy of the hierarchy, the final version reflected a transformed self-understanding of the church as the community of believers.[18]

In his development of the priesthood of all believers, Küng includes dimensions of that priesthood that empower the laity. He discusses "direct access to God," in showing how, "in *faith, all* have through Christ direct access to grace, all make spiritual sacrifices, all are engaged in the preaching of the Word, which is entrusted to all." Even more, "All are called to preach the Gospel in the sense of their personal Christian witness, without being all called to preach in the narrow sense of the word or to be theologians." Küng also points out the power of any baptized Christian to baptize. In all of this, Küng wants to make clear that the priesthood of all believers "is far from being just a theological slogan or an empty title."[19]

Küng then details the ways the church became increasingly institutionalized during the years following the apostolic period, and how the central meaning of the priesthood of all believers was lost as priesthood became associated with a clerical caste. He pays some, but not extensive, attention to the development of the priestly office in the patristic, medieval, and early modern periods. It is only after this review that Küng asks, "Given that the exclusive and particular names like priests and clergy have no basis in the New Testament, is it not difficult to find a suitable name for those who hold office in the Church?" Küng's answer is that the essence of the priesthood, for both the people of God and those in church office, is service, *diakonia*. Rejecting any understanding of church office as involving law, power, or enhanced dignity, Küng stresses that service arises out of love for others. And in a long, Barthian-style note, Küng concludes:

> If we look at the Churches of the New Testament we can see what a very perceptible weakening and impoverishment of the charismatic structure of the Church in general and of the diaconal structure in particular their disappearance signified.[20]

It is clear that Küng regards the priesthood of the postapostolic church as failing to live up to the standards set in the New Testament and early church. This development only increased over time.

As Küng works his way through New Testament texts, looking for the ways in which the early church exercised ministry and how church offices developed, one point that he seems to emphasize repeatedly is what is *not* there: no monarchial episcopate, no presbyter, no mention of ordination. While the church developed somewhat differently depending on whether it had a Gentile or Jewish context, much of what is taken for granted in the present—the elevation of clergy over laity, the unique quality possessed by the ordained—is simply absent. What *is* present is a diversity of ministries—preaching, reconciling, prophesying, teaching—that is characterized by its fluidity. And he comments, "Nothing is to be gained from concealing the fact...that a frightening gulf separates the Church of today from the original constitution of the Church." He sums up his attitude toward ordination:

> Ordination is not the handing on of a complete authority which glorifies him who receives it without binding him to any responsibilities; the authority which is given is one of service, and it demands from him a corresponding attitude, a corresponding life and work.[21]

When Küng turns (somewhat briefly) to the question of how ministries are exercised in the present, he refers to the "pastor" of a church rather than the priest. When he does mention ordained ministry, he cautions that those "who are empowered to exercise a particular pastoral ministry in the Church are not, at least as far as the New Testament tells us, a separate caste of consecrated priests, as they often are in primitive religions." While always emphasizing the foundation of the priesthood of all believers, he does say that the one who serves in a pastoral role "is marked by a special commission."[22]

In sum, Küng's theology of priesthood in *The Church* is really a theology of ministry based almost exclusively in the New Testament and, in particular, the church of St. Paul. All are priests, some are called to specific roles of service in the community depending on their gifts, but priesthood is not something that only a few are called to: it is the vocation of *every* Christian to be a priest. Some Christians are pastors, some are teachers, some are prophets, but all share in Christ's priesthood.

Reviews of *The Church* were decidedly mixed. Some commented that *The Church* could have been written by a Protestant, as Anthony Hoekema notes in *Calvin Theological Journal*.[23] But many Catholic reviewers were far more critical of Küng. In *The Catholic Biblical Quarterly,* Joseph Zalotay, while saying that this is "a book that will never be forgotten" and that it "radiates freedom, intelligence and loyalty to the true ideals given his Church by Christ himself," nevertheless laments that the book has "more problems than can even be mentioned here."[24] Maurice Bévenot, in *The Heythrop Journal,* while noting the "outstanding achievements" of the book, is critical of the way that Küng "pays scant attention to Tradition" and that he barely mentions *Dei Verbum,* the Constitution on Revelation. The book, he writes, "is marred by a great number of impassioned passages, hitting again and again on exposed nerves."[25] George Tavard, in *Continuum,* is stronger, even scathing, in his critique of Küng's biblical hermeneutics: "There seems to be no room, in Hans Küng's church, for anything that can have happened between the proclamation of the kerygma by St. Paul and the proclamation of the secular city by Harvey Cox."[26]

Why Priests? A Proposal for Church Ministry (1971)

In 1971, Küng published *Why Priests? A Proposal for a New Church Ministry.* In comparison to his two previous books on the church, this is a brief (118 pages) treatment of the topic. In the preface, Küng describes the "emergency," facing the church, as the departures from the priesthood and the decline in vocations have increased. He acknowledges the opposition his writing has met and argues that the "only worthwhile answer is an ecumenical one." The first section of the book is entitled "The Church as Community of Liberty, Equality, Fraternity." This means, for Küng, a "nuanced democratization of the Church." In his development of this point, Küng turns, as he did in *Structures* and *The Church,* to the New Testament as his guide. And repeating ideas developed in those two books, he says that "unlike the pagan or Jewish cult, the Christian needs no priest as mediator at the innermost part of the temple, with God himself." The church consists of the "whole believing community"; all are called to preach the gospel. With liberty, "faith effectively subsumes law and power and completely relativizes them." Equality means that "the Church may and should be a community of fundamentally equal people."[27] And fraternity means that "all members of the Church are [God's] adult sons and daughters and they must not be reduced to the status of minors."[28]

As he demonstrated in the two previous books, the New Testament basis for ministries shows that they were "pluriform, mobile, and flexible." And again, Küng insists that the correct way to understand any form of service in the church is with the term "ministry, not office." He calls for abandoning the term *hierarchy* ("holy domination") "because it is misleading." Jesus, he points out, was a layman. He discusses apostolic succession as a "complex historical process" that cannot be traced back to a "divine institution" by Christ. And as before, Küng describes as a "decline" the development of institutional forms of ministry in the postapostolic period. The New Testament remains normative.[29]

This book then moves into a relatively short description of the historical development of church offices. The language of "priest" began to be used, as did sacrificial language relating to the Eucharist. Clerics began to occupy a particular social class, celibacy was introduced, and ministry was "sacramentalized," as the priest was now seen as the one who offered the eucharistic sacrifice. Küng again argues that "no claim can be made that they [these developments] are normative,"[30] since they were not there from the start.

When Küng turns to the development of the sacraments, he notes, correctly, that the number of seven sacraments "is a product of history."[31] And as other scholars, notably Gary Macy, have established, what "ordination" meant at one or another time in the church's history is not uniform.[32] While the criterion of "institution by Christ" has been the traditional standard for claiming sacramental status, Küng argues that the Council of Trent took the opportunity to name certain sacraments (confirmation, extreme unction, marriage, and ordination) although they were not "instituted by Christ" in the strict sense. In addition, Küng blames Trent for assuming what became the doctrine of sacramental character "without any serious discussion." Küng's argument is that there is no adequate distinction between the activity of the Holy Spirit and some kind of "spiritual stamp" that inheres in a person from certain sacraments; he argues that the idea of sacramental character can be traced back to Augustine, and its point is that the repetition of a sacrament of initiation does not make sense, not that it refers to an "indelible character."[33]

Similarly, Küng is critical of the Tridentine idea, challenging the Protestant reformers, that the Mass is a sacrifice. He counters, "The Eucharistic celebration is not itself a sacrifice but continually directs our attention anew to Christ's unique sacrifice of the cross and makes it present and effective." Thus "the one who presides at the Eucharistic celebration must not be considered a sacrificial priest."[34] As in *The Church*, ministry is Küng's preferred term for leadership in a church community.

In the final chapter, "The Shape of the Church's Ministry of Leadership," Küng sets out his own vision of what church ministries of leadership should look like—or, perhaps, what ministry does *not* require. There is more freedom in how one ministers than one might think, he argues, and goes on to say that leadership need not be full-time, lifelong, based on rank or education. "Training for the Church's ministry of leadership does not have to be academic; it need not be scholarly." Nor should the minister necessarily be celibate or male. When it comes to women's role in ministerial leadership, Küng is clear: "Full participation of women in the Church's life, on the basis of equal rights, is something that belongs to a suitably renewed Church today."[35]

What does remain is a "functional-ecclesiological" understanding of ministry, although just after this sentence, Küng defines ministry this way: "The Church's ministry of leadership is a permanent (or in certain instances a temporally limited) function which arises from a vocation (charism) that really and permanently defines the person." Throughout the book, he is critical of any form of domination or power accruing to ministry. While he does acknowledge that ordination, as it has developed over time, should be seen as "a completely legitimate development, and not as a deviation," nevertheless "it should not be said that ordination...was instituted by Christ."[36]

Küng's use of the New Testament as the sole criterion for authenticity of church leadership is also another point of difficulty, since again, as he did in *Structures* and *The Church*, he basically dismisses the developments in the theology and practice of ministry since apostolic times. His emphasis is, as always, on service. Since for him, "all Christians are empowered to carry out baptism and the Eucharist," the role of the ministerial leader is to ensure that "the congregation assembles again and again...in grateful remembrance and praise of the Lord."[37] *Why Priests?* received decidedly mixed reviews from its scholarly readers. In *Theological Studies*, Ray Robert Noll described the book as "a longish, provocative, overpriced essay" that was "both praiseworthy and disappointing."[38] The brevity of the book did not allow for the extensive scholarly apparatus included in the two prior books dealing with priesthood. Since Küng is particularly critical of Trent on the priesthood, Noll's response is that Küng "needs to do better than pose a few questions."[39] In *Theology Today*, Gregory Baum observed that it was "obviously written in a hurry" and described it as "a polemical essay."[40] In *New Blackfriars*, Jerome Smith describes the book as "strong in assertions but weak in evidences, full of sweeping conclusions but empty of the detailed arguments and citations necessary to sustain them."[41]

Küng, the Priesthood, and the Present

In 2001, forty years after *Why Priests?*, Küng published *Women in Christianity*, which came out of a research project undertaken by his Institute for Ecumenical Studies.[42] The brief book contains an overview of the churches' views of women since biblical times. In the book's last chapter, Küng makes his position regarding women and ordination clear: "By what right do the Orthodox and Roman Catholic Churches still refuse women an equal share in their activities, to the point of excluding them from the ministry of the Church?" He challenges the claim that women cannot image Christ, argues—as he did in *Why Priests?*—for democracy in the church, and makes the case that celibacy should be dropped as a requirement for the priesthood—indeed, that equality for women and a married clergy are issues that go together. The diaconate should be open to women, he argues, but ordination to the diaconate is "not enough":

> Unless the admission of a woman to the diaconate also at the same time makes her admission to the presbyterate possible, this would not lead to equal rights for women but rather to a postponement of their ordination.

Küng laments that he first made these proposals twenty-five years before the publication of this book and concludes with the words *Speramus contra spem*—we hope against hope.[43]

Küng's theology of the priesthood is remarkably consistent over time: the early church had a diversity of ministries, none of them bearing the title of "priest"; the development of the office of the priesthood is a historical development, if not devolution, from the egalitarian and charismatic style of leadership in the early church; there ought to be no barrier to a married clergy or to the ordination of women; the church is in a crisis over the priesthood and should return to its biblical roots.

With all that Küng has to say about clericalism and the hierarchy, however, he approaches it as a historical theologian and does not really address the multiple effects of clericalism. While he is very critical of how power is used as a clerical "weapon," he does not touch in any detail on the way it affects seminarians, priests, and laity, or how it permeates the culture and is not just a historical phenomenon due for an update. The enormous difficulty of eradicating clericalism, which has existed for nearly as long as the church has, is not really addressed. It is clear that clericalism is at the heart of the clergy sex abuse crisis: that is, the idea that priests "stand apart" from the laity and have a privileged position. The important report, "Beyond 'Bad Apples,'" funded by the "Taking Responsibility" project centered at Fordham University,[44] defines clericalism in these terms:

> a structure of power that isolates clergy and sets priests above and apart, granting them excessive authority, trust, rights, and responsibilities while diminishing the agency of lay people and religious.[45]

Küng would no doubt agree with this definition. The authors of the report make a series of recommendations for clergy and lay formation that focus on the integration of sexuality and vocation, gender inclusion, critiques of power and, for our purposes in this essay, one that "center[s] on theologies of the priesthood that emphasize the Spirit's guidance of ministry and collective discernment rather than the authority of the ordained."[46]

The "Bad Apples" report, along with fifteen other research reports in the project, offers a powerful critique of the current structures of seminary education, relationships between clergy and laity, the complicity of both laity and clergy in maintaining silence about abuse, and the multiple ways that bishops and other clergy systematically silenced and denied the voices of victims. The project focused on the impact of the clergy sex abuse crisis on Jesuit colleges and universities, but the findings of the research projects are applicable even more to diocesan institutions which, unfortunately, largely declined to participate in the "Bad Apples" qualitative survey as well as in other projects.

In 2010, Küng was quoted in an article in the *Christian Century*: "Vatican critic Hans Küng has warned against 'condemning the church and its priests wholesale' for the current spate of sexual abuse allegations. 'It would be a bad generalization to place the whole clergy and Catholic Church under suspicion,' the Roman Catholic priest said in an interview with *The European*, a Berlin-based online news service."[47] But here, I would venture to guess that Küng may have grossly underestimated the impact of the revelations of clergy sex abuse on the church as a whole.[48]

It is interesting to compare Küng's *Why Priests?* with Garry Wills's book of the same title, but with a different subtitle: Wills's subtitle is *A Failed Tradition*.[49] Like Küng, Wills turns to the New Testament to show that the early church did not use the title of priest for its leaders; Jesus is the one (and only) High Priest. The title is given to Jesus seven times in Hebrews. While Küng discusses apostolic succession and sacrifice in both *Structures* and in *The Church*, Wills ties the problems of the priesthood both to those and to additional issues: the theology of real presence and the ransom theory of atonement that supports the idea of the Mass as a sacrifice. Wills's main argument is that priesthood is a development of the later church that goes against the attitude of Jesus: "The priests were the men most dangerous to Jesus." Using personal anecdotes—he is a cradle Catholic, a former altar server, and a former seminarian—Wills emphasizes the power that the priest has to consecrate the Eucharist as a way of being "set apart" and considers himself to belong to "a higher order of being." But unlike Küng, Wills does not offer an alternative vision of ministry, other than to say that Catholicism does not have a monopoly on the sacred, and that "all those acting in the name of Jesus are our brothers and sisters."[50]

In February 2022, the Vatican hosted an international conference on the priesthood. Pope Francis's remarks to the participants reflect some of the issues and concerns that Küng emphasized throughout his writings on the priesthood. One major point is that the priest is, first, a member of the baptized: "The life of a priest is above all the salvation history of one baptized person."[51] While acknowledging the difference between the ministerial and baptized priesthood, Pope Francis observed that this foundation is often forgotten, which is "a tragedy." What is needed is more "closeness": to Jesus, to the bishop, to other priests, and to the people he serves. Like Küng, Pope Francis emphasizes the pastoral dimension of the priesthood and its New Testament roots. But the changes that Küng embraced, such as a married clergy or the ordination of women, were not on the table. Indeed, Pope Francis praised clerical celibacy as a "gift" that needs to be lived out with "healthy relationships."[52] Although various church groups have called for a relaxation of the requirement of clerical celibacy, such as the Synod on the Amazon and the German Synodal Way, no changes appear to be in sight for the Roman Catholic priesthood.

Küng's vision of the priesthood remains relevant for the present despite its idealism. There is no question that the priesthood in the global north remains in crisis as priestly vocations continue to decline. In the global south, vocations are increasing, notably in Africa and Southeast Asia.[53] Clericalism, however, remains a problem, even in countries that were colonized by the global north. Küng's focus on global ethics in his later years shows how he saw the church changing with a greater focus on the church's international dimensions and on the crises facing the world. His vision of Christian ministry, focused on service and shared by all the baptized, remains an unfulfilled hope.

Notes

1. https://www.synod.va/en.html.

2. James F. Keenan, "Hierarchalism," *Theological Studies* 83, no. 1 (March 2022): 84–108.

3. Hans Küng, *Structures of the Church*, trans. Salvador Attanasio (London: Burns and Oates, 1965), *The Church*, trans. Ray and Rosaleen Ockenden (New York: Sheed and Ward, 1967), and *Why*

Priests? A Proposal for a New Church Ministry, trans. Robert C. Collins, SJ (Garden City, NY: Doubleday, 1972).

4. Hans Küng, *The Council, Reform and Reunion*, trans. Cecily Hastings (New York: Sheed and Ward, 1962).

5. Küng, *Structures*, 1.

6. Küng, *Structures*, 71–72, 81, 84.

7. Küng, *Structures*, 85, italics original, 193–94.

8. Yves Congar, *Lay People in the Church: A Study for a Theology of Laity*, trans. Donald Attwater (Westminster, MD: Newman Press, 1957).

9. Küng, *Structures*, 123, 124.

10. Küng, *Structures*, 89, 90.

11. Robert McAfee Brown, Review of *Structures of the Church* in *Church History* 34, no. 2 (June 1965): 225–26, at 225.

12. Charles Lee Mitton, Review of *Structures of the Church*, in *The Expository Times* 78, no. 3 (December 1966): 66–67, at 66.

13. Küng, *The Church*, ix, x.

14. Küng, *The Church*, 363–64.

15. Küng, *The Church*, 370; italics in original.

16. For an extensive treatment of the Vatican II discussions on the Constitution on the Church, see Giuseppe Alberigo and Joseph A. Komonchak, eds., *History of Vatican II*, vol. 2 (Maryknoll, NY: Orbis, 1997), 391–412.

17. Avery Dulles, SJ, in *The Documents of Vatican II*, ed. Walter Abbott, SJ (New York: Hill and Wang, 1966), 10.

18. See *History of Vatican II*, n16 above.

19. Küng, *The Church*, 373, italics original, 377, 382.

20. Küng, *The Church*, 387, 398.

21. Küng, *The Church*, 402, 413, 427.

22. Küng, *The Church*, 438, 439.

23. Anthony Hoekema, review of *The Church*, in *Calvin Theological Journal* 5, no. 1 (1970): 110.

24. Joseph Zalotay, review of *The Church* in *The Catholic Biblical Quarterly* 31, no. 1 (1969): 102.

25. Maurice Bévenot, review of *The Church* in *The Heythrop Journal* 9, no. 3 (1968): 328–31.

26. George Tavard, review of *The Church* in *Continuum* 30 (1968): 110.

27. Küng, *Why Priests?*, 30.

28. Küng, *Why Priests?*, 15, 24, 28, 29, 30, 32.
29. Küng, *Why Priests?*, 37, 39, 41, 47–48.
30. Küng, *Why Priests?*, 55–57.
31. Küng, *Why Priests?*, 60.
32. Gary Macy and Bernard J. Cooke, *A History of Women and Ordination* (Lanham, MD: Scarecrow Press, 2002).
33. Küng, *Why Priests?*, 63, 65, 64, 66.
34. Küng, *Why Priests?*, 68–69.
35. Küng, *Why Priests?*, 78, 79–82.
36. Küng, *Why Priests?*, 82–83, 89.
37. Küng, *Why Priests?*, 104.
38. Ray Robert Noll, review of *Why Priests?*, *Theological Studies* 34, no. 1 (1973): 133–36, at 133.
39. Noll, Review of *Why Priests?*, 135.
40. Gregory L. Baum, review of *Why Priests?*, *Theology Today* 30, no. 1 (1973): 102.
41. Jerome Smith, review of *Why Priests?*, *New Blackfriars* 53, no. 630 (1973): 523.
42. Hans Küng, *Women in Christianity*, trans. John Bowden (New York: Continuum, 2001).
43. Küng, *Women in Christianity*, 96, 101, 103.
44. https://takingresponsibility.ace.fordham.edu/.
45. Julie Hanlon Rubio and Paul J. Schutz, "Beyond 'Bad Apples': Understanding Clergy Perpetrated Sexual Abuse as a Structural Problem & Cultivating Strategies for Change," Report for "Taking Responsibility," https://www.scu.edu/ic/programs/bannan-forum/media-publications/beyond-bad-apples-/.
46. Rubio and Schutz, "Beyond 'Bad Apples,'" 47.
47. Interview with Hans Küng, *Christian Century*, June 1, 2010, 18.
48. See https://www.aa.com.tr/en/world/25-of-christians-consider-leaving-church-in-germany-over-abuse-scandals-survey/2764582 on the numbers of German Catholics considering leaving the church; https://www.washingtonpost.com/religion/2019/03/13/more-us-catholics-are-considering-leaving-church-over-sex-abuse-crisis-poll-says/ on U.S. Catholics.
49. Garry Wills, *Why Priests? A Failed Tradition* (New York: Viking, 2013).
50. Wills, *Why Priests?*, 142, 1, 80, 30, 258.

51. https://www.vatican.va/content/francesco/en/speeches/2022/february/documents/20220217-simposio-teologia-sacerdozio.html.

52. See https://www.ncronline.org/news/vatican/pope-francis-opens-vatican-priesthood-conference-upholding-celibacy-gift.

53. For Southeast Asia, see https://www.ucanews.com/news/the-rise-of-priestly-vocations-in-southeast-asia/97624; for Africa, see https://www.aciafrica.org/news/2610/inside-tanzanias-growing-vocations-to-the-priesthood.

7

HANS KÜNG

A Transitional Ecumenist

Jakob Rinderknecht

Hans Küng is remembered for many things. But for the latter half of his career, his official title was Professor of Ecumenical Theology and Director of the Institute for Ecumenical Research in the University of Tübingen. His works regularly frame themselves as ecumenical, either in scope, impact, or argument. A book on his work and its reception would therefore be lacking if it did not consider him as an ecumenist. While Küng himself talked about the shift to a global church,[1] his vision of the ecumenical task is inescapably rooted in his own time and place. He must be considered as a fundamentally twentieth-century Swiss or German ecumenist who spoke from and to this setting.

One central piece of framing for Küng's life is the way he is shaped by his relationship with Karl Barth. Küng was a long-time admirer of Barth, beginning in his student days. His doctoral dissertation, later published as the famous *Justification: The Doctrine of Karl Barth and a Catholic Reflection*, connected him to Barth's thought throughout his career.[2] This important work sets many of the trajectories of Küng's work and also highlights some important ways in which he understands the ecumenical project as a project, and so a significant portion of this essay will engage with it, even though it stands at the very beginning of Küng's corpus.

Hans Küng

Küng's deep respect for Barth is evident. Famously, Barth saw himself truthfully reflected in the book, penning the "Letter to the Author" that is prefaced to many editions of the work. In this letter, Barth makes three major points: First, he writes that Küng has "adequately covered all significant aspects of justification treated in the ten volumes of my *Church Dogmatics* published so far, and that [he has] fully and accurately reproduced my views as I myself understand them."[3] Second, Barth notes that Küng argues that these opinions "objectively concur on all points with the correctly understood teaching of the Roman Catholic Church."[4] And finally, he reads Küng to have argued that he has misunderstood the Catholic tradition due to an ahistorical reading of the sources. While Barth expresses some wonder at these conclusions, he is certainly hopeful that it might be the case and that there would therefore be hope for increased reconciliation between Catholics and Protestants. Remember, this book was published during the papacy of Pius XII, two years before John XXIII announced his plans for the Second Vatican Council.

Barth's letter provides powerful reason to attend to *Justification* and impressive evidence of Küng's possessing an important ecumenical skill: that of being capable of reading another author, especially one from another ecclesial tradition, with such care that one's description of their thought is recognizable to them. To be able to do it to the level that Barth describes is impressive. It also highlights an ecumenical difficulty to which I will return: the difference between adequately understanding another single author (itself difficult) and speaking normatively for an entire tradition (which is impossible). Unless one is in a position of authority within that community, the best that one can hope to do is to speak in such a way that the majority are convinced.[5] Even when a church speaks in its own name, and with its own authority (as in the *Joint Declaration on the Doctrine of Justification*[6] [JDDJ]), some authors will go to great lengths to argue that these documents are not authoritative.[7]

Several things can be said about *Justification* and the way in which Küng's relationship to Barth frames his ongoing understanding of the ecumenical project. At Barth's funeral, Küng said the following:

> There was a time which needed the *doctor utriusque iuris*, the doctor of both laws. Our time urgently needs

the *doctor utriusque theologiae*, the doctor of both theologies, Protestant and Catholic. And if anyone in our century has offered an outstanding example of this, it was Karl Barth.[8]

Apart from the question of whether Küng is right about Barth, this plaudit provides a definition of what the ecumenical project is for Küng. It is a vocation that he believes his friend to have fulfilled like no one else. While recognizing that Barth provided a challenge to both Protestant and Catholic theologies of his time and, in particular, rejected central traditions of Catholic thought (such as the *analogia entis*),[9] Küng describes Barth as the *doctor utriusque theologiae*, because Barth consistently argued that Protestants also needed to attend to theology prior to 1517, such that it "be permissible to refer to Anselm and Thomas 'without any signs of disgust.'" This, for Küng, was a good enough sign that Barth was possessed of both Catholic breadth and Protestant substance.[10]

Now, it must be noted that this is said in the context of a eulogy, which is not usually where people are at their most systematically precise. Moreover, it is in 1968, a decade before Küng lost his canonical mission, and several decades before his death. It is, therefore, a chancy pathway to choose into Küng's ecumenical thought. But I will argue that it is nonetheless apt, as it points to the personal regard Küng had for his interlocutor, to the role of a particular German-speaking sense of the relationship between Protestant and Catholic Christianity, to the type of role that Küng saw history playing in ecumenical thought, and to an early version of what he thought the tasks of the ecumenical project were (although these would change).

The Background of Ecclesial Structures in the German-Speaking Realm

While Küng's later work attended directly to the importance of the global church, his thought is marked in inescapable ways by the place of his own formation. This is not a critique; it is true of all theologians. As David Turnbloom remarks regarding the goal of the *ressourcement* theologians, "The defining characteristic of true *ressourcement* is maintaining the object of study as a source to be transposed to the present, as a source from which to progressively develop a meaningful theology."[11] If Küng is to be a resource for new generations of theologians, then we must interpret him within his own heritage, even if he himself sought to reach beyond it.

The unique ecclesial inheritance of the so-called German-speaking area (*deutschsprachige Raum*), especially when it is expanded to include the whole of Switzerland, is magnified by the important role that these areas have had in both the ecclesial division of the sixteenth century and in the project of ecumenical theology today. As the birthplace of the sixteenth-century reforms and the location of major events of this reformation, these regions and their theologians have an understandable sense of ownership of both Europe's dogmatic and ecumenical projects. But that history has its own unique circumstances also, including, for example, the union of Protestant churches that took place during the nineteenth century in various German-speaking countries. Without attending to these features, we will misinterpret both historical and contemporary figures in this context. In 1817, for example, the Prussian King Frederick William III ordered the unification of the various Protestant confessions within his domain.[12] While this unification (like others following it) met with strong opposition at the time, it was eventually successful. As Germany was united under Prussian influence in the late nineteenth century, the pattern spread, leading to today's *Evangelische Kirche in Deutschland* (EKD), a pan-Protestant church consisting of twenty independent State Churches (*Landeskirchen*), each of which has a unique religious makeup. Some *Landeskirchen* are members of the *Verein Evangelische-Lutherische Kirchen Deutschlands* (VELKD), a Lutheran organization. Others belong to the *Union Evangelischer Kirchen* (UEK), which describes itself as a "union of uniting, Reformed and Lutheran churches."[13] Some *Landeskirchen* belong to both or are members of one and associated with the other. One *Landeskirche* (Würtemberg) belongs to neither, but is an associate of both.[14] Similarly, the Protestant Church in Switzerland is a union of the twenty-four Reformed Cantonal churches and the United Methodist Church, which includes primarily Zwinglian, Calvinist, and, of course, Methodist emphases. Switzerland also has a small separate Lutheran Church, the *Bund Evangelische-Lutherische Kirchen in der Schweiz und im Fürstentum Liechtenstein* (BELK).[15]

Austria has a similar arrangement to Germany, with an overarching Protestant organization, the *Evangelische Kirche der Augsburgische und Helvetische Bekenntnisses* (EKA.u.H.B), within which there are separate subgroups for Lutherans and Reformed.[16]

Within this complex landscape, "Protestant" has a different valence than it does in other parts of the world. "Protestant" here not only names a kind of general catch-all category, it also names an organizational structure within which various historically divided communions are more or less reconciled. Individual belonging can be somewhat murky, as clergy and faithful shift fairly easily between traditions as they move from one place to another. Küng's own move from Lucerne to Rome and Paris, then to Münster and to Tübingen, brought him from primarily Roman Catholic and Calvinist spaces to a university with both Roman Catholic and Protestant faculty (in a primarily Calvinist area of Germany) to another university with double faculties in an area composed of more of a mix of Lutherans and Calvinists. In both universities, the clear division between Catholic and Protestant faculties was made—without similar divisions being in place among Protestants as might happen elsewhere, as, for example, in the US.

Within this framework, the young Küng's taking Barth as a representative of all Protestants, and the elder Küng naming him as emblematic of "the two theologies" is more sensible.[17] But it also speaks to a particular location for Protestant and Catholic encounter that is not replicated in much of the rest of the world. It leads, perhaps, to the difference between Küng's expansive sense of what *Justification* accomplished and its actual effect on the interecclesial dialogue on justification in the second half of the twentieth century.

This pattern of dissonance between German and global structures of church organization continued to exert a direct effect on the dialogue on justification that can be seen in the history of the JDDJ itself, where the shift from projects of the EKD, represented by *Lehrverurteilungen-Kirchentrennend?*,[18] to the Lutheran World Federation's leadership on the JDDJ led to a number of public protests from Protestant professors who did not feel that the new document adequately reflected their understanding of their tradition.[19]

Hans Küng

Structural Differences and the Ecumenical Project

Ecumenical difference always includes situations in which the structural or habitual patterns of separated communities do not easily map onto each other, making both comparison and dialogue difficult. As an example, we might consider the discussion leading up to the 1999 JDDJ. One of the questions with which the dialogue had to deal, and with which not all parties were satisfied during its reception, was the question of the place of justification within church doctrine. For many Lutherans, the traditional saying that this doctrine was "the article by which the church stands or falls" makes it *the unique criterion* of the church,[20] to which others may not be added. As an example, consider the formal response of the Lutheran Church—Missouri Synod, which writes:

> Lutherans confess that justification is the article that integrates all faith and theology. This centrality of justification is lost in JDDJ. The Vatican insisted on changing a draft of JDDJ that said this article should be seen "as a criterion" which "constantly serves to orient all the teaching and practice of our churches to Christ." The Pontifical Council for Promoting Christian Unity would go no further than to say that "the doctrine of justification is *an* indispensable criterion" [emphasis added]—which is the final wording of JDDJ.[21]

Here, the Catholic Church could not say that justification should be considered "*the* indispensable criterion which constantly serves to orient all the teaching and practice of our churches to Christ" because to say this would make other criteria, such as the Nicene Creed, superfluous. But this seems to be a question of applying a different meaning to the same expression because of history and culture.

Confessional Lutherans also hold the Nicene Creed to be necessary to a true Christian faith. Nor are Catholics unwilling to grant a special place to justification. The intention of the JDDJ in its final form offers a "differentiated consensus" on the question, a consensus accompanied by an explanation for why the different Lutheran and Catholic modes of thought and speech do not undo the consensus reached. The JDDJ continues:

> When Lutherans emphasize the unique significance of this criterion, they do not deny the interrelation and significance of all truths of faith. When Catholics see themselves as bound by several criteria, they do not deny the special function of the message of justification. Lutherans and Catholics share the goal of confessing Christ in all things, who alone is to be trusted above all things as the one mediator (1 Tim 2:5f) through whom God in the Holy Spirit gives himself and pours out his renewing gifts.[22]

These differences in framing mean that oftentimes ecumenical partners disagree more about the questions that need to be answered (here, something like "the uniqueness of justification" versus "the place of justification within Christian dogma") more than they do about the answers. However, five hundred years of division about these questions has sharpened these answers, often misunderstood as the answers to my set of questions, as communal markers of identity. Ecumenical work must always be on the lookout for such situations if it is to find a new way forward.

Another classic example would be the Lutheran sense that Catholics believe that their works save them, while Catholics were trained to think that Protestants did not see growth in holiness as important. Of course, neither of these stereotypes is at all recognizable when viewed against actual communal practice—consider the many texts of the Mass that talk about my unworthiness to receive and Christ's free gift, or the major emphasis put on practices of holiness by so many Lutherans. But the difference in how questions were asked and answered provides ample room for mutual misunderstanding. Differentiated consensus and related forms of ecumenical engagement, including George Lindbeck's proposal for a cultural-linguistic model, offer other understandings of how consensus works. Along with contemporary proposals including receptive ecumenism, they seek to attend to these kinds of difference in a way that need not overcome disunity only through univocity or sameness.[23]

These nonparallels show up in Küng's fundamental design both in *Justification* and in his later works, although he does not generally consider them directly. In *Justification*, he is comparing the thought of a single (important) Protestant thinker to the Catholic tradition writ large. Assuming for a moment that his project were universally acceptable to the exceedingly high bar set by Barth's own reception, what would be the outcome? On the one hand, Barth seems to be convinced that this Catholic teaching is at least possibly acceptable to this particular Protestant thinker and perhaps to those affected by him. And on the other, Catholics might believe that the teaching on justification contained in the *Church Dogmatics* would be acceptable to Catholics. But while this would be a colossal step forward, it would be a step forward on one of several major divisions. Barth, in his "Letter," names "Transubstantiation, the Sacrifice of the Mass, Mary, and the infallible papacy," along with other aspects of the received Catholic faith as inhibiting further agreement or unity.[24] Of course, Küng would write on many of these questions over the years, although with less of a single-minded focus on Barth. But on the Catholic side, other issues predominate in the wake of *Justification*—especially church order and sacramental validity.[25]

The status of the doctrine of justification is itself, in addition to being a clear example of nonparallels between ecclesial theologies, an example of a place where Küng's attachment to Barth led him to believe he has "overcome" the differences between Catholics and Protestants but does so in a way that merely ignores the concerns of many actual Protestants. And so, the discovery of a possible compatibility between Barth and the Roman tradition leads Küng to say of his own work (in the new introduction written for the 1964 edition), "at that time almost twenty-five years ago [i.e., 1957], the foundations were laid for a common Christian understanding of the doctrine of Justification; the fundamental question at issue between the Roman Catholic Church and the Reformation may now be regarded as settled."[26] This opinion was not widely shared, although there was much hope that a settlement on justification was possible. The Lutheran-Catholic dialogues, for example, would conduct several rounds of discussions after 1964 touching on the question. These eventually led to the famous agreement between the Lutheran World Federation and the Roman Catholic Church in 1999.[27] While this agreement would eventually receive approbation from other Protestant groups, including the World Alliance of Reformed Churches, the question of how this document resolves differences between these other groups' traditional language and that of the original Lutheran/Catholic agreement remains open.[28]

During the process leading to the JDDJ, Küng's *Justification* was consulted and engaged (most explicitly in discussions of *simul iustus et peccator* and on the centrality of justification as *articulus stantis vel cadentis ecclesiae*),[29] but because the primary theological dialogue leading to the *Joint Declaration* is between *Lutherans* and *Catholics*, Küng's engagement with Barth is somewhat peripheral to the issues at hand. So, while Küng joins Barth in insisting on a christocentric frame in which justification cannot be the primary criterion of faith, Lutherans in the '70s, '80s, and '90s did not find this argument to be convincing, seeing justification as defining the proper relationship to Christ and not as something secondary.[30]

The Priority of Doctrine or Kerygma

Second, Küng's insistence on the priority of doctrine in ecumenism requires some attention. As George Lindbeck writes, summarizing rather than quoting Karl Rahner, "ultimately, as Rahner has noted in his essay on Küng's book on justification in Barth, the only proof of the compatibility of diverse doctrines is the establishment of communion between the churches that adhere to them."[31] In other words, while Küng can proclaim that Barth's positions are not contradictory to Catholic teaching, and while this position might gain general acceptance among Catholics, what makes a doctrinal difference to be church-dividing or not is not the doctrines themselves, but the communities' reciprocal recognition of each other as churches with all the actions that flow from that recognition. So, for example, the mutual recognition that exists between the Assyrian Church of the East and Roman Catholics is what allowed Pope John Paul II to rule that the Anaphora of Addai and Mari is a valid eucharistic prayer, not a textual analysis of the text itself. Recognition may require doctrinal reconciliation, but it is the actions of the churches that finally determine whether a difference is church-dividing. What may be divisive in one place and time may not be in another. This is a difficult truth for ecumenical theologians to accept, as we cannot and do not control the churches' mutual regard. But finally, if love is more central to Christianity than is faith or hope, then schism, as a sin against love, must be viewed as more damaging even than heresy. Even heresy gives testimony to the centrality of relationship, for only in division does falsehood develop into heresy. If Christian division is to be overcome, the final test will therefore not be doctrine, but relationship: are we willing to love one another and be in communion with one another?

The Role of History and Tradition for Theology

Finally, the role of a developing historical mindset for theology cannot be forgotten. As I have argued, Küng cannot be understood except as a product of this region, both as a child of Switzerland and as a theologian at Tübingen. Even his difficulties with the CDF and with other German-speaking theologians (including Rahner) are related to the questions posed by the frame in which he lived.

Within this frame, perhaps *the* question of European theology in the twentieth century is the question of history, and specifically the history of theological development and of the church as an actor in history. And, within ecumenical thought, this question was only heightened as churches came to grips not only with their own histories but also with the way those histories were both shaped by and contributing to division between Christians, and between Christians and others.

The number of thinkers who have worked on these questions is far too great to name—but the recognition that "historical self-consciousness is very likely the most important revolution among those we have undergone since the beginning of the modern epoch" can now practically be treated as a commonplace.[32] Twentieth-century Catholic thought in particular has focused on questions of interpretation and development and sought to describe how what is true can also be understood as that which develops in history and in culture. But, what exactly this means for Catholic theology has been up for debate. In the wake of Küng's perhaps most famous book, *Infallible? An Inquiry*, among the many debates in which he participated was one with Karl Rahner about the role of history. This was not an amicable disagreement and was one in which both parties felt there to be real stakes. It was, perhaps, made needlessly harsh by Rahner in his initial public response to *Infallible?*, where he wrote that Küng's account of development and truth was far enough afield that "the controversy over Küng's thesis can no longer be regarded on the face of it as an intra-Catholic controversy."[33] Küng and Rahner traded barbs and arguments about the question in several later publications.[34] What is interesting about this debate in the realm of ecumenism is precisely the question of what history is, and therefore what a "historical" theology should be. This is a particularly important question for ecumenical theology, as we need to understand not only what happened in history but also how this context shaped what divided Christians were able to say about themselves and each other.

While Küng can say that he has learned more from Karl Rahner than anyone else about the importance of interpreting dogma historically,[35] in his response he also argues that Rahner is excessively "speculative and unhistorical" in his approach to dogma.[36] What exactly this historicity means is precisely the question, although the two men do not formulate the issue exactly that way in this series of articles. Küng, it seems, ties a truly historically aware dogmatics primarily to the church's beginnings, while Rahner leans more on a notion of development that sees historically aware theology as conscious participation in a process in fidelity to Jesus toward the kingdom, rather than as primarily looking backward to the first-century Levant.[37] This is more starkly stated as a difference here than either thinker would probably allow, but it illuminates a real distinction in their thought, and one that is important to understanding their very different approaches to the ecumenical task.

Throughout his works, Küng calls the churches *back to* unity in terms of fidelity to an original *kerygma*, or more often in service to the Christ of history, whom Küng always holds up as the criterion of faith. He explicitly names his reform project as a radical one, in the sense of "returning to the roots" in his 1994 *Christianity: Essence, History, and Future*, and ties this to overcoming the scandal of ecumenical division:

> But if Christianity is again to become more Christian, conversion will be necessary: a radical reform which is more than the psychologizing or remythologizing of Christianity. A reform is radical, it "goes to the roots," only if it brings something essential to light again. But what is this essence of Christianity? Here one cannot just appeal to religious experiences and dispense with all thinking. Every possible means must be used to investigate the question: what holds together all these Christian churches, so varied and intrinsically different, all these Christian centuries which differ so much? Is there—despite all the abuses and violations—something like a recognizable essence of Christianity on which one can reflect in the different churches?[38]

Küng then points to the scriptures as *norma normans sed non normata*,[39] and to fidelity to Christ as the measure of this faith. There is nothing, on the face of it, wrong with these—indeed, they should be uncontroversial among Christians—but just what each claim means and how it is applied is precisely the question. Within this structure, Küng repeatedly stresses the difference between the church and the reign of God, in which that promised *basileia* is something in the future for which the church hopes.[40] Here, to say that scripture is historical is understood best as relating to the church's imperfection, its continual falling away from its original gift and calling. Within this schema, the ecumenical call is in a sense *backward* toward the origins of the church, but also forward, as it is something that will be made perfect only in the future as a pure gift of God.

On the other hand, while Rahner also points to the Gospel and to Christ as *norma normans*, he is clearly usually pointing to the eschatological Christ in whom the churches will find the unity that they have lost in history. As one example, consider this paragraph, which Rahner wrote in 1974:

> If and insofar as there are also legitimate ministries and valid sacraments "outside of" the Catholic Church, they are not coopted by this concrete church, but it is instead said that these offices and sacraments are historical-ecclesiastical embodiments of the Spirit and have an inner

ordering from this Spirit toward the church, according to the Catholic understanding of the church as the "full" embodiment of this Spirit. Wherever it blows, it creates ecclesiality. Even if it is now still scattered, it is directed toward that full unity toward which all ecclesiality is aligned and moves. If the Protestant Christian and theologian is convinced of the importance of this yet-to-be achieved unitary church, and also recognizes valid ministry and right sacramental administration, and does not see in it merely a "synagogue of Satan," then he cannot think otherwise in the last word about this scattered ecclesiastical tradition, even though he thinks that in this unified church, these ecclesiastical structures need not be given a Petrine and episcopal structure, as they must according to Catholic ways of thinking.[41]

Here, to say that doctrine is historical is to say that it exists in history *as part of the movement of the Spirit toward the eschaton*. That does not mean that history is perfect, or even good. The pattern of human fragility is clear. But it means that the ecumenical call is *forward*, that is, in development toward the eschaton, where the unity of the church will be perfect.

This mirrors a pattern of difference between traditional Catholic and Protestant concerns about justification. Some Protestant thinkers see justification as a kind of new creation, a return to the primordial order of the Garden, or to humanity as *it should have been* had the fall not taken place.[42] However, Catholic theologians have generally worried that in such a scheme, that which is saved is not us. If God is to save human sinners who are recognizably themselves, there must be some redemption of their actual history in continuity with the life they lived.[43]

Within ecumenical circles, this difference is important. Küng's model is in many ways that of the early twentieth-century ecumenical movement, especially as it was practiced among Protestants. At the time, the primary model was multilateral, with attempts to overcome Christian disunity with the formation of single "union" churches. Some of these churches were formed, most notably in India, including both historically episcopal and nonepiscopal groups with structures not dissimilar to the nineteenth-century unions made in the German-speaking lands discussed above.⁴⁴ These union churches were often looking for a Christian essence around which they could gather that would allow some diversity within community. The detractors of these models call them "least-common-denominator" ecumenism, and because these models often see difference and historical development as a barrier to union, it has not been the primary model of union in recent years. However, it did produce many of the structural unions between churches that have actually occurred.

Over the course of the twentieth century, the primary model of ecumenical engagement has shifted to the bilateral dialogue in which two particular communions discuss questions pertaining to their relationship, whether that be theological, moral, or practical. Within these dialogues, the emergence of "differentiated consensus" or other descriptors of consensus that allow for difference have been central to ecumenical process, while always remaining controversial.⁴⁵

Alongside this, a commitment to models of union that do not require understanding unity as being a kind of "return" to a prior church (whichever church may play that role) has led to a growing sense that the history of division cannot be, and perhaps should not be, undone, but rather redeemed. The unity toward which Christ calls the church, therefore, might look something like the relationship between Orthodox churches, or like that between the Roman Catholic Church and the various Eastern Catholic Churches, or like the Evangelical Lutheran Church in America and the Episcopal Church in the USA, in which each recognizes the other as being church and this communion is signified in intercommunion, some (controlled) exchange of ministers, and remembrance of the other's leaders in the Eucharistic prayer. These models of redemption, rather than return, have tended to produce models of union in which churches come into communion without losing their distinctiveness. Or, as in the *Joint Declaration*, descriptions of "differentiated consensus" in which the actual and historically developed differences are recognized as not requiring a break in communion and that leave room for the differentiated churches to come into communion as different churches that maintain their histories.⁴⁶

One of the things that this means, however, is that the earlier vision of a unified global theology that is ecumenical in itself (and that Küng often called theologians to seek) will be replaced by a chorus of voices, each coming into harmony. This will have to go well beyond the broad categories of "Catholic, Orthodox, Protestant" that we find, for example, in *Christianity*. The sheer multiplicity of Christian communions, often bemoaned by Catholics in the past, comes to be seen as a divine gift, and one in which more differentiations, including, for example, the distinctive contributions of Black Catholic theologians, Black Protestant theologians, Latinx theology and Queer theology, German theology, Polish Catholic and Lutheran theologies, and Nigerian Anglican and Catholic theologies in all their glorious variations can *add* to the vision of the gospel that has been gifted to them in their unique situation. And each will receive the questions, challenges, and critiques of the others, hopefully in a situation in which truly receptive ecumenism can occur.[47] No one person can, in such a system, write an ecumenical theology, although everyone, writing from their own tradition, should be writing theology that is for the sake of—and in dialogue with—the *oikoumene*.

Ecumenism and Interfaith Dialogue

As a final note, it is important to engage briefly with Küng's regular and repeated call that ecumenical work remember the need for interfaith engagement. This is found throughout his later work and is particularly notable in *Christianity*, where he calls Christian reformers to deal with the questions their work might pose particularly for Jews and Muslims. This is important, but to avoid replicating the focus of another chapter in this volume, I will say only that while ecumenical work must be *aware* of the interfaith impact of its work, we must keep the two tasks formally and clearly separated. They have entirely different goals. While ecumenical work seeks the union of the churches (in diversity), interfaith work seeks understanding, but does not attempt to unite the religions. Keeping these goals separate, without forgetting that the work of each will necessarily be cognizant of the progress of the other, will allow each to approach its own goals. Here we see a yet bigger field in which, if we are not careful, the twentieth-century modern desire for global unity can lead to uniformity rather than unity.

Hans Küng

Conclusion

Hans Küng's contribution to the ecumenical movement should not be undervalued. He kept focus on ecumenical questions throughout his career. Especially toward the end of his life he edited a number of volumes, primarily in *Concilium*, on ecumenical topics. These brought major, primarily Continental, thinkers together to consider major ecumenical questions.[48] These volumes contributed to the ongoing development of ecumenical thought, as did Küng's own works beginning with his dissertation. While some of his contributions can be seen to have not been as comprehensive or decisive as he sometimes hoped or proclaimed, his attention to particularly Barthian Calvinist thought is a real achievement, as is his willingness to call his fellow Catholics to do theology with more attention to the thought of other Christians. May his hopes for Christian unity be fulfilled.

Notes

1. See, for example, the chapter "Not an Epilogue," in Hans Küng, *Christianity: Essence, History, and Future*, trans. John Bowden (New York: Continuum, 2000), 792–96.

2. Hans Küng, *Rechtfertigung. Die Lehre Karl Barths und eine katholische Besinnung* (Einsiedeln: Johannes, 1957). Citations from Küng, *Justification: The Doctrine of Karl Barth and a Catholic Reflection*, trans. Thomas Collins, Edmund E. Tolk, and David Granskou (Philadelphia: Westminster, 1964).

3. Karl Barth, "Letter to the Author," in Küng, *Justification*, xxxix.

4. Barth, "Letter to the Author," xxxix.

5. It is clear that *Justification* reaches this milestone. As Karl Rahner comments, "Küng's presentation is Catholic. Not in the sense that everything it says is defined or universal doctrine, but in the sense that none of it is in contradiction to any doctrine of the magisterium. More one cannot ask." (Rahner, "Questions of Controversial Theology on *Justification*," *Theological Investigations* [Baltimore: Helicon, 1966], 4:189).

6. Lutheran World Federation and the Roman Catholic Church, *Joint Declaration on the Doctrine of Justification, 20th Anniversary Edition* (Geneva: Lutheran World Federation, 2019); https://www.lutheranworld.org/sites/default/files/2022-02/joint_declaration_2019_en.pdf.

7. For an example of this, see Christopher Malloy, *Engrafted into Christ: A Critique of the Joint Declaration* (Frankfurt: Peter Lang, 2005), 4–8. For my response to this argument, see my *Mapping the Differentiated Consensus of the Joint Declaration* (New York: Palgrave, 2016), 35–37.

8. Hans Küng, "Tribute to Karl Barth," *Journal of Ecumenical Studies* 6, no. 2 (Spring 1969): 233.

9. Küng, "Tribute to Karl Barth," 235; *Church Dogmatics* I.

10. Küng, "Tribute to Karl Barth," 235; *Church Dogmatics* I.

11. David Turnbloom, *Speaking with Aquinas: A Conversation about Grace, Virtue, and the Eucharist* (Collegeville, MN: Liturgical Press, 2017), xxix.

12. See Henry Renaud Turner Brandreth, "Approaches of the Churches toward Each Other in the Nineteenth Century," in *A History of the Ecumenical Movement, 1517–1948*, 2nd ed., ed. Ruth Rouse and Stephen Charles Neill (Philadelphia: Westminster Press, 1968), 286–90.

13. https://www.uek-online.de/.

14. https://www.ekd.de/evangelische-kirche-in-deutschland-14272.htm.

15. https://luther-schweiz.org/.

16. https://evang.at/kirche/wir-ueber-uns/.

17. Another example of Küng's prioritization of Calvin over Luther is the titling of his sections on them in his book *Christianity*: "The Problematical Results of the Lutheran Reformation" (C.IV.5) and "The Consistent Reformation: 'Reformed' Protestantism" (C.IV.6). Küng, *Christianity: Essence, History, and Future*.

18. Karl Lehmann and Wolfhart Pannenberg, eds., *Lehrverurteilungen–Kirchentrennend?: Rechtfertigung, Sakramente, und Amt in Zeitalter der Reformation und Heute* (Freiburg im Breisgau: Herder, 1986).

19. See Protestant Professors of Theology, "Kein Konsens in der Gemeinsamen Erklärung," *Frankfurter Allgemeine Zeitung* (January 29, 1998), Politik 4, and "Stellungsnahme theologischer

Hochschullehrer zur geplanten Unterzeichnung der Gemeinsamen Offiziellen Feststellung zur Rechtfertigungslehre," *Frankfurter Allgemeine Zeitung* (September 25, 1999): 67. A fuller description of the controversy can be found in Pieter de Witte, *Doctrine, Dynamic, and Difference: To the Heart of the Lutheran–Roman Catholic Differentiated Consensus on Justification* (New York: T & T Clark, 2012) and Rinderknecht, *Mapping the Differentiated Consensus of the Joint Declaration*, 11–38.

20. On this, see especially section 4.5 in Joint Evangelical Lutheran–Roman Catholic Commission, "Church and Justification, 1993"; http://www.christianunity.va/content/unitacristiani/en/dialoghi/sezione-occidentale/luterani/dialogo/documenti-di-dialogo/1993-church-and-justification.html; Michael Root, "Continuing the Conversation: Deeper Agreement on Justification as Criterion and on the Christian as *simul justus et peccator*," in *The Gospel of Justification in Christ: Where Does the Church Stand Today?*, ed. Wayne C. Stumme (Grand Rapids: Eerdmans, 2006), 42–61. For discussion of this question in the JDDJ, see my *Mapping the Differentiated Consensus*, 30–35 and 183–86.

21. Lutheran Church–Missouri Synod, *The Joint Declaration on the Doctrine of Justification in Confessional Lutheran Perspective*, Summary, §8; http://www.ctsfw.net/media/pdfs/CTSFWJointDeclarationontheDoctrineofJustification.pdf.

22. JDDJ §18.

23. See, for example, Anthony Godzieba, "'...And Followed Him on the Way' (Mk 10:52): Identity, Difference, and the Play of Discipleship," *CTSA Proceedings* 69 (2014): 1–22; Minna Hietamäki, *Agreeable Agreement: An Examination of the Quest for Consensus in Ecumenical Dialogue*, Ecclesiological Investigations 8 (New York: T & T Clark, 2010); George Lindbeck, *The Nature of Doctrine: Religion and Theology in a Postliberal Age* (Louisville, KY: Westminster John Knox, 1984); Harding Meyer, *Versöhnte Verschiedenheit: Aufsätze zur ökumenischen Theologie*, 3 vols. (Frankfurt/M: Otto Lembeck, 1998–2009); Wolfgang Thönissen, *Dogma und Symbol: eine ökumenische Hermeneutik* (Freiburg im Breisgau: Herder, 2008).

24. Barth, "Letter to the Author," xxxix.

25. On this question, see especially Congregation for the Doctrine of the Faith, Responsa "Responses to Some Questions Regarding Certain Aspects of the Doctrine on the Church," June 29,

2007; https://www.vatican.va/roman_curia/congregations/cfaith/documents/rc_con_cfaith_doc_20070629_responsa-quaestiones_en.html. In the wake of the JDDJ, much of Catholic attention has turned to the question of ecclesiality, although direct attention to the validity of orders has received less attention, perhaps because of the political difficulty of attending to the question of the ordination of women as presbyters and bishops.

26. Hans Küng, "Justification Today: An Introductory Chapter to the New Edition," in *Justification*, ix.

27. Justification is specifically dealt with in many of the dialogue documents, most importantly: Joint Lutheran–Roman Catholic Study Commission, "The Gospel and the Church" (1972); http://www.christianunity.va/content/unitacristiani/en/dialoghi/sezione-occidentale/luterani/dialogo/documenti-di-dialogo/en4.html; Roman Catholic/Lutheran Joint Commission, "All Under One Christ" (1980); http://www.christianunity.va/content/unitacristiani/en/dialoghi/sezione-occidentale/luterani/dialogo/documenti-di-dialogo/en12.html; Roman Catholic/Lutheran Joint Commission, "The Ministry in the Church (1981); http://www.christianunity.va/content/unitacristiani/en/dialoghi/sezione-occidentale/luterani/dialogo/documenti-di-dialogo/en6.html; American Lutheran/Catholic Dialogue, *Justification by Faith*, ed. H. George Anderson, T. Austin Murphy, and Joseph A. Burgess (Minneapolis: Augsburg, 1985); *Ökumenischer Arbeitskreis evangelischer und katholischer Theologen, Lehrverurteilungen–kirchentrennend?*, ed. K. Lehmann and W. Pannenberg, 5 vols. (Freiburg: Herder, 1986–1994); Arnoldshainer Konferenz, *Lehrverurteilungen im Gespräch* (Göttingen: Vandenhoeck & Ruprecht, 1992); Lutheran/Roman Catholic International Dialogue, "Church and Justification" (1993); http://www.christianunity.va/content/unitacristiani/en/dialoghi/sezione-occidentale/luterani/dialogo/documenti-di-dialogo/1993-church-and-justification.html; and Lutheran World Federation and the Roman Catholic Church, *Joint Declaration on the Doctrine of Justification*.

28. On this, specifically for the JDDJ, see my "Receiving the Joint Declaration: A Test-Case in Bilateral and Multilateral Engagement," *Ecumenical Trends* 49, no. 3 (May–June 2020): 11–15, 26.

29. "The article by which the church stands or falls" is a commonplace among Protestant thinkers for referring to justification.

See, for example, U.S. Lutheran Catholic Dialogue VII, *Justification by Faith* (Minneapolis: Augsburg, 1985).

30. See Robert W. Bertram, "Recent Lutheran Theologies on Justification by Faith: A Sampling," in *Justification by Faith*, 241–55.

31. George Lindbeck, "A Question of Compatibility: A Lutheran Reflects on Trent," in *Lutherans and Catholics in Dialogue VII: Justification by Faith*, 231. Here he footnotes Rahner's essay "Questions of Controversial Theology on Justification," in *Theological Investigations* 4:189–218.

32. Hans-Georg Gadamer, "The Problem of Historical Consciousness," *Graduate Faculty Philosophy Journal* 5, no. 1. H.-G. Gadamer Special Issue (1975): 8.

33. "Die Kontroverse über Küngs These kann man von der Sache her nicht mehr als eine inner-katholische theologische Kontroverse betrachten," K. Rahner, "Kritik an Hans Küng: Zur Frage der Unfehlbarkeit theologischer Sätze," *Stimmen der Zeit* 186, no. 12 (December 1970): 365.

34. For Kung's response see Küng, "Im Interesse der Sache: Antwort an Karl Rahner," *Stimmen der Zeit* 187, no. 1 (January 1971): 43–64; and *Stimmen der Zeit* 187, no. 2 (February 1971): 105–22. Rahner replied in "Replik. Bemerkungen zu: Hans Küng, Im Interesse der Sache," *Stimmen der Zeit* 187 no. 3 (March 1971): 145–60 and again in his *Vorfragen zu einem ökumenischen Amtsverständnis*, available in English as *K. Rahner, An Ecumenical Priesthood: The Spirit of God and the Structure of the Church*, trans. and ed. J. K. Rinderknecht (Minneapolis: Fortress, 2022), 3. For a good overview of the argument there, see J. J. Hughes, "*Infallible? An Inquiry* Considered," *Theological Studies* 32, no. 2 (1971): 183–207.

35. Küng, "Im Interesse, I," 43.

36. Küng, "Im Interesse, II," 113.

37. There is a second primary difference demonstrated in this debate regarding the role of theological "sentences" (Sätzen), both in terms of what it would mean for them to be infallible or to be in error, and in terms of whether there is room for the kind of sophisticated differentiation among kinds of church teaching within the "school theology" of the time. But that is beyond the scope of this chapter.

38. Küng, *Christianity: Essence, History, and Future*, xxii–xxiii. Emphasis original.

39. That is, "The norm that norms, but which is not itself normed," a slogan of Protestant theology regarding the role of scripture, as opposed, for example, to the creeds, which are norms that are themselves normed by scripture.

40. See, for example, Küng, *The Church* (Garden City, NY: Image Books, 1976), 131: "While ekklesia is something essentially in the present, something finite, basileia is something which, although it has irrupted into the present, belongs fundamentally to the future. Ekklesia is a pilgrimage through the interim period of last days, something provisional; basileia is the final glory at the end of all time, something definitive. Ekklesia embraces sinners and righteous, basileia is the kingdom of the righteous, of the saints. Ekklesia grows from below, can be organized, is the product of development and progress and dialectic, in short is definitely the work of man; basileia comes from above, is an unprepared action, an incalculable event, in short is definitely the work of God. God is the subject of this reign, he himself as the Lord and Father acting in kingly freedom and sovereignty. The reign of God is his kingly dignity, his act and his domain."

Notice how this description emphasizes the difference, even the separation, between the two, whereas, for example, a more Rahnerian description, or that of *Lumen Gentium*, while still noting the distinction, sees them as existing more as *sacramentum et res*, as interpenetrating realities in which the final is present in history, as work of both God and human.

41. Rahner, *An Ecumenical Priesthood*, 77.

42. See, for example, Gerhard Forde, *Justification by Faith: A Matter of Death and Life* (Minneapolis: Fortress Press, 1982). For a Lutheran counterargument, see David S. Yeago, "Lutherans and the Historic Episcopate: Theological Impasse and Ecclesial Future," *Lutheran Forum* 26, no. 4 (1992): 36–45.

43. On this question, see my *Mapping the Differentiated Consensus of the Joint Declaration*, esp. 232–45.

44. See Stephen Charles Neill, "Plans of Union and Reunion, 1910–1948," in *A History of the Ecumenical Movement, 1517–1948*, 445–95.

45. For an excellent overview, see Minna Hietamäki, *Agreeable Agreement: An Examination of the Quest for Consensus in Ecumenical Dialogue* (New York: T & T Clark, 2010).

46. There is more work to be done on this question, but it may be that the difference between the two is not a question of "redemption" insofar as all would recognize that unity will be God's gift to the church. It may be that the difference is between a two-pole—Sin–Redemption—versus a three-pole—Progress–Decline–Redemption—as in Bernard Lonergan. See Lonergan, "The Human Good as Object; Differentials and Integration," in *Collected Works of Bernard Lonergan*, vol. 10: *Topics in Education*, ed. Robert M. Doran and Frederick E. Crowe (Toronto: University of Toronto Press, 1993), 49–78. If this is the case, the question at stake would be whether there are authentic developments in the various churches that will be maintained (or themselves developed) in the various churches that are in final communion of the One Church of Christ. It might also potentially mirror the shift that took place in the invention of the Theorem of the Supernatural.

47. See here Margaret O'Gara, *The Ecumenical Gift Exchange* (Collegeville, MN: Liturgical Press, 1998); Paul D. Murray, ed., *Receptive Ecumenism and the Call to Catholic Learning: Exploring a Way for Contemporary Ecumenism* (Oxford: Oxford University Press, 2008); Paul D. Murray, ed. *Receptive Ecumenism as Transformative Ecclesial Learning: Walking the Way to a Church Re-formed* (Oxford: Oxford University Press, 2020).

48. Notable examples include Hans Küng, ed., *Apostolic Succession—Rethinking a Barrier to Unity* (New York: Paulist Press, 1969); Küng, *The Future of Ecumenism* (New York: Paulist Press, 1969); Küng, *Post-ecumenical Christianity* (London: Burns & Oates, 1970); and Hans Küng and Walter Kasper, eds., *Polarization in the Church* (New York: Herder & Herder, 1973); Hans Küng and Jürgen Moltmann, eds., *An Ecumenical Confession of Faith* (New York: Seabury, 1979); Hans Küng, ed., *Conflicts about the Holy Spirit* (New York: Seabury, 1979); Küng, *Fundamentalism as an Ecumenical Challenge* (New York: SCM Press, 1996).

8

HANS KÜNG'S GLOBAL ETHICS PROJECT

A Revaluation

Hille Haker

Introduction

Between the summer and the autumn of 1989, the Iron Curtain was slowly lifted and the Cold War ended with the collapse of the Berlin Wall on November 9, 1989. The border that cut through Europe, separating families, countries, and political systems, had been the symbol of the postwar order: neither war nor peace. It separated the West from the East, capitalist democracies from socialist regimes and dictatorships, and societies that integrated and embraced religion from politically imposed atheism.

In theological circles, the Swiss Catholic priest Hans Küng had been a well-known figure since the Second Vatican Council in the 1960s. Because he had lived in Rome for seven years, from 1948 to 1955, he knew the Vatican like few others did, and his critique of the church originated as much from his intimate knowledge of the inner workings of the Curia as from his own convictions as a systematic theologian. For most of his adult life, however, Küng had lived in Germany, teaching as professor of dogmatics in Tübingen since

1960. Together with some other scholars, Küng founded the journal *Concilium*—a global theological endeavor to accompany the reform of the church in form of a public theology journal translated into six languages. Until 1979, when he lost the *missio canonica* and could no longer teach at the Theological Faculty of Tübingen, Küng's work centered on dogmatic issues: he could explain what religion might mean, what Christianity is about, how the church ought to be reformed, how one can be Catholic without declaring other denominations or other faith traditions to be truthful, without using too much theological jargon. Küng also never stopped encouraging all Christians to encounter modern life, to claim their rights within the church, and to think as well as meet people of non-Christian religious traditions with open eyes. Finally, he saw himself as a public intellectual who eagerly engaged in the social and political realities of his time. Küng certainly cherished his Swiss nationality and the country's natural beauty, its economic pride, and its political prudence. But living and working in Germany, he wholeheartedly embraced the European Union. And, as much as he loved the rich and pluralistic religious history of Europe, he loved the freedom he had as a citizen of the western part of Europe. The freedom to travel, in particular, which was denied to millions of Eastern Europeans, allowed Küng to visit whatever country he liked, and from the 1970s onward, he traveled to almost every country in the world, including Eastern European countries and Russia. On these trips, he encountered the global diversity of religions and cultures in and beyond Europe. Recognized as a gifted speaker and "church reformer," he insisted that freedom is a right that comes with responsibilities, applicable to the right to religious freedom as well as any other human right.

After 1980, the direction of Küng's theological research changed considerably. He turned his attention to ecumenical issues within the church. At the newly established Ecumenical Institute, he hosted projects on feminist theology and began to engage in interreligious dialogue. As he had done in his struggles with the Catholic Church, he now insisted on taking the ecumenic endeavor more seriously. He never accepted arbitrary boundaries, not those between priests and laity, Catholicism and Protestantism, Catholic doctrine and Orthodox Christianity, or between Christianity and all other religions. Instead, the differences sparked his curiosity, challenging him to explain and to reckon with the foundations of the Catholic and Christian faith. His open-mindedness and humor were legendary. In his autobiography, Küng recalls the difficulties he encountered in engaging with theologians from Eastern Europe during the Cold War.[1] Küng loved the Orthodox tradition, and a symbol of the paradigm shift he saw in the "fall of the Berlin wall" was the concelebrated Eucharist with the Orthodox Patriarch in Moscow's Cathedral in 1991, while at his first visit to Moscow in 1971 it had still been a museum. In Eastern Europe, religion had never disappeared, it had merely been repressed.[2]

1989 became a watershed moment in many respects, not only globally, transnationally for Europe, and nationally for Germany but also for the direction of Küng's own work. For Europeans, 1989–90 was the beginning of the reordering of their social identity as Europeans—the European Union quickly embraced new member states from the East (though it hesitated to create a pathway for Turkey), broadening the free trade and labor market considerably. Beginning in 1990, globalization became a hotly discussed issue especially in the West, but also at the United Nations. Academically, identity questions were newly debated as multiculturalism and cultural diversity. This was the environment in which the Global Ethic Project emerged.

The Global Ethic Project

THE ORIGINS OF THE GLOBAL ETHIC PROJECT[3]

In February 1989, nobody expected the year to end as it did, and Küng was certainly not thinking of participating in a new global balancing act between the superpowers when he gave a lecture at a UNESCO meeting in Paris. The colloquium was based on his book on Christianity and world religions, and it would not have been so noteworthy had it not become so important in retrospect. Küng's lecture was titled "No Peace among the Nations without Peace among the Religions," a topic that would later serve as one of the principles of the Global Ethic Project. Coincidentally, at the time of the Velvet Revolution (as some of the nonviolent protests that led to the collapse of the USSR were later known), Küng was in

Hans Küng's Global Ethics Project

the Netherlands, speaking in Amsterdam, Nijmegen, and Tilburg—coincidentally, because the Dutch theologian Erasmus of Rotterdam, humanist and church reformer, had long been a role model for Küng's own modernist and humanist theology. In the fall semester of 1989–90, Küng held a seminar on the topic: "Does a common ethos exist among the religions?"[4] Then, in spring 1990, Küng spoke at the World Economic Forum in Davos on the topic "Why do we need global ethical standards to survive?" Later, he would state that he had always envisioned the "global ethic" as a common basic morality for all humans, religious or nonreligious. But in the beginning, a global ethic was clearly situated in his own explorations of ecumenical theology and interfaith dialogue. For both endeavors, Küng wanted to provide criteria to circumvent two pitfalls: the threat of supremacy of one religion (or culture) over others, and the threat of relativism that dismissed the possibility of making truth claims at all. He began a research project on the three Abrahamic world religions, and this work, too, oriented the Global Ethic Project. The UNESCO paper, the Davos paper, and the developing thoughts on the commonalities among religions became part of the first book on the Global Ethic Project, published in 1990.[5]

In 1990, a friend and colleague in the United States, Leonard Swidler, professor of religious studies and editor of the *Journal of Ecumenical Studies*, asked Hans Küng to co-draft a declaration of Global Ethic.[6] This was published as an "appeal" and signed, among others, by the two Catholic ethics professors of the Tübingen Faculty of Theology, as well as by several non-Christian scholars of international reputation.[7] Küng was then asked to draft a Declaration for the Parliament of the World's Religions, which adopted it at its meeting in Chicago in 1993. This Declaration, correctly called Küng's because there was almost no discussion of the text among the delegates, embraced the United Nations framework of human rights, made the other side of rights, namely, human responsibilities, more explicit, and tied it to the moral visions of religions. The Global Ethic Project in Tübingen took clearer shape now, too, aiming at providing a minimal value consensus to orient people and peoples in the transformation of the global political and economic order. Funded by the Karl Schlecht Foundation, Küng could establish the project as a larger endeavor, and it was finally transformed into a foundation in 2012.

Beyond these external events, there is, however, also a genuinely theological origin of the Global Ethic Project. If the humanism of Erasmus of Rotterdam may have served Küng as a model for the internal reforms of the Catholic Church, Gotthold Ephraim Lessing's understanding of tolerance among the world religions and, as Küng argued, his vision of reconciliation between the religions, could serve as a model for the Global Ethic Project. Lessing's famous ring parable, embedded in his play *Nathan the Wise*, envisioned the peaceful cohabitation of the religions in their common goal to seek the truth of their respective religions. For Lessing, this truth was not about doctrinal questions but would manifest itself in the practice of love. Thus, this Enlightenment thinker paved the way for the priority of orthopraxis over orthodoxy, and at the same time, he showed how religions could be newly interpreted without sacrificing reason.[8] Küng follows Lessing insofar as he rejects any preordained claim of superiority of one religion, but he insists on the central role of religion for the foundation of morality.[9]

THE CONCEPT OF A GLOBAL ETHIC

Küng envisioned a global ethic primarily as an ethical project, complementing the human rights approach with a value-based ethic. In German, global ethics is called *Weltethos*. Aristotle's *Nicomachean Ethics* introduces the two Greek terms of *ethos* that have informed the theory of ethics: on the one hand, actions that become habitual shape a person's character (ἦθος).[10] Morality in this sense can be learned and perfected, and a person's moral identity is shaped in a continuous, reflective, and practical formation (Nietzsche, Freud, and Foucault would call it "disciplining") and self-formation process. Second, however, ethos (ἔθος) is the environment in which habits (or virtues) are formed, and they entail not only the organization of the polis but also a moral culture with its embedded values. Aristotle points to the traditions and customs of a polis, countered in modern moral philosophy by Kant's focus on *autonomy* as the capability to determine for oneself the moral norms. Küng's use of the term *ethos* was technical and decidedly Aristotelian. Furthermore, Küng may have been inspired by the concept of the overlapping consensus, introduced by John Rawls in his *Theory of Justice*, although he does not refer to Rawls in his interpretations.[11] Rather, Küng followed his own intuitions, informed by the interreligious dialogue he envisioned (and had experienced): the basic global ethic was not to be exclusively a religious ethic, but it was also not meant to replace the religious moral tradition with a secular ethics. The Global Ethic Project aimed at developing a value-based, interreligious and intercultural ethic, reaching out to all people in good faith to gather around the basic values that make a peaceful cohabitation of the world possible. The Global Ethic built upon four major theses that reveal Küng's background as an ecumenical theologian:

1. No peace among nations without peace among religions.
2. No peace among the religions without dialogue among them.
3. No dialogue among religions without some global ethical standards.
4. No survival of the earth without a global ethic, connecting religious and nonreligious people.

Like Rawls, Küng is certain that there is some basic traditional ethos (ἔθος) that can be found in multiple cultures throughout human history. But at the same time, it comes with a normative outlook that is embodied and/or must be fostered as a particular attitude or habitus (ἦθος). Both dimensions are summarized in the Golden Rule that can be found in multiple religions. Küng therefore insists: the Global Ethic Project is not a Western project but a general, consensual starting point for dialogue under the conditions of globalization. Therefore, peace that rests upon dialogue first requires the recognition of plurality and diversity of worldviews between and among religions and cultures as well as the commonalities.

For the 1993 *Chicago Declaration of the Parliament of World's Religions*, naturally, the role of religion is highlighted:

> We are persons who have committed ourselves to the precepts and practices of the world's religions. We confirm that there is already a consensus among the religions which can be the basis for a global ethic—a minimal fundamental consensus concerning binding values, irrevocable standards, and fundamental moral attitudes.[12]

Given the resistance of several religions, not least Christianity and Catholicism in particular, it was no small thing to declare that human beings have dignity, are subjects of rights, and all "possess reason" and therefore moral agency:

> every human being without distinction of age, sex, race, skin color, physical or mental ability, language, religion, political view, or national or social origin possesses an inalienable and untouchable dignity and everyone, the individual as well as the state, is therefore obliged to honor this dignity and protect it. Humans must always be the subjects of rights, must be ends, never mere means, never objects of commercialization and industrialization in economics, politics and media, in research institutes, and industrial corporations....Possessed of reason and conscience, every human is obliged to behave in a genuinely human fashion, to do good and avoid evil![13]

With this precondition of morality as part of the human condition, the Declaration formulates three principles that serve as guides for the further elaboration of a new ethos:

> Principle 1: No New Global Order without a New Global Ethic!
>   This principle responds to the paradigm shift that Küng and others sensed was taking place, changing the global order from the age of colonization to an age of global responsibility to fight for the survival of the planet. The cultural and economic globalization is at risk of entering into a new phase of reification, exploitation, and ecological destruction. It therefore requires all cultures—and the religions—to revisit their traditional approaches of what it means under these conditions to be moral agents, that is, "do good and avoid evil." Echoing Hans Jonas's *Principle of Responsibility*, the new global ethic is formulated as an ethics of responsibilities.[14]
> Principle 2: We Express a Fundamental Demand: Every Human Being Must Be Treated Humanely.
>   The second principle echoes the preamble of the *Universal Declaration of Human Rights*, emphasizing

that human dignity must be spelled out in terms of "humaneness." The global ethics is an ethics of human dignity and human rights that centers on the individual person as a moral agent, in the tradition of Immanuel Kant's categorical imperative.[15]

Principle 3: We Commit to a Set of Irrevocable Directives.

The third principle declares a commitment to the normative dimension of morality, thus emphasizing that moral cultures, though rooted in factual customs, come with moral claims that require the development of moral values. Pointing to this dimension of morality therefore does not merely repeat what is captured in the human rights framework but rather highlights the connection between commitment and normative rules. Turned into a minimal consensus concept of global values, global ethic entails a culture of nonviolence and respect for life, a culture of solidarity and a just economic order, a culture of tolerance and a life of truthfulness, a culture of equal rights and partnership between men and women, and a culture of sustainability and care for the earth.[16]

THE RECEPTION OF THE GLOBAL ETHIC PROJECT

It is not the place or task of a Declaration to reason about the underlying theoretical framework. Thus, the Parliament of World Religions' Declaration was meant to bring together multiple people and groups under an umbrella concept with an ethical outlook, guiding future people in the commitment to interreligious and intercultural dialogue. The delegates of the Chicago Convention inserted the word *toward* in the Declaration, alluding to the fact that much work needed to be done—which had not happened in the preparation for the meeting.[17] Yet, after 1993, "global ethic" became almost a trademark term, countering Huntington's "clash of civilization" rhetoric at a time when multiculturalism became the symbolic term for major social transformations.[18] The importance of the Global Ethic Project was clearly seen by Kofi Annan, then Secretary-General of the United Nations. In a short time, the Global Ethic became a household name for different international programs at the U.N., be it Annan's Building Bridges initiative, Our Global Neighborhood Initiative, or the Commission on Global Governance.[19] The Global Ethic Project has been the subject of countless lectures and conferences, it has been introduced in a television documentary, it offers an exhibit that can be loaned, and it has developed teaching material about the world religions and their ethical underpinning (ethos) that can be used in German religious education classes at high schools.[20] Over the last decades—and perhaps in part due to the funding by the Schlecht Foundation—the Global Ethic Institute has more and more turned to economic issues, integrating global economy into its program of interreligious and intercultural dialogue. With its more recent status as a foundation and its integration into the University of Tübingen, its long-term establishment is secured. Ironically, Küng has left an institutional footprint that goes far beyond what he might have been able to achieve had he merely maintained his position as professor of Catholic dogmatic theology.

The Critique of the Global Ethic Project

ETHIC OR ETHICS?

Scholars of intercultural theology or philosophy, religious studies, and ethics have mostly kept their distance from the underlying concept of a global ethic, and this not only because of its overdetermined emphasis on religion. For instance, the philosophical approach of "global ethics" is explicitly designed as a theory of morality—*ethics* in the common use of the term—and not, like Küng's ethic, as an ethos.[21] Likewise, important protagonists of intercultural philosophy such as Enrique Dussel or Raúl Fornet-Betancourt have taken a different path. They point to the difficulty in any polylogue to acknowledge one's own worldview while at the same time relativizing it in the encounter with others.[22]

From an ethical perspective, Küng's project sounds naïve and arbitrary in the choices of both the principles and the directives. A few examples may suffice: when one takes a closer look both at the "principles" and the "directives," they are far from self-evident: for instance, the statement that there cannot be peace among nations without peace among religions is not a principle but an assertion. It may be obvious to a theologian who looks at the history of religious conflicts and the political-theological power that religions have in different settings—but for the paradigm of global affairs it is questionable whether peace among religions is as important as the recognition of the separation of political and religious power. Or the choice to highlight an "ethics of life" begs the question why life should be prioritized over freedom or justice. The "directives" state that a "culture of equal rights and partnership between men and women" is a part of the basic consensus and commitment of the world's religions—while at the same time, Küng claims that he deliberately left out any contested questions. But what gender equality means is a question in a number of religions, and to explain its normative character, a different normative theory is necessary than that which the "ethos" concept provides. While it is certainly wrong to say a normative claim is erroneous because it lacks the factual implementation—a mistake often made with respect to human rights—it is a category mistake to conflate values and norms. These examples point to conceptual problems that have been raised from the beginning but were never corrected. In the following, I will address two substantial critiques and comment on them from my own perspective.

THEOLOGICAL-ETHICAL CRITIQUE

In his critical response to the Global Ethic Project, Johann Baptist Metz articulated its blind spot: it bases moral universalism upon a minimal consensus. But from a strictly theological and not just from a religious and political perspective, ethical universalism is not a product of consensus. Indebted to the Critical Theory of the early Frankfurt School, Metz insists that the only universal claim that can be justified is negative:

> [Ethical universalism] is rooted in the unconditional recognition of an authority—which can certainly be appealed to in all great religions and cultures, too: in *the recognition of the authority of those who suffer*.[23]

While Küng often aligned himself with the political and economic leaders of world affairs, Metz emphasizes compassion, the sensitivity for the suffering of others, as the point of departure.

His emphasis on suffering individuals as subjects takes their moral agency seriously.[24] Metz agreed with Küng and the Global Ethic Project that the resources of all religions are needed, but he emphasized *the dangerous memory* of those who pay the price for our inaction, for the global political, economic, and technological order.

With Metz, I hold that ethics must critique the infliction of moral injuries, any denial of agency, and the damage it does to those who are often already structurally vulnerable. Following Metz, global responsibility cannot mean to gather around values but, rather, to practice *solidarity* with those who are the victims, those left behind by modernity's scientific, technological, and economic progress, even when this is counterfactual and goes against the consensus in a given value system. But there is a more systematic point to be made: connecting the attention to suffering individuals with justice grounds ethics in moral experiences and a moral sense for injustice. But experiences or intuitions must be subjected to the reflective *moral reasoning* that justifies the demands on others, for example, to end oppression or exploitation, or to treat others fairly. Subjecting moral claims to reflective scrutiny and, vice versa, confronting the normative imperatives of morality with the demands to effectively change unjust practices, a critical dialectical movement between *values* and *norms* on the one hand and moral praxis and ethical theory on the other becomes possible. In focusing on the ethical praxis and shared values, Küng undermines the power of ethical critique.

PHILOSOPHICAL-ETHICAL CRITIQUE

The philosopher Annemarie Pieper pointed to the fact that Aristotle's ethics is not and ought not to be used as a model for a global ethics, and certainly not for a global ethic. She rests her objections on the incomparable conditions of a closed-group "polis" such as Athens and modern cultures. More importantly, however, she points to the fundamental difference regarding modern ethical reasoning that fosters intercultural dialogue and subjects any ethic to critique:

> The classical concept of ethos assumes relatively closed group structures, which seem obsolete in modernity and postmodernity: Obviously, the Aristotelian doctrine of

ethos cannot be easily transferred to modern times, since it was conceived in the narrow context of a polis community, whose structures cannot simply be extended to a global society that knows itself bound by a common global ethic. This is already impossible because Aristotle considered the ethos unquestionable in terms of its validity....*It derives its validity and thus its general binding force from tradition, so that a radical critique of norms, such as modern ethics has made possible for moral subjects on the ground of autonomous self-determination, is inconceivable* from Aristotle's point of view.[25]

In a similar vein, philosopher Agnes Heller has pointed out that modern ethics may not only question any given tradition, but it is defined by the acknowledgment of epistemic and existential contingency. Thus, ethics has become a reflective and self-reflective endeavor—without therefore losing its normative force.[26] Küng aimed at a common global ethic in order to overcome claims of supremacy and/or superiority of one religion or culture over others. This is indeed laudable. But it is questionable whether the Global Ethic Project is well equipped to make this argument. With its conflation of values and moral norms, the Global Ethic Project loses the possibility to distinguish between descriptive and evaluative statements. If the common values are meant descriptively, the "search" for the minimal consensus ought to be left to cultural anthropology, which is equipped to conduct empirical studies. If it is meant as a normative statement, it is essential to distinguish between factual values and obligating norms. Descriptively, "lists" of cross-cultural values may help better to understand moral cultures; these are, however, deprived of their practical embedding and therefore lack any action orientation.[27] I am not saying that it is not useful to formulate an overlapping consensus. I am only warning against overestimating its practical relevance when it is abstracted from any context or practice. Moral conflicts arise mostly when concrete situations, obligating demands, or appeals to act are interpreted differently by different actors. The above-mentioned dialectic, the corrective movement between values and norms, and moral practice and ethical theory, is necessary because there is no simple transition from moral convictions (or commitment) to a moral culture (or vice versa), and no easy transition from moral culture to morally justified demands or, vice versa, from justified demands to the transformation of social practices and moral cultures. The superiority claim of one culture over another must be identified and critiqued directly. The turn to a shared ethos is too weak to fight against injustice.

Küng rejects the acceptance of moral relativism which, he fears, is a consequence of postmodern moral pluralism. Here, scholars who defend moral universalism will agree with him, but one must still make the effort to spell out what universalism means in relation to moral truth, and I doubt that the political term *global* in Küng's global ethic will suffice. Seyla Benhabib's distinctions between an essentialist, justificatory, moral, and juridical universalism may be useful to understand better what moral relativism is, why it is problematic, and how it may be countered. Here, I can only allude to one option with which I agree, namely, Benhabib's take on cultural dialogue, democratic participation, and human rights:

> There is a fundamental relationship between complex cultural dialogues among peoples in a global civil society and processes of democratic iteration. Only when members of a society can engage in free and unrestrained dialogue about their collective identity in free public spheres can they develop narratives of self-identification that unfold into fluid and creative re-appropriations of their own traditions. By contrast, totalizing discourses about "our culture" versus "theirs" seek to inhibit the free flow of individual and collective cultural narratives that might produce so-called "subversive" effects, in that they question the legitimizing collectivities in whose name power is exercised. Cultures are narratively constituted through contentious accounts of self-other differentiations. The other is not outside culture, but constitutive of it. Intercultural conversations and intracultural ones are deeply intertwined.
>
> One way to look at human rights is to consider them as enabling conditions, in the legal and political senses, of "uncoerced democratic iterations" among the peoples and cultures of the world.[28]

Hans Küng's Global Ethics Project

Here, Benhabib clarifies the role of different cultural—and we can add religious—narratives for the self-interpretation of cultures and identities among other identities that rest upon a self-other relationship. Whereas a global normative ethics—namely, in the declarations of human rights—is already spelled out, a cross-cultural common ethic may not only be impossible but also may not be desirable exactly because it rests upon a common identity concept rather than utilizing the self-other dynamic that rests upon openness to the other. Many scholars of global ethics argue that, on the one hand, what we need today is a translation of the ethics of human rights into a *politics* of human rights so that they can finally be implemented practically and not only serve as rhetorical phrases. On the other hand, they call for the recognition of difference, plurality, and diversity of cultural identities, especially under the conditions of economic and cultural globalization, and they argue that this cultural diversity does not at all imply moral relativism.

I would add to these debates on cultural diversity that one element of civil society's participatory political deliberations is public moral discourses that accompany the formalized political discourses resulting in legislation and governance. Here, the dialectic of moral experiences and moral reasoning, and moral practices and ethical theory, could (and must) be fostered by a renewed global *ethics* project. Religious, cultural, socioeconomic, and political practices require a self-reflective stance and the possibility of critique as means of correction. In addition to freedom as the condition for equal standing regarding rights claims, truthfulness is a normative condition of dialogue. Truthfulness in the encounters with others is a *moral* condition because without trust that the other will not exploit one's vulnerability, openness is impossible. A global ethic is either an abstraction from these necessary conversations, or it is a concealed particularistic ethos that is only masked as universal. But Benhabib says something else that is of equal importance, concerning the narrative mediation of identities, especially collective identities. They rely upon genealogies and stories of collective experiences. In addition to events, they include cultural or religious rituals that bring people together, praise of landscapes and nature as aesthetic environ, and so forth. All this shapes the customs, as Aristotle rightly stated. Diversity does not deny the fact that humans share some features of the *conditio humana*, among them natality and mortality. But pointing to the more recent bioethical debates on the beginning and end of life may suffice to demonstrate that even these seemingly unambivalent commonalities require interpretation when they are correlated with human actions and practices.

In sum: values and norms are interrelated, and they must be reflected upon in their dialectical, reciprocally corrective relationship: worldviews and life forms must be open to critique in order to improve or correct practices. And vice versa, norms must pass the practice test in order to fulfill their prescriptive task, namely, to guarantee that moral agency of agents can be realized under the conditions of ontological, moral, and structural vulnerability.[29] Aristotle was certainly right to integrate his ethics into his political theory: ethics is indeed necessarily *political* because it aims at goodness and justice. But in order to realize this goal, ethics must be *critical* with respect to both factual values and normative claims. Negative universalism takes the concrete, historical experiences of moral injuries and structural injustice as criteria of what ought *not* to be. Universalism in this sense does not equal a global perspective, just as particularism does not equal a local perspective.[30] Rather, universalism marks a categorical binding that defines "evil" and, respectively, "good." Second, a decentering, diatopical (or polytopical) epistemological critique, as well as an intercultural and interreligious dialogue (or polylogue), is needed that takes the diversity of worldviews seriously on all levels.[31] Here, the voices of women and minorities must become much louder, and their contributions must be recognized as equally valid as those of men—religions, in particular, have to catch up with secular cultures regarding women's rights and justice. The capability to "speak" in the public sphere is a condition for any political participation, the motor of any democratic governance. Narratives provide negative models of the damaged life as well as visions of the good life.

Conclusion: The Continuing Value of the Global Ethic Project

Today, the Global Ethic Project, together with the *Declaration of the Parliament of the World's Religions*, inspires many people and continues to spark discussions on morality and ethics. Likewise, the Global Ethic Project has generated a new interest in the world's religions and given people a pathway into studying and encountering their rich traditions. Within Catholic theology, however, Küng has been pushed into the background—and I believe this is a mistake. Still, his oeuvre convinces me more as contribution to a reform program for the Catholic Church than in its Global Ethic Project.

Leonard Swidler was correct to emphasize that Küng always understood the Global Ethic Project in political-spatial terms. In contrast to this concept of *Welt*, an alternative viewpoint may complement this with a more existential and phenomenological reading. Then, the political interdependence that is captured by the term *globalization* is complemented by the "being in the world," the existential experience of embeddedness in a particular environ, in a particular, contingent culture and religion, at a particular time. Modernity emphasized this as freedom but also as the risk of separation, to the point of self-alienation for the lack of connectedness with others and/or the world. Paradoxically, freedom is an experience that points to the transcendental-existential conditions of human interdependence and the need of "resonance" that enables humans to connect to other humans, animals, plants, nature, and to the divine.[32] When the Parliament of World's Religions added the "directive" sustainability and care for the earth, it meant it as a political claim. Underneath the normative claim, however, lies the promise made of another world that we cannot see yet—and that can only be expressed in narrative, poetic, or religious terms. Aesthetic, ethical, and spiritual experiences of "resonance" may signify a deeper connection among the inhabitants of planet earth than any norm can capture. Perhaps we need to learn—or relearn—to attend to such experiences, because they may entail the motivational energy that moral agents need to follow through with what is demanded of all humans—the care for oneself and the other, as the common caretakers of a shared common home.

Notes

1. Sometimes the difficulties were also ideological, as was the case with regard to Karol Wojtyla, the Archbishop of Krakow who

became Pope John Paul II in 1978. Küng had come to know him at the Second Vatican Council, where Wojtyla sided with those who tried to maintain the ecclesial and dogmatic *status quo ante*—the opposite of what Küng and the group of reformers fought for.

2. Cf. Hans Küng, *Umstrittene Wahrheit: Erinnerungen* (Munich: Piper, 2007); Hans Küng, *Disputed Truth: Memoirs*, vol. 2 (New York: Continuum, 2014).

3. For a comprehensive documentation of the history, the conceptualization of the ethical outlook, and the different declarations that complement the "project" in Tübingen, see Hans Küng, *Weltethos. Sämtliche Werke* (Freiburg im Br.: Herder, 2019).

4. Hans Küng, *Erlebte Menschlichkeit: Erinnerungen* (Munich: Piper, 2015). The Greek word *Ethos* is usually translated as "ethic." In the philosophical context, however, it is mostly translated as "ethical life."

5. Hans Küng, *Projekt Weltethos* (Munich: Piper, 1990). Hans Küng, *Global Responsibility: In Search of a New World Ethic* (New York: Crossroad, 1991). Küng easily moved among politicians, church leaders, and managers of large corporations. This was exceptional, at least in the German theological context.

6. Swidler's role is rarely mentioned in Küng's publications. Cf. Leonard Swidler. "Toward a Universal Declaration of a Global Ethic," *Journal of Ecumenical Studies* 42, no. 3 (2007): 337ff; Leonard Swidler, "The Movement for a Global Ethic," *Journal of Ecumenical Studies* 53, no. 1 (2018): 1–11.

7. My teacher, Dietmar Mieth, Professor of Social Ethics in Tübingen and, like Küng, coeditor of the journal *Concilium*, was among the first signatories of this declaration. But even though the Global Ethic project entailed a genuinely ethical theory, it developed rather separately from the ethics unit of the theology faculty. In hindsight, this created some tensions, especially regarding the simultaneously founded International Center for Ethics in the Sciences and Humanities at the University of Tübingen, which pursued a different approach to ethics. The tensions may well have originated from Küng's former colleague Alfons Auer, moral theologian (and Mieth's teacher) in Tübingen: Auer had not shown solidarity in 1979 when Küng was silenced, and to me, as academic assistant to Mieth in the 1990s and early 2000s, it sometimes seemed as if the tensions

between Küng and the Faculty of Theology were, in some ways, transgenerational.

8. Gotthold Ephraim Lessing, "Nathan der Weise: ein dramatisches Gedicht in fünf Aufzügen," in *Werke in 3 Bänden*, ed. G. Göpfert (Hamburg: Hanser, 1982 [1779]), 539–736; Gotthold Ephraim Lessing, *Nathan the Wise: A Dramatic Poem in Five Acts* (New York: Ungar, 1955). Küng recalls his long-lasting interest in Lessing in a book that explicitly connects *Nathan the Wise* with the Global Ethic Project. Cf. Hans Küng, Karl-Josef Kuschel, and Alois Riklin, *Die Ringparabel und das Projekt Weltethos* (Göttingen: Wallstein-Verlag, 2010).

9. Küng, et al., *Die Ringparabel und das Projekt Weltethos*.

10. Aristotle, *Nicomachean Ethics* (Oxford: Oxford University Press, 2020).

11. John Rawls, *A Theory of Justice* (Cambridge, MA: Belknap Press of Harvard University Press, 1999 [1970]).

12. Parliament of World's Religions, *Towards a Global Ethic: An Initial Declaration* (1993).

13. Parliament of World's Religions, *Towards a Global Ethic*.

14. Hans Jonas, *The Imperative of Responsibility: In Search of an Ethics for the Technological Age* (Chicago: University of Chicago Press, 1984).

15. Immanuel Kant, *Groundwork of the Metaphysics of Morals* (Cambridge: Cambridge University Press, 1998 [1785]).

16. This last "directive" was added in 2018.

17. Cf. for the story of the circumstances, Leonard Swidler, "Toward a Universal Declaration of a Global Ethic," 342–43.

18. Cf. among many others Charles Taylor, *Multiculturalism and the Politics of Recognition: An Essay* (Princeton, NJ: Princeton University Press, 1992).

19. For documentation see Hans Küng, Stephan Schlensog, and Günther Gebhardt, *Handbuch Weltethos: Eine Vision und ihre Umsetzung* (Munich: Piper Verlag, 2017); Küng, *Weltethos. Sämtliche Werke*.

20. In Germany, religious education is part of the public school curriculum.

21. Cf. for an overview and literature Heather Widdows, *Global Ethics: An Introduction* (London: Taylor & Francis, 2014).

22. Cf., for example, Nicole Note, Raúl Fornet-Betancourt, Josef Estermann, and Diederik Aerts, *Worldview and Cultures: Philosophical Reflections from an Intercultural Perspective; An Introduction* (Berlin: Springer, 2009).

23. Johann Baptist Metz, "In the Pluralism of Religious and Cultural Worlds: Notes toward a Theological and Political Program," *CrossCurrents* 49, no. 2 (1999): 227–36. Emphasis is mine (translation corrected). Metz elaborated further on the Global Ethic in "Compassion. Zu einem Weltprogramm des Christentums im Zeitalter des Pluralismus der Religionen und Kulturen," in *Compassion. Weltprogramm des Christentums. Soziale Verantwortung lernen*, ed. Lothar Kuld and Adolf Weisbrod, and Johann Baptist Metz (Freiburg: Herder, 2000), 9–20. For a thorough analysis see my own essay: Hille Haker, "'Compassion als Weltprogramm des Christentums'—Eine ethische Auseinandersetzung mit Johann Baptist Metz," *Concilium* 37, no. 4 (2001): 436–50. More recently, Hille Haker, "Decolonizing Religion(s). A New Catholic Direction for the Global Ethic," in *Multi-religious Perspectives on a Global Ethic: In Search of a Common Morality*, ed. Myriam Renaud and William Schweiker (New York: Routledge, 2020), 165–84.

24. In my own works, I have reformulated this subject status as vulnerable agency and aimed to complement Metz's political theology with a critical political ethics. Hille Haker, *Towards a Critical Political Ethics: Catholic Ethics and Social Challenges* (Basel: Schwabe Verlag, 2020).

25. Annemarie Pieper, "Vom Sinn eines Weltethos im Zeitalter der Globalisierung," in *Weltwirtschaftsethik. Globalisierung auf dem Prüfstand der Lebensdienlichkeit*, ed. Hans Küng (Bern: Paul Haupt Verlag, 2000), 61–75. (My emphasis).

26. Agnes Heller, *A Philosophy of Morals* (Oxford: Blackwell, 1990).

27. Cf. the compilation based on surveys in more than eighty countries in Ronald Inglehart, Miguel Basañez, et al., *Human Beliefs and Values: A Cross-Cultural Sourcebook Based on the 1999–2002 Values Surveys* (Mexico City: Siglo XXI, 2004).

28. Seyla Benhabib, "Another Universalism: On the Unity and Diversity of Human Rights," *Proceedings and Addresses of the American Philosophical Association* 81, no. 2 (2007): 7–32.

29. For a discussion of the relationship between the narrative-hermeneutical and the normative dimension of ethics see Hille Haker, *Moralische Identität. Literarische Lebensgeschichten als Medium ethischer Reflexion. Mit einer Interpretation der "Jahrestage" von Uwe Johnson* (Tübingen: Francke, 1999).

30. In his otherwise thorough study, David Hollenbach recommends that the Global Ethic Project ought to reconsider the relationship between the "universal" and the "local." But moral universalism means that a claim can be justified independent of one's own desires or values: it comes with an obligation for anyone under the same condition of action. See David Hollenbach, "Religious Nationalism, a Global Ethic, and the Culture of Encounter," *Theological Studies* 83, no. 3 (2022): 361–78.

31. See Boaventura de Sousa Santos, *Epistemologies of the South: Justice against Epistemicide* (Boulder, CO: Paradigm Publishers, 2014).

32. See Hartmut Rosa, *Resonanz. Eine Soziologie der Weltbeziehung* (Berlin: Suhrkamp, 2017); trans. James C. Wagner as *Resonance: A Sociology of Our Relationship to the World* (Hoboken, NJ: Wiley, 2019).

9
HANS KÜNG VISITS THE WORLD RELIGIONS

Francis X. Clooney, SJ

Hans Küng was a respected Catholic theologian, learned, bold, and often insightful in his Catholic and ecumenical theology. He was erudite and passionate in his view of what the church was and could be. Later in life, he was notable, too, for his determination to learn seriously from the religious traditions of the world, highlighting common ground without covering over differences. Küng's view of the church overflowed into his view of how the world religions needed to be understood, engaged, if they were to be at their best. Küng's writing regarding the world religions adds up to a significant body of work, and perhaps never has there been a Christian systematic theologian who has in midcareer turned so impressively to learning about the world's religions. I readily acknowledge and commend Küng's overall project. But I will also notice its major limitation: it is primarily a learning about religions that fits them into Küng's already mature worldview, but without that learning transforming him or his thinking as a staunchly Catholic theologian.

This essay has three parts. First, I offer an overview of Küng's capacious learning about traditions, a learning that must be respected and commended but also assessed for what it was and was not able to achieve. Second, drawing on the third of his autobiographical volumes, I inquire into whether he was deeply changed by his interreligious learning; I argue that while he arguably did outgrow any narrow ecclesial frame, his view of religions was in essence a matter of fitting them into his overall worldview as progressive Catholic. He always remained master of what he learned, in control, but less affected by the opportunities the religions might have presented to him. His option for breadth of learning, though impressive and not without some rationale in his mind, sacrificed the power that comes with the depth of more focused learning. Third, however, the real benefit of his work is evident in his tireless efforts toward a consensus on the basics of a global ethic.

Breadth of Learning

After his confrontation with the Vatican and loss of status as a Catholic theologian, Hans Küng made the best of the unhappy event by stepping onto a much wider stage, beginning to explore the religions of the world. At the end of *My Struggle for Freedom: Memoirs*,[1] Küng writes,

> Had I turned to the Roman system at that time in the 1960s and put myself at the service of a world church, I would have been limited to the church world and would by no means have been involved so intensively with the themes of world literature, world religions, world peace and a global ethic as I would be forced to do *Dei providentia hominum confusione*— through God's providence and human confusion. (463)

The result, perhaps unexpected even to himself, was, by a rechanneling of his energies, a fresh investment in learning about world religions, from the early 1980s on.[2] This writing is wide-reaching and intended by Küng to create firm basis for the theological exchange among believers. But it gained its most notable focus in *A Global Ethic for Global Politics and Economics*,[3] a quest for a common ground among religions that continued for thirty years or so. The project was updated by Küng toward the very end of his life, in *Walls to Bridges*.[4]

HANS KÜNG

The first major writing by Küng in his venture to master the world religions was *Christianity and the World Religions*.[5] The volume is a solid achievement, as Küng begins his study of the religions. The book covered Islam, Hinduism, and Buddhism. To Küng's credit, it was a collaborative work, with experts van Ess (Islam), Stietencron (Hinduism), and Bechert (Buddhism) providing information for Küng's subsequent reflection. Stietencron, for example, offers a very thorough, fair presentation of the complexities of Hinduism—a set of traditions notoriously hard to summarize. Küng responds with his own elaborate reflections, showing us what he thinks about what Stietencron has shown him, but as if talking to himself. We don't really see a back-and-forth conversation with Stietencron or van Ess or Bechert.

By way of contrast I point us to a series of conferences on Hinduism, Buddhism, and Islam in relation to Christian faith, which in turn resulted in six paired volumes edited by Andreas Bsteh, with these titles for the English translations: *Hinduism Questioning Christianity*, and *Christian Faith in Dialogue with Hindu Religious Traditions*; *Buddhism Questioning Christianity*, and *Christian Faith in Dialogue with Buddhist Religious Traditions*; *Islam Questioning Christianity*, and *Christian Faith in Dialogue with Islamic Religious Traditions*.[6] The first volume in each pair intends that intellectual challenges and questions be posed by each of the three religions to Christian faith and theology; the second volume in each set displays Christian resources and constructive theological thinking relevant to the issues raised by Hindu, Buddhist, and Islamic thought by Christian theologians who have read the first volume and now reflect back again on elements of Christian faith. What is distinctive is that each volume contains the record of the conversations that followed the individual lectures. We see in these accounts the complexity of interreligious learning when the inquiry is pursued at a deeper level, with a back and forth among experts in the religions and theologians. By contrast, while we see Küng learning from scholars, we do not witness a further back and forth of him in conversation with these scholarly peers.

In any case, *Christianity and the World Religions* sets the pattern for the very large, tradition-focused volumes that follow. Scholars would explain the religions to Küng, Küng then synthesized and wrote, so that others could then learn from Küng. He does not respond to smaller details, but looks to the big picture, noticing what he thinks of in relation to one or the other. As I will argue below, his strengths

Hans Küng Visits the World Religions

pertain to great breadth, not great depth. He himself seems to do little reading of primary texts, and he seems to expect little primary study of his readers. Relying on experts also meant that Küng remained at a distance from the non-Christian traditions regarding which he wished to theologize; this is a dynamic operative throughout his career of interreligious learning.

After the 1986 book, Küng does little more work on Hinduism and Buddhism, and so his views on them do not develop greatly. The Asian religions do not seem to be of great interest to him after he has dutifully taken notice of them and reflected on them in the 1986 volume.

Soon after *Christianity and the World Religions*, however, Küng went on to fill out his picture of religions, complementing what he calls the prophetic stream and the mystical stream, with the Chinese stream. This additional study appears as *Christianity and Chinese Religions*, with Julia Ching.[7] His treatment of Chinese religions or systems of thought is worthy of attention, particularly since he realized the importance of East Asian religions. Chinese systems of thought, too, did not become central to his way of thinking and seem not to have had any effect on the content or method of his theology.

Küng returns thereafter to his focus on Judaism and Islam in relation to Christianity, with three very large volumes: *Judaism: Between Yesterday and Tomorrow* (753 pp.);[8] *Christianity: Essence, History, Future* (934 pp.);[9] *Islam: Past, Present, and Future* (761 pp.).[10] These books, too, are the product of a capacious inquiring thinker, progressive and able to learn widely of several religions which had previously been unfamiliar to him.[11]

He correctly wanted to have a sound basis for his assessment of the religions and to share with potentially interested readers his learning and opinions on the religions, what they mean for Catholics, how they are to be corrected, and so forth. Seeking comprehensiveness rather than depth, he could move quickly, expanding and modulating the breadth, saying more and more. He rarely stops to consider the traditions more particularly by, for example, studying key passages in their scriptures; it is themes he is interested in. But even if Küng's goal was a certain ideal of completeness, none of these volumes needed to be so long. Even as he was writing these volumes, there had been a proliferation of more and higher quality books offering insight into every religion large and small; no reader would need

Küng's large volumes to find out what the religions say, though they remain pertinent for theological reflection. His volumes' distinctiveness of course lies in the theological reflection that is evident in them, Küng thinking capaciously about similarities and differences in what he is learning, and how it relates back to his Catholic theology.[12]

Küng on Islam

For a more fine-tuned analysis, I now look a bit more closely at Küng's treatment of just one religion, Islam, as portrayed in *Islam: Past, Present and Future*. I do so as someone who is not expert in Islam and is not qualified to comment in detail on this generally well-received volume.

Küng treated Islam first in the 1986 book, but later he more properly places it after Christianity. Recognizing the importance of the fact that Islam comes after the New Testament, he honors the religion as offering a purifying critique of notable limitations of Christianity. In his preface to Islam, Küng speaks of the importance of a real understanding of Islam today that old stereotypes might be put aside and a real rapprochement occur. The goal of the book is to show the complexity, with attention to points of similarity and rapprochement with the Christian, for the sake of a more complex—and benign—mutual understanding. He does so by a coherent overview, with an eye, in the last two parts, to the present moment and to what is possible in the future if Christians and Muslims truly understand one another. The book combines a historical perspective with comparative and theological insights. All of this seems quite well-informed, even if not the work of an expert attuned to the subtleties and complications that scholars face each day.

These are the book's main headings and subheadings:

Origin: I. A Controversial Religion; II. Problems of the Beginning

Centre: I. God's Word Has Become a Book; II. The Central Message; III. The Central Structural Elements

History: I. The Original Paradigm of the Islamic Community; II. The Paradigm of the Arab Empire; III. The

Classical Paradigm of Islam as a World Religion; IV. The Paradigm of the Ulama and Sufis; V. The Paradigm of Islamic Modernization

Challenges of the Present: I. Competition between Paradigms; II. What Kind of Islam Do Muslims Want?; III. The Middle East Conflict and a New Paradigm; IV. New Approaches to Theological Conversation; IV. Speculative Questions; V. From Biblical Criticism to Qur'anic Criticism?

Possibilities for the Future: I. Islamic Renewal; II. The Future of the Islamic Legal Order; III. The Future of Islam State Order and Politics; IV. The Future of the Islamic Economic Order; V. The Future of the Islamic Way of Life

Each of the major parts is further divided, a few pages each on various topics of interest. For example, D. IV includes "After One Empire, Many States," "The Ulama: Legal Schools Become Popular Movements," "The Sufis: Mystics Form Themselves into Brotherhoods," "Sufis as a Mass Movement," "Normative Theology," "Theological Summas (Comparing al-Ghazali and Thomas Aquinas)," "The Rise and Fall of Arabic Philosophy," and "The Crisis of Medieval Islam." This breathtaking array of topics is covered in pages 305–88.

As a text scholar myself (though with respect to Hindu traditions), what I find most notably missing from Küng's volume is any serious engagement with the Qur'an or later poetic works or philosophical treatises of Islamic literature. Such primary texts are, of course, hard to read, even in the many excellent translations that exist today. When they are read closely, texts resist systematization and slow down the reader. But the rewards are great, as classic religious texts, especially scriptures, draw in and transform their readers in unexpected ways. One can only wish that Küng had carefully read a surah of the Qur'an, or a chapter of the Bhagavad Gita, or some other normative sacred text of another tradition.

Of course, Küng's work, even on Islam in the third great tome on a religious tradition, does not compete with the much more detailed and fine-tuned work of theologians who have studied Islam in depth.

Scholars from the time of Louis Massignon (1883–1962) to Christian Troll (1937–) and Klaus von Stosch (1971–), just to name a few, have long brought deep learning on Islam into direct dialogue with Christian theology.[13] It would not be fair to expect Küng, who turned to such learning only in mid-career, to rival their depth of learning. But they do show a solid alternative to his great ambition of comprehensive learning. If only Küng had settled down and spent years studying Islam, or some other single tradition, his work would have been more fruitful in the long run.[14]

Keith Ward shows us how a nonexpert might proceed, if he or she wanted to cover the range of religions in a more focused, limited manner. Between 1991 and 2004, Ward was the Regius Professor of Divinity at the University of Oxford. Largely during that period, he published a series of studies by which to engage religions in a sustained fashion: *Religion and Revelation* (Oxford: Clarendon Press, 1994); *Religion and Creation* (Oxford: Clarendon Press, 1996); *Religion and Human Nature* (Oxford: Clarendon Press, 1998); *Religion and Community* (Oxford: Clarendon Press, 2000); *Religion and Human Fulfilment* (London: SCM Press, 2008). In each volume, he first treats of the theme in Judaism, Islam, Hinduism, and Buddhism, and then turns to Christian theological reflection, now in light of the views professed in other traditions. Ward is explicit regarding his indebtedness to scholars of the traditions. These modest volumes forego the goal of comprehensiveness and focus rather on smaller scale theological considerations of similarities and differences. This kind of reflective consideration cannot match the capacious larger swathes of knowledge for which Küng is known, but Ward's more modest volumes have succinct and enduring value and are no less interesting than Küng's massive tomes.[15]

Küng chose, in keeping with his self-image as global theologian, to write about a great array of religions, sacrificing depth for the sake of comprehensiveness. Yet his books are rarely those to which one would go for in-depth insights on any given religion. We can go to other sources to learn more deeply about Islam. Theologically, of course, the volumes do show us Küng thinking through the religious themes and shedding light on Küng's Catholic theology.

Hans Küng Visits the World Religions

How Did This Learning Matter for Küng Himself?

Did Küng's learning get "inside him"? Did his mind change over time?[16] For these questions, the third of his volumes of autobiography is valuable. *What I Believe* (2010) offers a retrospective on the whole of his life. Here Küng offers ten meditations on life—trust in life, joy in life, way of life, meaning in life, foundation of life, power of life, model of life, suffering in life, art of living, vision of life. Treating these themes with attention to each of the religions he has studied, he gives witness to his basic Christian commitment, which, he hopes, remains firm but is also informed about the other religions. Küng writes in a confessional tone, speaking of his faith, his insistence on knowing the truth and therefore on raising questions, and his steadfastness as a progressive Catholic Christian. Early in the book, he explains: "Since the Second Vatican Council and corresponding initiatives by the World Council of Churches, Christians have worked hard to gain an undistorted look at the world religions. They no longer want, as was customary for centuries, to judge by Christian dogmatic criteria. They want to understand them as they understand themselves." Eager to find common ground, he does not want to ignore differences: "I had always been aware that in spite of all the agreements among the religions there are fundamental differences, many opposing views, despite all the similarities." For example,

> There are countless gods of the religions in history and the present, the divine nature figures and forces of nature, the plant, animal and human gods, gods of equal rank and gods in hierarchies. We have to face the question: Which is the true God? Is he to be found in the original tribal religions that still have a simple structure, or in the highly-developed religions? In those which have grown up slowly or those which have been founded? In the mythological religions or the enlightened religions? And there are other questions: Are there many gods, polytheism, or an individual supreme God among many gods, henotheism? Or is there only one God, monotheism? Is God to be thought

of above or outside the world, deism? Is God completely included in the world, pantheism? Or is the world completely in God, panentheism?

These are weighty questions, but they are to be resolved through amicable and relevant dialogues:

I realized long ago that to examine these questions at every level and within all religions we need to have friendly and pleasant discussions together, having provided ourselves the necessary factual knowledge. The more I read, travel, speak, listen, experience, the clearer it has become to me that dialogue between the religions is no remote academic affair. Rather, dialogue is a political and religious necessity—a foundation for peace between the nations. (*Power of Life*, 97)

But it is not clear to me what that dialogue would be like, among representative Christians, Muslims, and Hindus, nor how such dialogue would lead to the resolution of the questions. It seems unlikely that amicable dialogue would lead everyone to a consensus that there is only one God. "Factual knowledge," surely a good thing, would nonetheless be only a starting point on much deeper study such as would lead to some understanding of how people worship and what they mean by the one, many, no deities involved. Küng is eager to resolve all the questions, in dialogue with all the traditions, but his hope in this regard outreaches his prospects for success.

In chapter 7, "Model of Life," Küng considers various "paths to the summit" where the transcendent God can be met. In a disarmingly idiosyncratic manner, Küng contemplates serially what it would mean to have been born into this or that religion: "When I stayed on other continents, I often reflected what would have become of me had I not been born in Europe but in another cultural circle. Perhaps I would then have shaped my life according to a quite different model, a quite different pattern of feeling, thinking and acting" (124). He takes up the traditions in what seems to be both a matter of a timeline, and by an ascending order of interest, according to his personal preference: Hindu, Buddhist, Confucian, Jewish, deficient Christianity, true Christianity, and Islam. Here too he moves quickly. He begins with Hinduism. In the one page he devotes to Hinduism, he mentions that he would have been a believer in the cycle of rebirths, his state in life now affected by deeds from previous lives; that he would have studied the Vedas, or at least believed in the enduring (sanatana) dharma (which condenses the Veda's theoretical and ethical teachings) including caste.

These seem to be descriptive of what he takes to be the standard Hindu beliefs and self-understandings, and of how he himself would think, should he find himself for a moment a Hindu. But he does not seem to have a feel for what it would mean to be a Hindu, for instance. He is imagining "Hindu" in some generic sense rather than "Hindu" in any of the myriad traditions of India, ancient or modern. He asserts, too, that he would have felt no strong attention to dogmas and formal orthodoxy, but rather to right action, in accord with the customs of family. He assumes then that he will be educated—reading the Vedas, as most Hindus do not; he will be a liberal, enlightened, critical of abuses:

> As in Christianity, if I was educated to the same degree, presumably in Hinduism too, I would be dissatisfied with some rites and teachings, precepts and practices. I would be one of today's Hindu critics. I would have no time for the social elites preferred by the eternal order who all too readily—with a reference to the eternal law—insist on their given rights and privileges and miss out on social involvement. Without any tendency towards fundamentalism, I would certainly be one of the critical thinkers and reformers of India who fight the caste system which, though officially abolished, in practice still functions, and I would fight for an improved position for women and the around 150 million out-castes. (125)

But this expectation about "Küng the Hindu" seems rather fanciful. Küng seems to imagine finding himself, just as he is, for a moment in a Hindu body. He concludes by saying that being antipathetic to the caste system, he might well "turn his back on Hinduism" and incline toward Buddhism. He imagines being a Buddhist, soon dissatisfied with that too, and then a Confucian, and so forth. Each falls short in terms of his restlessness for more.

The overall impression is that even in the imaginative exercise of imagining himself to be a Hindu, a Buddhist, or a Confucian,

HANS KÜNG

Küng remains Hans Küng, born in 1918 in Germany, finding himself for a time in this or that Hindu or Buddhist body, and so forth, but with the same progressive attitudes and critical prophetic voice. His worldview seems not to change at all. I myself can imagine, in a way, what it would be like to dwell in a Hindu body. But in that body, I would no longer be the Clooney I am now, no longer able to look out on the world with the dispositions of a Catholic identity formed long ago. I would be different, deeply so, not merely Clooney in a different body.

In turning next to Judaism, Küng drops the visitor motif and moves quickly to highlighting Judaism's common ground with Christianity and his own efforts to engage in dialogue with Jews—he goes on to reflect in two sections on what it means, on the one hand, to be a Christian in name only or in a distorted fashion and, on the other, the ideal of being a true Christian, inclusive, progressive, entirely rational.

The overall impression one gets from this chapter, and from *What I Believe* as a whole, is that Küng has not deeply entered into any of the religions other than his own, and simply imagines himself visiting the various religions as Hans Küng for a time a Hindu, a Buddhist, or a Confucian. He knows the traditions in some detail but, it seems, from the outside. He remains always a Catholic and a theologian of the progressive kind, and such he would be, in any body, in any religion.

Küng closes the chapter with a short section on Islam. Though this comes after his consideration of Christianity, there is no indication that Küng considers converting to Islam; the imaginative experience of trying out the various traditions has fallen away. He simply wishes to honor Islam's place as a religion taking shape after Christianity, as a righteous tradition that chastises Christianity and purifies it of errors about God, Jesus, and the human. Here too, he turns out to be an educated, thoughtful, progressive Muslim—again, a Hans Küng in Muslim garb. Remarkably, on the one hand, he would be a Muslim who would "emphatically affirm Jesus's exaltation to God," but a few lines later on the same page, he adds that "I would have had objections to the elevation of Jesus to God" (141). He resolves this contradiction by appealing to a more nuanced Christian understanding of "God" and Jesus as the Son. He concludes by stressing how Islam serves as a corrective; it is useful as an instigation for

Christians to return to the true roots of a progressive enlightened Christianity.

The chapter is a good example of the extent to which Küng personalizes—at arm's length—the religions about which he has written. On one level, it is no business of mine to question his report on religions, since this is his personal witness; I respect his narrative of how he thinks. But with respect to his learning from traditions, as viewed by a reader, his approach seems extraordinarily deficient in terms of imagination and empathy—he can only be Hans Küng, whatever body in whichever culture he might inhabit. He has not crossed over in any deeper, empathetic way, by serious study or sustained learning from just one tradition. Yet it would have been in that depth of introspection that Küng, a respected Catholic theologian, would have made an enduring contribution.

So how does his labor in learning traditions affect him more generally? It is hard to say. His other books written in the latter part of his life, in his arguments with church leaders and for reform in the church, are largely silent on religions. His projects "in the church" stand at a distance from projects "engaging world religions." For example, *Can We Save the Catholic Church?* (2013), even as it calls for reform of the church, gives no hint that in other volumes Küng has studied many religions or has been inspired by Islam's reforming critique. Perhaps his treatment of religions is but another example of the enlightened humanistic perspective he thinks Catholics too should have of their church. But this was a missed opportunity, since it would have been very interesting indeed to see how Küng might have changed his ecclesial critique precisely by becoming a comparative theologian, rethinking older and familiar Catholic topics because of his study of Hinduism, Islam, and so forth.

The Global Ethic

Surely most enduring in its influence is Küng's quest to identify common ground among traditions, for the sake of a sharable ethics that might guide life in an increasingly interconnected world. He is intensely interested in making a difference, given that through his studies he now appreciates how a recognition of common ground among religions is both possible and worthwhile. His real strength with respect to religions may well be detectable in the realm of a kind of applied ethics, where the implications of the recognized commonalities among religions bear fruit practically. Hille Haker's essay in this volume very ably traces the history of the Global Ethics and situates it within Küng's overall achievement, and I will add only several comments here.

A Global Ethic: The Declaration of the Parliament of the World's Religions (1993)[17] focuses on shaping a shared ethic that he thinks will be positively received by enlightened and progressive members of every tradition. The admirably slim volume identifies "four irrevocable directions," commitments to "a culture of non-violence and respect for life," "a culture of solidarity and a just economic order," "a culture of tolerance and a life of truthfulness," and "a culture of equal rights and partnerships between men and women." All this is very fine, and has real force to it, and we cannot dismiss the importance of this Declaration, nor deny Küng's part in realizing it.

In *Walls to Bridges: The Global Ethic* (2019), Küng offers a retrospective on what he has learned about religions. He stresses that while the differences among religions are obvious, the way forward is for people of good faith to engage one another and learn from one another, in a mutually corrective process. His appeal for mutual understanding remains rather general and, as noted above, does not anticipate that some believers might become deeply immersed in the other faith traditions around them, that mingling making the larger difference. Küng's brave hope captures how he saw his project late in life: knowledge leads to a realistic grasp of commonalities, and that leads to a recognition of shared values and programs of action.[18]

But still, few experts would want to emulate how Küng and his colleagues seize upon general points of agreement—"nonviolence," "solidarity," "justice," and so forth—without worrying about the weight and impact of these words in any of the traditions.[19] At issue is not merely experts' love of details. Rather, it is arguable that the good and the true subsist most vitally in the details and likewise the points of tension and real difference. Küng's laudable project does not trace the generalized virtues to their deep sources in faith traditions, and as a result it lacks some of the intellectual and affective force required to bring his hopes to fruition.

Hans Küng Visits the World Religions

In Conclusion

Only as smart and comprehensive a thinker as Küng could synthesize so much regarding the religions of the world and, with such breadth, have something to say about so many religions, and with a clear message, that we must know each other's faiths for the sake of living together in peace and working together. Küng's vision of understanding opening into mutual respect and collaboration is admirable and an impressive application of mutual understanding, grounded in Küng's confidence that the religions have enough in common to seek and find common ground.

From my perspective, inevitably, Küng's work appears too broad and too much on the surface, and lacking in the force that would make a deeper difference in the theologian's life. But I am sure my work would seem too narrow to him, had he read anything I've written. Küng is making sense of the religions alongside his Christian faith, by knowing much about them—coming to terms with them as a believer. It is edifying that a theologian of his generation invested so much in so much new learning. But the paradigm is set: an intelligent encounter, learning, questions, but without any murkier boundaries, clouds of confusion, uncertain rethinkings of the boundaries of the Christian. But it is in those areas of uncertainty, where the spiritual imagination outstrips the rational mind, that the most interesting interreligious engagements take place.

His books can certainly be useful for people wishing to know the religions, even if there are so many sophisticated volumes introducing various religions available today, and they will be of interest even now, for insights into how a traditional systematic theologian such as Küng ventured so impressively to learn from other religions. It seems to me that Küng's books are too large for introductions, too secondary to be of interest to scholars of the religions, and, with respect to theological engagement, less useful that the works of scholars I have mentioned, such as Troll or Oberhammer.

It would surely be grudging to be unwilling to recognize the impressive work Küng did in learning about religions, producing large books containing impressive research and all kinds of theological reflections, as Küng works out his view of the religions. His manner of learning cannot be taken as a singular best model for the interreligious, comparative theological learning that we need in the twenty-first century. The required future theology needs to be less ambitious, smaller scale, rarer and deeper, more intimate. Or, again, it may simply be in his global ethic that his legacy will live on, since he wanted to make a difference in terms of how people know one another, live in peace, and work together on issues of common concern.

Notes

1. Hans Küng, *My Struggle for Freedom: Memoirs* (Grand Rapids, MI: Eerdmans, 2003).

2. Here is a list of the major books related to world religions: *Christianity and the World Religions*, with Josef van Ess, Heinrich von Stietencron, and Heinz Becheert (1986); *Christianity and Chinese Religions*, with Julia Ching (1989); *Judaism: Between Yesterday and Tomorrow* (1992); *Christianity: Essence, History, Future* (1995); *Tracing the Way: Spiritual Dimensions of the World Religions* (2002); *Islam: Past, Present, and Future* (2007).

3. Hans Küng, *A Global Ethic for Global Politics and Economics* (Oxford: Oxford University Press, 1998).

4. Hans Küng, *Walls to Bridges* (Mesa, AZ: iPub Global Connection, LLC, 2019).

5. Hans Küng, *Christianity and the World Religions* (Garden City, NY: Doubleday, 1986).

6. *Hinduism Questioning Christianity*, trans. Ingeborg Bogensberger with John Mercer and Adrianne Nagy DaPonte (Mödling: St. Gabriel Publications, 2007); *Christian Faith in Dialogue with Hindu Religious Traditions*, trans. Ingeborg Bogensberger with Adrianne Nagy DaPonte (Mödling: St. Gabriel Publications, 2007); *Islam Questioning Christianity*, trans. Ingeborg Bogensberger with Carol Bebawi (Mödling: St. Gabriel Publications, 2007); *Christian Faith in Dialogue with Islamic Religious Traditions*, trans. Ingeborg Bogensberger with Carol Bebawi (Mödling: St. Gabriel Publications, 2007); *Buddhism Questioning Christianity*, trans. Ingeborg Bogensberger with Adrianne Nagy DaPonte (Mödling: St. Gabriel Publications, 2010); *Christian Faith in Dialogue with Buddhism*, trans. Ingeborg Bogensberger with

Hans Küng Visits the World Religions

Adrianne Nagy DaPonte, Cynthia Peck-Kubaczek, and Carol Rowe (Mödling: St. Gabriel Publications, 2010).

7. Küng, *Christianity and the World Religions*.

8. Hans Küng, *Judaism: Between Yesterday and Tomorrow* (London: Continuum, 1992).

9. Hans Küng, *Christianity: Essence, History, Future* (London: Continuum, 1995).

10. Hans Küng, *Islam: Past, Present, and Future* (London: OneWorld Publications, 2007).

11. Küng ventured even into the world of film, as in the filmed episodes later turned into the book *Tracing the Way: Spiritual Dimensions of the World Religions* (2002). Related to a TV series, it is a much smaller work (280 pp.). Here Küng meditates his way through the religions—now beginning with the indigenous religions (mainly) of Africa, and then Hinduism, Chinese religions, Buddhism, Judaism, Christianity and then Islam.

12. In most of these writings Küng reminds us that he was not merely a library scholar. He was seemingly a constant traveler, flying around the world, lecturing, meeting dignitaries of all kinds. He had many conversations in all these places and was always pleased to find himself welcomed, listened to, appreciated, confirmed in his beliefs.

13. On Massignon, see Christian Krokus, *The Theology of Louis Massignon: Islam, Christ, and the Church* (Washington, DC: Catholic University of America Press, 2017). On Troll, see Joseph Victor Edwin, SJ, *A New Spirit in Christian-Muslim Relations in India: Three Jesuit Pioneers* (Hyderabad, India: Henry Martyn Institute, 2021). Klaus von Stosch has dedicated himself to the study of Islam in relation to Christianity in a specialist manner, but always with an eye to implications for Catholic theology. Solidly Catholic, in collaboration with Muslim colleagues, he has done genuinely constructive work in Catholic-Muslim theology. Among von Stosch's books (in their English translations): *The Other Prophet: Jesus in the Qur'an*, with Mouhanad Khorchide (London: Gingko Library, 2019); *Divine Action: Challenges for Muslim and Christian Theology*, ed. John Sanders and Klaus Von Stosch (Paderborn: Brill Schöningh, 2021); *Mary in the Qur'an: Friend of God, Virgin, Mother*, ed. von Stosch, Muna Tatari, et al. (London: Gingko Library, 2022).

14. We can also take note of the sustained work of Küng's contemporary, Gerhard Oberhammer (1929–). This is a scholar who has

consistently and over many decades enriched learning of another religion—Hinduism—with clear theological perspectives, attentive to Hindu theology, with an Indological yet also Christian and Catholic perspective on Hinduism. He has edited, for instance, nine volumes in a series on the tradition of the Hindu theologian Ramanuja, *Materialien zur Geschichte der Rāmānuja-Schule* (Vienna: Austrian Academy of Sciences, 1996–2008). These are, to be sure, Indological volumes, showcasing Oberhammer's own expertise, of a kind to which Küng could not aspire; but they are also deeply sensitive to the theological issues at play in Ramanuja's writings and the wider theological implications of Ramanuja's works. Oberhammer also edited volumes with Christian theological import, such as these: *Offenbarung, geistige Realität des Menschen: Arbeitsdokumentation eines Symposiums zum Offenbarungsbegriff in Indien* (Leiden: Brill, 1974); *Relevanz des historischen Jesus für die Begegnung des Christentums mit dem Hinduismus*, coedited with Nikolaus Kehl (1974); *Transzendenzerfahrung, Vollzugshorizont des Heils: das Problem in indischer und christlicher Tradition* (Vienna: Indologisches Institut der Universität Wien, 1978). Again, we cannot expect Küng to be a specialist of the depth and quality of Oberhammer; but neither was Küng unique in bringing the study of a religion and theology together.

15. Ward admits (https://www.keithward.org.uk/books-all/) the modest and realistic nature of his project in the five volumes: "This, I suppose, is my major academic contribution to the study of religions and to theology. These volumes compare and contrast [the] doctrines of Hinduism, Islam, Judaism, Buddhism and Christianity on each topic. The aim is to present the doctrines accurately, but to let them interact and influence each other. The books are written from within a Christian tradition, and a Christian systematic theology is developed throughout the series. But this is a theology radically influenced by a global religious perspective. The intended result is both a Christian systematic theology in a global context, and an attempt to show how the world's major religious traditions can interact positively and fruitfully in the modern world." See also his *Religion in the Modern World* (Cambridge: Cambridge University Press, 2019), which focuses on this problem: "The initial problem is raised by increased knowledge of the wide diversity of competing religious views, and the question of how a reasonable decision about the truth of any one tradition can be made." It seems that Ward and Küng do not refer to one another's work.

16. I suspect his mind did not change as much as one would hope; the learning did not get inside him, because he did not take the time to let that happen, and because his robust Catholicism did not allow for such vulnerability.

17. *A Global Ethic: The Declaration of the Parliament of the World's Religions* (1993); later editions of the same, and *Walls to Bridges: The Global Ethic*, a late career (2019, 2020) revision.

18. See particularly pages 74–81.

19. In the 1993 volume, Küng does address some specific issues, such as the Buddhist refusal to use the word *God*, for instance.

10

KÜNG AND THE SECULAR WORLD

Johanna Rahner

A Sensibility for the *Sensus (In)fidelis*

"Hans Küng has an alert sense for contemporary issues and a great talent for communication."[1] This brief characterization highlights the essential orientation of Hans Küng's way of doing theology and being a theologian, namely, having a sensitivity to the very heartbeat of his time. Küng did not invent the questions he raised, but he appreciated them as the result of "an open discomfort among the People of God" and made them public by highlighting them in the media. Actually, it was not only discomfort among the people of God that forced Küng to raise his questions, but it was also high time for these topics because they represented what a "theology sensitive to the times cannot ignore." His questions—if one takes a close look— "indicate the unresolved conflict between modernity and the Catholic Church,"[2] meaning they constitute part of the core problem: how to be a church for the twentieth and the twenty-first centuries. No one can be surprised that for "many believers, those who search for and ask about the faith...and for those who are interested in the faith but also critical or doubtful," Hans Küng has become "the symbol of an open church which manages to cross its confines again and again to encounter people's modern consciousness and at the same time not lose its identity as a church."[3] Medard Kehl speaks vividly of the "missionary power" of Küng as a theologian and writer. For a wide circle of readers this power was evident in his famous classic *On Being a Christian*.[4]

Published in 1974, this book had a deep impact. It appeared in several editions within a short time and was translated into quite a few languages within a year of its first publication. Reactions to the book, though, were mixed from the beginning and stretched from euphoric enthusiasm to scathing criticism. Some readers warmly welcomed Küng's endeavor to seek a new language in proclaiming the great themes of Christianity, which the book covers in a *tour d'horizon*, examining humanism and the various world religions, addressing the question of God's existence, the future of faith, looking at Jesus Christ, his history, message, uniqueness, death, and resurrection, and discussing the church, the Christian ethos and discipleship. For some readers, Küng's concern to convey the core of Christianity to his contemporaries while using a new language, different forms of thinking, and the results of historical-critical exegesis, was radically disturbing. From the point of view of his critics,[5] such an attempt sacrificed the truth of Christianity to the spirit of the age and constituted an endeavor to pander to the "relativism" of a secularized society that does not believe nor wants to and thus ultimately abandons faith, replacing it with anthropological plausibility or trivial humanism. They measured the truth of faith against the standard of the traditional dogmatic language the Catholic Church had used over the centuries and that Küng in his book explicitly and consciously contrasted with historical-critical skepticism and a way of arguing oriented to the most basic questions of human existence. This method was, of course, exactly the reason so many other readers found the book so liberating. Their feeling of relief was the result of Küng's deliberate break with the tradition of habitual language patterns and old models of thought, thus opening new paths to faith. For his opponents, however, Küng's method destroyed faith altogether.

Interestingly, the slant of criticism remained the same right up to Küng's death in 2021. Michael Karger, for example, in his obituary of Küng for the *Tagespost*—the traditionalist German Catholic weekly—wrote on April 7, 2021:

> What does Küng actually teach? Nothing else than the program of modernity, which is why it was so favorable to

him: progressiveness in itself is his all-encompassing standard of value. Beliefs are downgraded to hypotheses. They are no more than non-binding suggestions for interpretation that must be continually surpassed in the interest of progressiveness. Statements of essence are replaced by functionalist equivalents and thus made to disappear. The doctrine of the Trinity, the doctrine of the God-man Jesus Christ, of his vicarious sacrificial death, the sacrament of marriage, the ordained priesthood, are all dissolved. Claims of truth in themselves are seen as intolerant and fundamentalist. God becomes a function of the human.[6]

Such assessments show a narrow understanding of Küng's concerns, for one, and also hardly take seriously the existential need of Küng's worldwide readership—which was always a concern and challenge for Küng. His books try to address what moves people of today insofar as they are "religious seekers" (Charles Taylor),[7] or interested but "tone deaf when it comes to religion" (Jürgen Habermas).[8] Books such as *On Being a Christian* were written with such people in mind. In Küng's own words: "The book is written for all those who, for any reason at all, honestly and sincerely want to know what Christianity, what being a Christian, really means....It is written then for Christians and atheists, Gnostics and agnostics, pietists and positivists, lukewarm and zealous Catholics, Protestants and Orthodox."[9] And Küng meets all of them with the respect of one who knows that "even believers carry doubt in their luggage."[10] He had a deep sense for their need to have their doubts and their deep existential questions be taken seriously: "Respect those who in the present situation frown upon hearing the word 'God,' but by no means avoid the word. Instead of no longer talking about God, or instead of simply talking about God as before, what matters to me is talking about God in a new way, in respect, even in humility."[11] Hans Küng met the challenge squarely, by writing for those who cannot trust an ecclesiastic language of faith "which does not take into account the absence of God, the unanswered cries for him, or, indeed, doubt."[12] Küng, then, cannot simply ignore the fact that there are "whole landscapes of lives that…are not sometimes visited or even inhabited by the church"[13]—let us call them skeptics, seekers, those who are shaped by a scientific worldview and way of thinking; the "tone-deaf when it comes to religion," or people of different traditions and faiths who want to know what being a Christian is all about. For these people, the traditional language of faith no longer works; not because they are hard of hearing or even obdurate, but because traditional rhetoric fails to speak their language or strike a chord in their hearts. For them, and with a view to their questions, new ways of speaking of God, of believing (even of just getting ready to believe) have to be tested[14] so that eventually a free decision can be reached that is necessary to become a believer: "Every person should decide freely, with no pressure exerted on their intellect, and with access to rational arguments. Atheism as well as belief in God therefore presents a challenge—and a risk....You need to decide to believe in God, and deciding is another word for 'believing.'"[15]

A Sense for the "Signs of Our Time"

The controversy about what is meant by a church in a modern world did not end with the Second Vatican Council (1962–1965), and it has continued to shape the church way into the turbulence of the twenty-first century. The question still prominent in the wake of the Council is about the unfinished "turn" of the Council, a turn that has led to a new definition of the relationship between the church and the world, and to the question of how the church must understand its own identity within this newly defined relationship. Here, the fathers of Vatican II seemed to have voted with a clear option (cf. *Gaudium et Spes* 1), that was, however, received quite differently in the postconciliar period. The questions concerning the boundaries of the church, the existence of faith (or even the church) beyond these boundaries, and what might in the long run be the real difference between those who are inside and those who seem to be outside the church meet with different answers, which in turn seem to delineate a decisive watershed for two different ways of interpreting what being church in the modern world actually means.

Küng is unambiguously on one side. The starting point in his survey of faith and his rethinking of the possibility of belief at all is the inalienable dignity and inherent worth of the world. He sees it filled with positive signals. Such a view encourages a very optimistic attitude; the world still presents a place for an authentic experience of God. Therefore, even secular history and a secularized world do not merely supply the material *against* which the church must define its identity by a demarcation line. On the contrary, they demand, urge, enable a pastoral solidarity *with* this world and its history. The world and its history are close to the heart and the very existence of the church. The regulative principle is the indispensable correlation between church and world. "No one without everyone" is now the principle on which to rely. The truth of the gospel is irrevocably interwoven with the requirements of our times. One cannot define what it means to believe in God, or what is actually the point of being a Christian, without factoring in the value of the world or without developing a deep and serious solidarity with it. Such renewed ecclesial identity draws its criteria from an interconnection regarded as a good thing, a *missio ad mundum*, a mission into and for the world. Don't just proclaim the truth, but listen to all that might be truthful within this world. The appropriate method for doing so is engaging in dialogue. Entering into a proper dialogue means acknowledging that the others might also have a point, perhaps a better one than I, and as a result I might learn from the others. The traditional way of "proclaiming the truth" must be reversed, then, because now the church also has to listen and perhaps learn from the others.

Actual contemporaneity characterizes this option. Neither "being a Christian," nor faith, nor believing in God can be taken for granted today. New questions need to be asked: What is the deepest meaning, the real sense of my life? Can a religious answer to this question still convince a person in our age? Why still believe in God? What is the point of being a Christian in the twenty-first century? What is the sociopolitical potential of religions for a globalized world and its longing for peace, freedom, solidarity? All this also implies a sensitivity to the question why resonance for theological language, ecclesiastical jargon, even, indeed, for religion as a horizon of understanding seems increasingly on the wane. Hans Küng was always concerned with these questions when facing a rapidly and fundamentally changing world. He never avoided the crucial basic questions such as "Does God exist?" or "Is there eternal life?" He aimed at a reflective, capable, and informed type of faith rooted in life as it is, and in which the questions of this life and the answers of faith are mutually enriching: "I try to hold together and structure the overabundance of questions and topics that arise through the multicolored, comprehensive concept of life as it is realized in the development of life in general, in the course of a single human life, in my own life story."[16]

1968—an Epochal Caesura, and Its Consequences

"1968 was [admittedly] not the year that changed everything.... But after '68 almost nothing was the same as before"—this is how the contemporary German historian Norbert Frei puts it.[17] The student riots starting in Berlin and Paris caused turmoil in Europe and North America and inspired the whole world with new ideas—such as global solidarity and mutual responsibility, the need for a fundamental shift to democracy and justice, for peace and freedom, and even the most personal issues now became a matter of politics. This was ultimately the starting point for a fundamental change in (at least) European societies. The generation of "'68ers" established new forms of communication such as sit-ins, go-ins, teach-ins, and happenings, deliberately relying on disruption and provocation as performative signs and mercilessly exposing the hidden discourses of power of those who invoke tradition and "the traditional." They ruthlessly dismantled a language that strategically concealed personal power interests, they critically questioned all authority and convention, they declared institutional critique and antiauthoritarian structures to be a principle of life, and they put into question all previously binding norms and values.

It is no coincidence at all that the last and disturbing attempt of the papal magisterium to place the formal authority of the ecclesiastical hierarchy above the conscience of the individual Catholic was issued in exactly this year. Thus, the publication of *Humanae Vitae*, Paul VI's encyclical letter on human sexuality and contraception issued on July 25, 1968, is rightly perceived by church historians as the moment when the dam broke. In the history of the reception of Vatican II, you might still argue about whether "reform," "(dis)continuity," or even "rupture" are appropriate metaphors to describe the process of change initiated by the Council.[18] Looking at the earthquake in ways of thinking that marked the Catholic Church in the wake of *Humanae Vitae*, one cannot help calling it a rupture that affected the deepest roots. It was not simply resistance that was stirred up; the "specter of revolution" (a phrase of German author and poet Hans Magnus Enzensberger) had now also seized Catholics, and it was to become a Catholic matter of principle. Obviously, a fundamental break with the tradition of obedience[19] had become palpable, therein resembling the '68 movement, and in quite a short time led to the controversies around the "Küng Affair." Like no one else, Hans Küng had a sure instinct for the explosive nature of the situation at that time. "It is…the ecclesiastical system itself that has lagged far behind the times in its development and still exhibits numerous traits of princely absolutism: the pope and bishops as the *de facto* sole ruling lords of the church, uniting legislative, executive, and judicial functions in their hands. Their exercise of power is still not subject to any effective control in many places, in spite of the now established councils. Freedom for the church is demanded externally, but not granted internally. One preaches justice and peace where it costs the church and its leadership nothing."[20] This summarizes a petition Hans Küng initiated in 1972 as a first reaction (and one hundred well-known theologians around the world signed on). A few years later, in *Infallible? An Inquiry*,[21] Küng would pose the crucial question even more explicitly and categorically: How valid and plausible can a structure and form of thought be that has led to a decision that ignores the sense of the faithful in a deeply hurtful way, resulting in a theological crisis of legitimacy from which the Catholic Church has not recovered to this day, and which must therefore be regarded as a legacy still to be overcome?

The Küng Affair made visible how theologically insufficient and unpromising is the traditional way of discernment and decision-making in the Catholic Church, namely, an autocratic structure that affronted and silenced not only the female half of Catholics but most of the laity as a whole, thus disregarding not only the sense of the faithful but seemingly making it impossible for people to be modern in their thinking and Catholic at the same time. The writing was on the wall: the march into an intellectual and social ghetto was imminent. An appropriate response now seemed to be a revolution, the final break with everything familiar, turning tradition and structure upside down, leaving no stone unturned and nothing unproven. A famous colleague of Küng at the University of Tübingen, Joseph Ratzinger, threw in the towel in the face of these disturbing modern times and from then on supported the idea of an unchanging tradition and the folk piety of his youth.[22] In the preface to his 1968 book *Introduction to Christianity* Ratzinger wrote a short passage that also could be understood as a comment on the above: He compared most of his contemporary colleagues in Catholic theology with that pitiful wretch in the German fairy tale of Clever Hans, "who in order to feel more comfortable changed his gold, in turn, for a horse, then a cow, then a goose, then a whetstone (the latter finally to be thrown into the water), and in the end was even happy about it." What subtle but also biting criticism! However, even Ratzinger couldn't solve the crucial hermeneutical problem: which tradition is worth keeping and which is not, and what are the legitimate criteria on which to base a decision? Referring only to tradition and the principle of "always the same" is not a satisfactory answer for the future. It remains a question that is debated publicly and permanently up to the present day.

How to Make Faith Possible—Even for Critical Contemporaries

In his review of *On Being a Christian*, none other than Karl Rahner had given a short but striking resumé of the benefits of Küng's hermeneutical program and epistemological method to open up faith beyond the hermetic language of ecclesial tradition and the narrowing medieval legacy of an ontology of metaphysics: "If one imagines the circle of readers realistically and takes into account educated Catholics who are not specialists in theology, one will have to say that what Küng seeks to convey to his readers in terms of insights and convictions of a Christian nature goes far beyond what one usually takes for granted in these readers."[23] Thus, Rahner appreciates the constructive function and positive mission of a "presentation of the substance of Christianity" for those readers "for whom...all this is neither self-evident nor certain....They find a proper and deeper access to Christianity than they have found before."[24] Being a Christian in the twenty-first century is a crucial heuristic task that has certainly become far more complex and challenging under the conditions of late modernity than it was when Küng wrote his book fifty years ago. It therefore does not seem far-fetched to assume that the very presupposition of the book, namely, that there are religiously interested and educated readers who are skilled in theological discourses and intellectually and existentially challenged by them, is far less plausible today than it was then. Not that our time no longer needs such an undertaking—perhaps it does even more so than ever—but the question of how to do this has become far more complex than it seemed half a century ago.

In *On Being a Christian*, Hans Küng deals intensively with the phenomenon of historicity, that is, the entanglement of time and the contingency of the history of ideas and thus also of all theological forms of expression and thought models to explain the Christian faith. In the past these forms and models might have helped to understand and deepen the faith, but today they cannot do this anymore. Reading Küng's classic after fifty years makes one thing quite clear: even Küng's historically-critically verified analyses—although in accordance with the common sense of his time—bear the character of their time, as does the (neo-Scholastic) sterile-abstract school theology that is always present as a negative foil. The latter explains the fact that Küng's way of thinking and speaking is characterized always by an effort to correct the old form of thinking and by dismissing it. This, in turn, often leads to a confrontational style of argument. So even Küng's impressive endeavor is one limited by history, and thus the problem of temporality ultimately also hovers over Küng's enterprise of finding a new language of faith for critical contemporaries.

Still, his book remains a classic, for Küng develops a novel way to do Christology, finding and defining a new language to speak of Jesus of Nazareth as the Christ, decidedly in the style of a "Christology from below" and compatible with historical and philosophical reasoning. Küng's Jesus Christ aims at being a reconstruction with practical significance for the lives of those who believe in Christ, and he therefore consistently starts with Jesus of Nazareth as a human being and as a challenging model of life and action. According to Hermann Häring, Küng "turns the classical metaphysical doctrine of Christ upside down and makes it comprehensible to those who are interested in the 'practice' of being a Christian and in the question which way of life might be adequate for those who want to follow Jesus."[25] In doing so, the "figure of Jesus…should come to light without naïve later interpolation," especially ecclesial deformations. All the different "transformations of the faith in Christ" should be "culturally classified," and above all the "core of the faith in Christ as 'discipleship' should be revealed in its practical consequences for life."[26] Jesus becomes a "life model in person,"[27] and so "by following Jesus Christ, man [sic] in the world of today can truly humanly live, act, suffer and die: in happiness and unhappiness, life and death, sustained by God and helpful to men."[28]

As a result, the old formulas of Christian dogmatics are not simply played off against a historically reconstructed image of Jesus, but Küng develops a new interpretation of the dogmas of the early church, paying attention to the significance of the historical Jesus of Nazareth. He knows—perhaps much better than those overzealous guardians of orthodoxy with their insistence on certain formulas and sentences—that just quoting a dogmatic formula does not automatically convey the truth but would always require further interpretation and mediation. Küng proposes "to try new ways of translation and understanding. For if, or better since, Hellenism is not the actual 'original' world of Christianity, why should further processes of inculturation be forbidden, especially if the symbolic power of the elementary words can remain the same?"[29] Thus, according to Hermann Häring's summing up, the "outdated classical-metaphysical concept serving as a framework...is transformed into an ontological concept that is no longer oriented toward the supratemporal ideas of 'being' and 'essence' but to its counterparts 'acting' and 'experiencing.'" Indeed, Küng's preferred theological ontology can be characterized as an "ontology of action and relationship."[30]

Küng presents an understanding of the core of the Christian faith that is consistently oriented toward the openness of biblical language in order to recover the historical, that is, the original christological perspective of the New Testament. Kung seeks to explain the meaning of Christian faith and dogma "narratively." Jesus's program is mapped out; his social context, his position in relation to the establishment and the transforming power of his actions, his dissociation from political revolutions as well as from an elitist shunning of social reality and the provocative power of his ethics. The heart of his message is of the coming reign of God breaking into the present, looking to the absolute future, and, above all, the humanizing power of God's universal will for salvation. Jesus's words and actions are the starting point of God's reign. Küng thus develops a functional Christology, based on the key word (which could be placed alongside a number of similar ones)—"God's representative"[31]: "Jesus is not merely an expert like the Pharisees and Scribes: He stands in the place of God."[32]

Küng presents a good example of how to put the existential search for God into an open space, a space allowing doubt, insecurity, the inability to believe and even despair. Further attempts were to follow on various levels. Küng was moved by insights that the Czech writer and Catholic priest Tomáš Halík describes in this way: "At certain moments, it is precisely the experience of God's absence, the incomprehensibility of the world and the tragedy of human fate that becomes the incentive to wait and thirst longingly for God. God himself awakens this longing and is already present in it in a way; God comes to us not only as an answer but also as a question. God comes to be understood through a longing that transcends all partial answers and is always opening up new questions. God stimulates a new search—and thus the character of pilgrimage is imprinted onto our existence."[33] Küng tried to meet the challenge of keeping his eyes and his ears open for the signs of the times. For believers and unbelievers alike in each new publication that was respectively addressed to different partners in dialogue, he reconstructed the Christian faith from different points of view, thus taking seriously his responsibility toward those who are spiritual seekers.

The Epistemology of a "Treasure in Fragile Vessels"

From the beginning, the epistemological challenges associated with such an approach and its consequences have triggered contradiction and questions: "Re-construction, even the most successful, is always construction," Joseph Ratzinger pronounces with reference to Küng's approach to a Christology from below, thus raising questions about the relationship between historical reconstruction and the claims to truth, between history and dogma, and about the relationship between plausibility and credibility.[34] Walter Kasper takes a critical look at Küng's central form of thought, "as a modern type of subjectivity that is critical of tradition and authority by principle," seeing this as a decisive criterion of credibility.[35] Both enquiries into Küng's approach point in the same direction. Do Küng's deconstructions and reconstructions take place in the forecourt of the pagans, that is, do they serve to make things believable to outsiders, or do they become the criteria of truth for Christianity as a whole? From today's point of view, one would probably rather ask whether and how both could be adequately distinguished. And is there really a theological difference between them?

The same applies to the basic hermeneutical approach of making the classical dogmatic thought forms and language patterns more understandable and acceptable for people in the twenty-first century by updating and raising the question of their deeper or "existential" meaning. About this even Karl Rahner had made some critical remarks when reviewing Küng's *On Being a Christian*: "It seems to me that between the Jesus Küng discovers and presents as a historical reality and us today there lies only a history of theology, but not an actual history of faith in the Church, and this 'mere history of theology' ultimately has no fundamental normativity for him, because normativity and truth are only measured by what Küng himself had discovered about Jesus."[36] Is it possible to simply skip over almost two thousand years of the history of faith? Is the crucial task of a critical theology that wants to be compatible with modernity already fulfilled by first asking about the biblical sources of the event itself and, second, by asking about the significance for the present to make "an immediate correlation between the biblical horizon and the presently retrievable possibilities of understanding"?[37] Is it possible to recover "a true, simple origin" only by "misappropriating every historical thinking and its efforts"?[38]

True, every development of tradition, every history of dogma, and every doctrinal definition (particularly in Christology) must be critically questioned—that is the responsibility of a theology that deserves its name. For every theologian, however, it is also true that the different epochs in the history of faith need to be understood as a never-ending struggle for an appropriate understanding of faith in which no epoch can simply be skipped over or neglected. It is precisely this genuine history of theology with all its ups and downs that shows that some questions only emerge "in the process of the transmission of faith with aggressiveness and logic," so that they are neither to be trivialized nor concealed if one really wants to take the historicity of faith seriously.[39] The history of faith itself belongs to the truth of faith. You can't have one without the other. Whoever tries to ignore or skip one side runs the risk of overlooking central aspects that were only recognized as relevant in the history of theology within a certain context or by a certain, that is, necessarily contingent, form of thinking. "We carry the treasure of faith only in fragile vessels" (cf. 2 Cor 4:7)—that is the basic principle of Küng's theology—and sometimes it needs to be used as a critical measure against itself, something a theology for the twenty-first century cannot avoid without denying its very role.

The End of the Hellenistic Epoch and the Crisis of Faith

Küng was always concerned with counteracting the language barriers of the classical theological formulas and their "ecclesiological encodings" (an expression coined by Johann Baptist Metz) in order to overcome the crisis of faith in modern times and to discover a new approach to a modern theological language. This makes Küng's theology relevant for today. For the crisis of language and of the proclamation of faith still represents the real "shadow theme" in the current crisis of the Catholic Church. Some might suspect it to be a kind of linguistic sclerosis, a religious and cultural exhaustion of immense proportion. "It seems," as Hubertus Halbfas put it provocatively,

> as if the time of the Church of Greek inculturation has expired. This refers to the Church that translated itself into Hellenistic thought patterns already in the first generation of its existence, even before it could develop its own identity vis-à-vis its Jewish sphere of origin. It is precisely the world of faith created by Greek ways of thinking and Greek imagination that now experiences a breakdown of language and understanding, with the result that the ecclesial language of faith and of proclaiming the gospel comes to nothing.[40]

Sometimes the language of the dead simply remains dead: "In the meantime, all fundamental and central concepts of the Christian faith are outside the regular framework of understanding of our time....The expiry date of such concepts of faith has long since passed," according to Ludger Verst.[41] The loss of the existential basis of the language it uses is at best ignored by the church, but as a rule—according to Johann Baptist Metz—it is laboriously dressed up as a catechetical language that is "shock-free" and ignorant of every kind of actual needs.[42] This type of rigorous orthodoxy, however, can obfuscate the theological abyss that the German lyricist Paul Konrad Kurz analyzed with unmistakable acuity in the 1990s: "The relationship between the (relatively) static church and the dynamic world generates of itself a problem of believing in God."[43] The "God of Abraham flowing into life" is "channeled" by its ecclesiastical proclaimers "into orthodoxy, narrowly guided, set up, shoehorned into ecclesiastical concretions. The God-on-the-Way is locked into schemes of thought and behavior. He had to settle down as a resident, with the Church administration looking over his shoulder."[44] Consequently, it may well be true that the crisis of belief in enlightened societies is (only/mainly) "the crisis of the God the church proclaims—fixed, catechetical, authority-monitored, censored, administered God."[45] It could therefore be solved by replacing that ossified, all too certain way of speaking about God with one that is saturated with experience, worldly, subjective, the language of someone on his/her way that takes its questionability just as seriously as its innate susceptibility to disturbance and fragility.

Küng's theology reacts precisely to these attempts to deal with modern metaphysical homelessness. Again and again, he confronts faith with the fundamental question of modernity; has the emancipation of reason from faith, which is necessary for all enlightenment, not also given up a viable basis for appreciating and valuing human beings by approving the biblical intuition that every human being is an image of God and by the idea of God's incarnation? It can hardly be denied that secular reason has had quite a challenge trying to meet, in other ways, the unsurpassable appreciation of the humanity that comes with the Christian confession of God's incarnation, and so far its attempts have not reached their goal. Every theologian must take this seriously today, because even today the question of God cannot be negotiated, and theological or religious solutions for the crisis cannot be sought below this existential level. In his foreword to *The Church*, Küng rightly noted that "the question of God is more important than the question of the Church. But often the second gets in the way of the first. That's not necessarily the case. We should try to show this."[46] The task that Küng then tackles can best be outlined by an almost euphoric sentence from the (albeit critical) review of *Die Kirche* by Hans Urs von Balthasar: "Küng does a good job cleaning out the stables, he resembles Hercules in the Augean stables."[47]

Beyond Christianity and the Church

The further developments in the Küng Affair and the resulting consequences are only too well known; the latter are perhaps even more painfully visible today at a distance of almost forty-five years, for the so-called "Crisis of the Church"—which is also structural—is gaining momentum unknown to previous generations. One can no longer ignore "what happens when the concrete social form of the Church makes it impossible for many people to set out on the path to God." Therein lies today "the really dramatic aspect of the Church's crisis."[48] It is the undeniable result of the changing perspective on what is necessary to make faith convincing in late modernity that also requires a different perspective on the church. It is because you can "only identify the Church with the question of God, indeed God himself with the Church if you can assume the Church to be a place where the question of God may be and is posed in all its ambivalences and thus is a question to be asked openly in view of the concrete realities of the lives of people today."[49] Here, the ecclesiological desiderata of a Catholic Church come to light, but also the increasing ecclesiastical incapability of speaking the language of our contemporaries, just as under a magnifying glass the ecclesiastical fear of contact with the modern world becomes visible here and threatens to let it slide into a sectarian mentality tantamount to a march into the ghetto. At best, it is laboriously dressed up by a zealously sharpened confessional language and a militant inability of communication with the modern world— still thinking that this is the only way of being (and remaining) truly Catholic.

In one of his last publications, Johann Baptist Metz, following Karl Rahner, spoke vividly of a "natural God-competence" in every human being.[50] That is the crucial point. This human gift must be taken seriously. However, this has to take place beyond or in a conscious break with the ecclesiological encoding, even appropriation, that is beyond the "ecclesial and theological trivialization" of speaking of

God.[51] We must develop a deeper sense for the "foreign prophecy" of an indispensable longing for authentic humanity. The new language of faith that is needed and the sensitivity for longings unheard before are determined by borderline experiences. As Pope Francis says, "The church is called to go outside of itself and go to the peripheries, not just geographic but also the existential peripheries....Those of the mystery of sin, of pain, injustice, ignorance, spiritual privation, thoughts and complete misery."[52] That is, of questions to which we no longer have an answer, where we are at the end of our tether, where we feel that the reality of human accounts does not add up. These are today's actual places of a true experience of grace or a gentle anticipation of the transcendent God. That is why those places are significant "where messianic healing of damaged lives is expected." It is a place of the church without the safety line of an institution that has become complacent: "I prefer a Church which is bruised, hurting and dirty because it has been out on the streets, rather than a Church which is unhealthy from being confined and from clinging to its own security."[53] The idea of a "Church on the streets" is not simply a spiritual hobbyhorse of the current pope; it actually describes a new ecclesiological model, not only for the Catholic Church. It is by no means innocuous but existentially and institutionally challenging, because the road on which Francis wants to lead the church is not the grand boulevard, but the gutter.

This leads to a different definition of where the place of the church has to be. It takes the confession of the incarnation as a measure. God is "in the flesh," in the wounds of the world. A pastoral ministry centered around the incarnation should be characterized by its sensitive mindfulness to the marginalized. Such an incarnation-centered ministry can, of course, be connected to the world through searching, not through knowledge. It is certainly not identical with a full-throated language of certainty that knows all about God and all about faith. On the contrary. Tomáš Halík describes the resulting necessities impressively in his latest book *The Afternoon of Christianity: The Courage to Change*: "The dialogue between believers and nonbelievers is no longer a matter of two strictly separate groups; it takes place in the minds and hearts of individuals." For, Halík continues,

> Faith, as I understand it in this book, is found not only in the lives of people who describe themselves as believers in a religious sense, but also in an implicit, anonymous form

in the spiritual quest of men and women beyond the visible boundaries of religious doctrines and institutions. Secular spirituality is also part of the story of faith. With this broad understanding of faith, however, I do not intend to blur the concept of faith into a vague shape by the banal statement that "everyone believes in something" and that even a non-believer is a believer in a sense. I speak of the "unbelief of believers" and the "faith of non-believers"; however, by speaking of the faith of unbelievers, I do not intend to arrogantly colonize the world of non-believers or deny respect to their own self-understanding by foisting upon them something that is alien to them. I only want to show another context of the phenomenon of faith: what faith is and what it is not must necessarily be sought again and again through a careful study of various forms of faith and non-belief.[54]

Against this background, Küng's prophetic sense for the secular world becomes all the more obvious.

An Unfinished Task

Contemporary culture and society are authentic *loci theologici*, that is, legitimate sources of theology and faith. This fundamentally calls into question the talk of "ingratiating oneself with the spirit of the age" that is so commonly used in some Catholic circles. "I believe," as Tomáš Halík puts it, "that God, who fully revealed himself in the *kenosis* (self-emptying) of Jesus, is so humble that he is also anonymously present in the expressions of human openness, longing and hope, even where he is not recognized and named—that is, in secular culture, if it is humanly authentic."[55] Thus, the basic truth of Christian faith, to believe that God became human, is irrevocably interwoven with the requirements of the time. The consequences for the Church are obvious; today not only a new ecclesiology is necessary, but also a new way of talking about faith. Or rather, the two are interdependent: "The Christianity of late modernity has fallen into a certain cultural homelessness, which is one of the causes of the present crisis. In this time of changing cultural paradigms, the Christian faith is still looking for a new form, a new home, new possibilities of expression, new social and cultural tasks and new allies."[56] These are the classic questions Hans Küng was always concerned with. Today, they are becoming increasingly fundamental existential questions for the Catholic Church and for "being a Christian" in the twenty-first century.

"Only a Church constantly transcending its own institutional boundaries towards the others and opening up its particularity to the others, in a broad universal approach, only a Church like that can exist as the *communio* constituted by the Risen One and making him present in the Eucharist."[57] Hans Küng's life option was and remains unmistakably directed toward this basic ecclesiological principle. This probably explains the brilliant and deep impact of the Küng Affair, for according to Kehl, the "great and probably not unjustified fear of many people in view of the Küng Affair goes precisely in this direction: whether the Catholic Church is not gradually putting this [missionary] dimension emphasized by the Second Vatican Council below the concern for its own identity and integrity."[58]

It cannot be denied that there is one crucial consequence that Medard Kehl already formulated in 1980:

> The institutional distancing that the *magisterium* carried out by withdrawing the permission to teach is in fact so serious and far-reaching that it hardly allows even a partial identification of the Church with Küng's missionary service. This does not diminish Küng's popularity and influence, but it does diminish the use of a rare talent as a charism in the Church. With all due respect for the decision of the *magisterium*, with all due understanding for the reasons for this decision—a stronger consideration of the second basic ecclesiological principle ("Church for the others") might have led to a decision that would have served the cause of the Church and its unity in faith better.[59]

There is nothing that needs to be added today to this summing-up.

Notes

1. Jan-Heiner Tück, "Die Wahrheit bleibt umstritten," *Neue Zürcher Zeitung*, December 12, 2007; https://www.nzz.ch/die_wahrheit_bleibt_umstritten-ld.451457.
2. Tück, "Wahrheit."
3. Medard Kehl, "Theologische Anmerkungen zum 'Fall Küng.' War der Entzug der Lehrbefugnis berechtigt?," *Stimmen der Zeit* 198 (1980): 376–84, 379f.
4. *On Being a Christian*, trans. Edward Quinn (Garden City, NY: Doubleday, 1976). Subsequent page references in the text refer to this edition.
5. As an example: Leo Scheffczyk, *Aufbruch oder Abbruch des Glaubens. Zum Buch H. Küngs 'Christ sein'* (Stein am Rhein: Christiana, 1976).
6. Michael Karger, "Hans Küng ist tot: Rückblick auf ein langes Leben im Konflikt mit der Kirche," *Tagespost*, April 7, 2021; https://www.die-tagespost.de/kirche-aktuell/weltkirche/hans-kueng-der-gegenpapst-art-217285.
7. Cf. Charles Taylor, *A Secular Age* (Cambridge, MA: Harvard University Press, 2007), esp. 505–38.
8. Cf. Jürgen Habermas, *Between Naturalism and Religion*, trans. Ciaran Cronin (Cambridge: Polity Press, 2008), esp. 209–47.
9. *On Being a Christian*, 19.
10. Magnus Striet, "Was ist 'katholisch'? Ein Bestimmungsversuch im Horizont der Moderne," in *Kirche 2011: Ein notwendiger Aufbruch. Argumente zum Memorandum* ed. Marianne Heimbach-Steins et al. (Freiburg: Herder, 2011), 58–70, 68.
11. Hans Küng, *What I Believe* (New York: Bloomsbury, 2010), 85.
12. Magnus Striet, *In der Gottesschleife: Von religiöser Sehnsucht in der Moderne* (Freiburg: Herder, 2014), 143.
13. Gotthard Fuchs, "Neuer Bedarf an Spiritualität," *Herder Korrespondenz* 59 (2005): 447–52, 449.
14. See especially *The Beginning of All Things: Science and Religion* (Grand Rapids, MI: Eerdmans, 2008), and *What I Believe*.
15. Hans Küng, *Was bleibt. Kerngedanken* (Munich: Piper 2014), 21.

16. Küng, *What I Believe*, 14.

17. Norbert Frei, *1968. Jugendrevolte und globaler Protest* (Munich: dtv-Verlag 2008), 228.

18. Cf. the discussion on Benedict XVI's speech to the Roman Curia on December 22, 2005, https://www.vatican.va/content/benedict-xvi/en/speeches/2005/december/documents/hf_ben_xvi_spe_20051222_roman-curia.html.

19. Cf. Ursula Krey, "Der Bruch mit der Gehorsamstradition. Die 68er Bewegung und der gesellschaftliche Wertewande," in *1968 und die Kirchen*, ed. Bernd Hey and Volkmar Wittmütz (Bielefeld: Verlag für Regionalgeschichte, 2008), 13–34.

20. Hans Küng, "Wider die Resignation," in *Kirchenreform. Sämtliche Werke*, vol 6, ed. Hans Küng and Stephan Schlensog (Freiburg: Herder, 2016), 54f.

21. Hans Küng, *Infallible? An Inquiry* (New York: Doubleday, 1983).

22. The English edition appeared in 1970 (New York: Herder & Herder).

23. Karl Rahner, Review of *On Being a Christian* by Hans Küng, *Theologie der Gegenwart* 2 (1975): 80–87, 82.

24. Rahner, "Review," 82f.

25. Hermann Häring, "Gehalten von Gott—engagiert für die Menschen—Eine Rückschau auf Hans Küng 'Christ sein,'" March 1, 2006, Introduction, https://www.hjhaering.de/gehalten-von-gott-engagiert-fuer-die-menschen-eine-rueckschau-auf-hans-kueng-christ-sein/.

26. Häring, "Gehalten von Gott," introduction.

27. Küng, *Was ich glaube*, 225.

28. Küng, *On Being a Christian*, 602.

29. Häring, "Gehalten von Gott," chap. 2.2.

30. Häring, "Gehalten von Gott," Conclusion.

31. Küng, *On Being a Christian*, 281.

32. Albert Raffelt, "Aspekte gegenwärtiger Christologie. Ein Literaturbericht," *Lebendige Seelsorge* 28 (1977): 34–40.

33. Tomáš Halík, *Der Nachmittag des Christentums* (Freiburg: Herder 2022), 49. English translation forthcoming in 2024 from the University of Notre Dame Press. See n54 below.

34. Joseph Ratzinger, "Wer verantwortet die Aussagen der Theologie?," in *Diskussion über Hans Küngs 'Christ sein,'* ed. H. U. v. Balthasar (Mainz: Grünewald, 1976), 7–18, 11.

35. Cf. Walter Kasper, "Christsein ohne Tradition," in *Diskussion über Hans Küngs 'Christ sein,'* ed. H. U. v. Balthasar (Mainz: Grünewald, 1976), 19–34, 31.

36. Rahner, "Review," 86.

37. Georg Essen/Thomas Pröpper, "Aneignungsprobleme der christologischen Überlieferung: hermeneutische Vorüberlegungen," in *Gottes ewiger Sohn. Die Präexistenz Christi*, ed. Rudolf Laufen (Paderborn: Ferdinand Schöningh, 1997), 163–78, 167.

38. Theodor Schneider, "Zur Trinitätslehre," in *Diskussion über Hans Küngs 'Christ sein,'* ed. H. U. v. Balthasar (Mainz: Grünewald, 1976), 95–104, 97.

39. Cf. Schneider, "Trinitätslehre," 97.

40. Hubertus Halbfas, "Traditionsbruch und Neubeginn. Paradigmenwechsel am Ende der überlieferten Kirchengestalt," in *Orientierung aus Religion und Gesellschaft. Rückblick über 30 Jahre theologische-Erwachsenenbildung*, ed. W. Pfeiffer (Noderstedt: Edition Hellweg 2011), 86–102, 92.

41. Ludger Verst, "Credo, ergo…Wortdurchfall," review of *Jargon der Betroffenheit* by Erik Flügge, http://www.feinschwarz.net/credo-ergo-wortdurchfall/.

42. Cf. Johann Baptist Metz, *Memoria passionis, Ein provozierendes Gedächtnis in pluralistischer Gesellschaft* (Freiburg: Herder, ⁴2011), 115.

43. Paul Konrad Kurz, *Gott in der modernen Literatur* (Munich: Kösel, 1996), 234.

44. Cf. Kurz, *Gott*, 231.

45. Cf. Kurz, *Gott*, 231.

46. *The Church* (New York: Sheed and Ward, 1967), xiii.

47. Hans Urs v. Balthasar, "Erbe als Auftrag," in *Hans Küng, Weg und Werk*, ed. Hermann Häring and Karl-Josef Kuschel (Munich: Piper 1978), 65–74, 65.

48. Cf. Ilse Müllner, "Das Memorandum 'Freiheit' und seine kommunikativen Horizonte," in *Das Memorandum. Positionen im Für und Wider*, ed. Judith Könemann (Freiburg: Herder, 2011), 134–41, 137.

49. Magnus Striet, "Was ist 'katholisch'? Ein Bestimmungsversuch im Horizont der Moderne," in *Kirche 2011: Ein notwendiger*

Aufbruch. Argumente zum Memorandum, ed. Marianne Heimbach-Steins et al. (Freiburg: Herder, 2011), 58–70, 68.

50. Metz, "Memoria passionis," 108ff.

51. Metz, "Memoria passionis," 115.

52. Jorge Maria Bergolio, Handwritten speech delivered before 2013 conclave, https://catholicherald.co.uk/handwritten-speech-delivered-by-pope-during-2013-conclave-is-released/.

53. Pope Francis, Apostolic Exhortation *Evangelii Gaudium* (November 24, 2013), 49.

54. Tomáš Halík, *The Afternoon of Christianity: The Courage to Change* (South Bend, IN: University of Notre Dame Press, 2024). The page references below are to the German language edition. This English edition is forthcoming.

55. Halík, "Afternoon," 47.

56. Halík, "Afternoon," 71.

57. Kehl, "Anmerkungen," 379.

58. Kehl, "Anmerkungen," 380.

59. Kehl, "Anmerkungen," 384.

11

DOES HANS KÜNG STILL MATTER?

Jonathan Keir

> The space that literature is busy losing must be reconquered, but that will require a resurgence of the humility which is proper to humanism at its best. Such humanism is not a glorification of a being more intelligent than her ape cousins, but of people who know that they need the texts of the past in order to understand the world and themselves.[1]
>
> Alain Finkielkraut

All New Zealanders suffer from a certain degree of imposter syndrome on the world stage, but this invitation to offer the last word on the legacy of Hans Küng in a volume full of eminent theological opinion represents a new peak—or trough—in my lifelong ocean of faking it. I am not even a theologian; my path to Küng and why he might "still matter" runs chiefly through the first atheist celebrity of the YouTube generation, Christopher Hitchens, and his 2002 book *Why Orwell Matters*. Like Hitchens, I was "energized," chaotically at first, by the attacks of September 11, 2001, and called to reflect on my utter ignorance of Islam (and much else about the world beyond New Zealand) at a time when I was making important decisions about my future (I had just turned nineteen when the towers in faraway New York, on which I had once stood, came crashing down on television). Eventually I won an Erasmus Mundus scholarship to study in Europe—academic tourism really, philosophy here and literature there—and by 2013, after a series of self-imposed and self-inflicted peregrinations, I finally found myself within sight of the PhD finish line. I had started off working on Egyptian novelist Naguib Mahfouz and the theme of *hadara* or "civilization" in his later novels. I gradually expanded the project to include Russian director Andrei Tarkovsky and Confucian philosopher Tu Weiming, who addressed the same theme (or so I argued) in similar ways. It was while reading about Tu's efforts to bring Confucian "civilization" into dialogue with the world that I first encountered the name Hans Küng and his Global Ethic Project. When my doctoral scholarship's mobility clause brought me to the University of Tübingen for my final year, however, I had no idea that Küng had built his career there. It was only when I physically walked past the *Weltethos Institut* in Tübingen's Old Town that I made the connection. A one-year postdoctoral stipend was on offer from the university to native English speakers in a bid to boost Tübingen's international ranking; exhausted from years of constant travel, I took it, and used the opportunity to learn more about Küng's work. The last decade of my life has ended up revolving around *Weltethos* worries in one form or another.

This long autobiographical preamble is meant as a *caveat emptor* to any readers expecting a further dose of academic theology here. I will argue that Küng matters well beyond the confines of religious studies (his importance within that field has been expertly discussed here by others, so I will not be replowing it with my rudimentary instruments). There is in any case a bittersweet irony, or perhaps divine justice, in the fact that I ended end up working with a reformist theologian on intercultural dialogue. I lived the Catholic-Protestant divide within my own family, so I know just how hard achieving an entire *Weltethos* will be. Assessing Küng's legacy in 2018 (on the twenty-fifth anniversary of the signing of the Declaration toward a Global Ethic in Chicago in 1993), I concluded that the Declaration itself was a dead letter; the Weltethos Project, however, was only just getting going, and still had a long and vigorous life ahead of it.[2] An intolerable degree of humbug surrounds the Declaration now; the easy optimism of the 1990s has given way to accelerating chaos in all areas of life following the greatest technological breakthrough of all time. It is no longer remotely enough to get Muslims and Buddhists and Jedi worshippers to agree with one another in public that lying, stealing, killing, and raping are wrong. Küng's "discovery" that these ethical precepts—reducible to the "Golden Rule" in some form—are common to the world's religions is so twee as to be beside the point to younger generations raised on a steady diet of polarizing social media content. Küng believed, honestly and innocently enough, that a Declaration toward a Global Ethic could be a useful document for the immediate post–Cold War world, a net addition to humanity in the genre of the Universal Declaration of Human Rights. Küng's colleague Karl-Josef Kuschel points out in his magisterial *Leben ist Brückenschlagen* (2011) that the history of interreligious dialogue is only really a century or so old; the twenty-first-century challenge, however, is no longer to state or elaborate these common ethical standards to one another like a newly discovered wheel, but rather to embody them in one's own behavior in a world of exponentially accelerating cheek-by-jowl interaction with other cultures. There is a hucksterish element involved in inviting members of established faiths to sign up to a global consensus on values while leaving the psychosocial roots of "faith" unthreatened by the very dialogue—and hence critique and self-critique—needed for Küngian peace in the first place. I have argued that one can and must decouple Küng's deeper *Weltethos* project from the 1993 Declaration, which has run its course and belongs in a history museum despite the best efforts of the Parliament of the World's Religions—and Küng's own Global Ethic Foundation—to keep it alive via addenda nods to the *zeitgeist* in the direction of identity politics and the environment.

"The major problem of our time is the decay of the belief in personal immortality," Orwell writes, suddenly and unexpectedly, in "Looking Back on the Spanish War" (1943), "and it cannot be dealt with while the average human being is either drudging like an ox or shivering in fear of the secret police."[3] Küng earns a place alongside Orwell and the other great antitotalitarian voices of the twentieth century—from Amado and Adonis to Zamyatin and Mou Zongsan—by offering proof of concept for a post-fascist Catholicism once thought impossible by observers of the church's largely abysmal war record. What Küng describes variously as *Grundvertrauen* and *Lebensvertrauen*—"Basic Trust in Life" in my combo rendition—is the beating heart of his *Weltethos* idea; by magnanimously admitting that "non-Christians, too, can say Yes to life,"[4] the doors of dialogue are thrown open to the world. As with any public figure, accusations of

Does Hans Küng Still Matter?

a double discourse are semi-justified in Küng's case; one should never forget that his first battle was internal reform of a fetid Vatican, and that he spent the first half of his life trying (and ultimately failing) to look less liberal than he really was to reactionary powerbrokers in Rome. Küng's rejection of the idea of "religious dual citizenship"[5] belongs in a bygone, preglobalization era (alongside the views of his contemporary Joseph Ratzinger, who maintained that interreligious dialogue "in the strict sense of the term" was not possible, since a true dialogue implied "putting one's own faith in brackets"[6]). And yet Küng, to his immense credit, at least recognized—as others around him did not—that one fact about the future is known:

> [A]t the end of humanity or the end of the world, there will be no Buddhism or Hinduism, no Islam and no Judaism. There will be no Christianity either. There will be no religion left, just the inexpressible ethos itself, towards which all religions strive. And in the end there will be no prophet or sage to stand between the religions and keep them separate from one another, no Muhammad or Buddha-figure, not even a Jesus, in whom Christians believe, but rather [will] God Himself—*ho theos* or however he may be called in the East—truly become, not just a part of everything, but everything in everything.[7]

It seems to matter enormously, however, when this post-history "end-time" might be expected to begin. Orwell explains:

> All that the working man demands is what…others would consider the indispensable minimum without which human life cannot be lived at all. Enough to eat, freedom from the haunting terror of unemployment, the knowledge that your children will get a fair chance, a bath once a day, clean linen reasonably often, a roof that doesn't leak, and short enough working hours to leave you with a little energy when the day is done.…Shall the common man be pushed back into the mud, or shall he not? I myself believe that the common man will win his fight sooner or later, but I want it to be sooner and not later—sometime within the next hundred years, say, and not sometime within the next ten thousand years.[8]

HANS KÜNG

Küng became involved in business ethics after the global financial crisis (GFC) of 2008, co-drafting a Global Economic Ethic Manifesto in 2009[9] and deepening his foundation's involvement with local business. One would not wish to compare these dalliances, Hitchens-style, with Mother Teresa's visits to the Duvalier dictatorship in Haiti, but they definitely divided Küng's supporters: such dialogical work is not actually done with money. Attempts to weaponize Küng for productivity gains—a condensed ethical formula as a means to the end of winning in global business—miss the point about culture: it must be valued for its own sake, not for its instrumental value. The most apt metaphor in this frequently sordid sphere of ethics and profitability is probably still the biblical one: "Those who find their life will lose it, and those who lose their life for my sake will find it" (Matt 10:39).

In the subsequent post-GFC decade of rudderless identity wrangling, however, Küng's love for Catholic tradition, giant warts notwithstanding, has shone as a beacon through all the froth of local *Weltethos* politics. Küng could not imagine his own *Lebensvertrauen* without either his stable attachment to his family in early childhood or, crucially, his discovery of Catholicism as a young man. I had every reason from pedophilia to pointless school prayer—not to mention my own eventual excommunication from one half of my own family on religious grounds—to loathe the very idea of the Catholic faith, and yet Küng found a way to make me (and a greater hater would have been hard to find) reevaluate the entire meaning of the Christian heritage:

> In [Christ] all people are confronted, without any form of compulsion but unavoidably and directly, with an Ultimate Reality which challenges them to make a decision regarding the final end and purpose of their lives. This Ultimate Reality seems to demand from them a critical attitude to their lives as a whole and their dealings in society, to the political structures and laws which have been handed down, to questions of worship and hierarchy, institutions and traditions, family ties and wider affiliations. This extends, naturally, to the victims of these systems, to the suffering, oppressed, guilty and failed people of all kinds, and calls them to take their side in compassion. This Ultimate Reality provides a guiding light for his life as a whole....In this Ultimate Reality, then, which he

Does Hans Küng Still Matter?

calls God, his Father and our Father, one finds anchored a principle which can be summarized in one word: his freedom....A radically new dimension opens up for the individual human being and for society as a whole: a real alternative with other values, norms and ideals, a truly qualitative jump to a new [individual, post-tribal] consciousness, a new goal in life, a new Lebenswelt, a new society of freedom and justice.[10]

Now I had first discovered this idea—religion as the opposite of the blind obedience most people think it is—in Naguib Mahfouz; in the novel *Dweller in Truth* (1985), Mahfouz depicts the Pharaoh Akhenaten as the world's first monotheist, a forerunner of later prophets with consciences (Mahfouz was stabbed in the throat by Salafists in 1994 for allegorizing this continuity of Abrahamic civilization in *Children of Gebelawi*). Küng, meanwhile, was the first Western thinker to situate Christianity and other world religions for me in this context. Of his various late-phase *Spurensuchen*, the eponymous DVD series has not aged well, but his 2004 tome on Islam (*Der Islam: Geschichte, Gegenwart, Zukunft*) remains a particular favorite, as do his concise retrospectives *Was bleibt* (2014) and *Was ich glaube* (2010): here Küng explains his "discovery," as if it had really been a secret, that the spark of individual freedom and conscience is recoverable in spiritual traditions everywhere. The figure of Jesus is not necessary to ignite it, but this was what lit Küng's fuse as a boy, culminating in something far more important than a Vatican career: namely, *Projekt Weltethos* itself.

But then, perhaps the existence of this Global Ethic—a synonym for antitotalitarian respect for individual life common to all spiritual traditions worth the name—really was a secret to Küng until the second half of his life, and perhaps it remains a secret to most people, who have yet to enjoy the privilege of travelling the world (physically or now virtually) and being forced to reevaluate their own prejudices. A certain chauvinistic pseudo-Confucianism, for example, looks down its twenty-first-century nose at the post-Enlightenment West and its apparent contempt for civilizational continuity of spirit (which only China might now provide). I know considerably less about the Indian situation, but one hears echoes of a similar critique emanating from there and elsewhere (Russia's neo-tsarist turn is perhaps the most acutely worrying contemporary example of this anti-*Weltethos* cultural nationalism). The raw lack of mutual civilizational knowledge is the common denominator here: if I think back to the state of my own knowledge of Islam circa 2001, I am reminded just how little it is possible to know about all those vital centuries of Middle Eastern cultural history when they are not properly taught. Was Küng perhaps right all along to assume zero knowledge of foreign cultures among 90-plus percent of the human population, and to start with the simplest possible Declaration as a trust-building exercise? Globalization, however, is happening before our eyes, unfairly and unevenly, but steadily; even my mother back in New Zealand has now watched Korean series like *Squid Game* on Netflix. Küng provides an excellent basecamp from which to endure the winds of this globalization by stressing, very simply, that self-critical openness to contact with foreign cultures, and hence to potential enrichment from them, is an integral part of what it means to be a good Christian, Muslim, Jew, Hindu, Confucian, Buddhist, agnostic, atheist, or member of any other cultural tradition to which one could ever be proud to belong. If all these traditions have also been abused and distorted down the centuries as sinister modes of social control, this does not absolve us of the duty—which is also a pleasure—of engaging critically with them and creatively adding to them in our own time: this is the only true path to human freedom and originality. Küng gives me a guilty conscience about how little I know about the history of Catholic-inspired thought and art, just as an author like Mahfouz (or a director like Tarkovsky, or a philosopher like Tu Weiming) do the same for their respective (Islamic, Orthodox, and Confucian) traditions; this very sense of shame at cultural ignorance is the sine qua non of the *Weltethos* project.

I dwelt for a long time on the status of the Bible in Küng's world; I was convinced that any form of literalism that granted an inalienable superhuman status to written texts—and that hence whisked such texts off the chessboard of philological critique and comparison—was symptomatic of a lack of basic trust in life (Bertrand Russell witnessed just this attitude in Lenin's faith in the "infallibility" of Marx[11]). The doctrine of *i'jaz* in Islamic theology, for example—the idea, roughly speaking, that the language of the Qur'an is so superhumanly beautiful and perfect that it could not possibly have been conceived by human beings—seemed to me to represent a knife held to the throat of any global republic of letters, a permanent source of tension and violence as long as believers and unbelievers in such a doctrine share the earth. I think I still believe that, but authors from Navid Kermani to Abdulhamid al-Ansari, not to mention Mahfouz himself and friends I have made from Egypt, Turkey, Pakistan, and beyond, helped me gradually to understand that even such doctrines, with dreadful histories overall, might be reworked in creative new ways in order to prevent future generations from throwing the baby out with the bathwater of Islamic civilization. While it may seem a stretch to see a poet like Adonis as a representative of Islamic civilization (or a philosopher like Nietzsche as a representative of Christian civilization), there is something in the old Northern Irish joke: a man is stopped at an Army checkpoint in Belfast at the height of the Troubles and asked: "Catholic or Protestant?" "I'm an atheist," the man replies. The bemused soldier retorts in a thick local accent: "Well are you a Catholic atheist or a Protestant atheist?" There is no point, in other words, trying to fight against a person's cultural heritage, only ever in seeking to promote, as Küng puts it,

> [a] Basic Trust in reality which, in view of the deeply questionable nature of this reality, demands both critique and active engagement with unjust social conditions: an art which from a foundational "Yes" to life, and precisely because of it, is able to represent all the terrible, ugly, wicked and destructive aspects of reality and gather them up in a higher aesthetic synthesis....For this we need, both as artists and as viewers of art, a mixture of fantasy, creative power, civil courage and intellectual integrity. Artists can, each in their own way, and in ways that activism alone seldom finds, help the otherwise helpless to enhance their conception of life and of reality as a whole, and thereby to confront their own alienation and to develop new senses of their place in the world.[12]

I met Hans Küng properly only once, in 2015, when he was already well into his eighties and riddled with Parkinson's. Grateful to talk for a whole hour with an unwell pensioner who had generously made time, I found our conversation drifting, to my surprise, away from *Weltethos* and toward the machinations of the Curia in Rome. This was a reminder to me of a man not with "roots" as such—human beings are not trees, after all—but of Küng's broadly monocultural background: he had invested the first half of his life in reform of his beloved church, and only in the second half (after the fulcrum of exclusion from Vatican politics in 1979) discovered the full richness of engagement with foreign cultures (before, at the very end, returning in spirit to where it had all begun for him). Paradoxically, Hans Küng was not quite cosmopolitan enough for someone of my generation; it was as if he ended up preaching what millions of us born since 1979 have been practicing with the help of air travel and the Internet. Indeed, Küng never quite seemed to believe what an author like Kazuo Ishiguro (1954–), a full generation younger than he, would clearly foresee:[13] the twenty-first century will be characterized by increasingly culturally mixed families. As I talk to my Italian friend's half-Japanese children (nine and seven) in a code-switching mixture of Italian, Japanese, and English on Zoom, I try hard to remind myself that this trend remains an elite, international-school phenomenon, but it is hard to avoid the feeling that such globalization is irreversible in the long run. The only question, by no means small, is how beautiful and just it will be.

Does Küng still matter? Beyond academic theology, I would venture, he matters above all, and more than ever, because he offers Christians and non-Christians alike—or people brought up at the margins of Christian culture (as even most "Westerners" now are)—a highly legible invitation to look beyond all the terrible press and discover names in Christian history from Bartolomé de las Casas to Karl Barth. His work on other religions, while necessarily lacking the incredible breadth and depth of learning he brought to bear on Christian theology, nevertheless succeeds in inviting readers to delve into foreign spiritual traditions too (his dialogues with Walter Jens make clear, moreover, that this curiosity extended beyond religion to embrace art in general and literature in particular[14]). Victory for Küng's *Projekt Weltethos* is far from assured—the early "Declaration years" (the quarter-century spanning Chicago in 1993 and Toronto in 2018) will probably go down as a burst of post–Cold War optimism, wedged in the annals somewhere between Fukuyama and Huntington in the long and bitter struggle for an institutional humanism with global teeth—but one does not diminish Küng's contribution by comparing it with others; on the contrary, a Global Ethic is by definition greater than the sum of its parts, and Küng played his with singular energy at a time when knowledge of the best of Christian tradition was existentially threatened on all sides. I would also like to add, on a personal note, that I taught myself German chiefly by reading Hans Küng. I mean this as an expression of personal gratitude for the inviting lucidity of his prose, but perhaps Küng will be seen by native experts to have reinvigorated the German language in the long run. If so, then that, too, surely matters.

Christopher Hitchens dismissed the famous fatwa issued against his friend Salman Rushdie as having been issued by a man—the Ayatollah Khomeini—who not only hadn't read the offending novel in question (*The Satanic Verses*) but couldn't read it.[15] Küng matters most urgently of all, I would conclude, because he offers a still accessible bridge to the entire heritage of Christian-inspired art and thought, a heritage that someone of my generation and background has had to fight clumsily for, and that someone born today—even in a nominally Christian country—might wholly struggle ever to appreciate without serious extracurricular guidance. In a world where ever-greater emphasis is placed on STEM learning and productive efficiency for a knowledge economy, students are given a smaller and smaller horizon of freedom within which to address Orwell's problem of "decay of the belief in personal immortality," or in Küng's idiom, the challenge of building a robust Basic Trust in Life, which can only come through a mixture of family care and contact with Matthew Arnold's "best that has been thought and said in the world." Paradoxically, an economy that liberated its participants to choose their preferred mode of productivity on their own unalienated terms, from a position of strength in *Grundvertrauen*, might well end up being more efficient than one in which captive wage slaves are told what to do (wealthy donors to Küng's Global Ethic Project have certainly thought so). We cannot all know everything about every cultural and spiritual tradition, or even experience the best of all these traditions in our own short lifetimes, and yet, *ceteris paribus*, the more we do absorb, the better equipped we will be as citizens and leaders in our desperately large and complex human zoo. But you have to want this knowledge for the sake of your own soul, not as a means to the end of status or wealth; this is perhaps what another leading Christian voice of our time, Christopher's brother Peter Hitchens, meant when he said that "love is the opposite of power."[16] The real reward of Küng's *Projekt Weltethos* is not even world peace; it is the promise of individual immortality via love in an age of dizzying cultural change. The peace among religions that will emerge from this dialogue among religions, in Küng's most famous formulation, is a collateral public byproduct of this delicious private curiosity. It is hard to think of anything that matters, or will ever matter, more than the cultivation of such spiritual taste.

Notes

1. Alain Finkielkraut, "Alain Finkielkraut dans Punchline le 9 novembre 2021," https://www.youtube.com/watch?v=h8gvB2m5SF8.

2. See my *From Global Ethic to World Ethos? Building on Hans Küng's Legacy of Basic Trust in Life* (Karl Schlecht Foundation, 2018), https://karl-schlecht.de/fileadmin/daten/Download/Buecher/Keir/From_Global_Ethic_Gesamt_PDF_Keir.pdf.

3. George Orwell, "Looking Back on the Spanish War" (1943), in *Homage to Catalonia* (Harmondsworth, UK: Penguin, 1974 [1938]), 245.

4. Hans Küng, *Wozu Weltethos? Religion und Ethik in Zeiten der Globalisierung* (Freiburg: Herder, 2002), 21.

5. Hans Küng, in Hans Küng and Julia Ching, *Christentum und chinesische Religion* (Munich: Piper, 1988), 306: "For all the possibilities of cultural and ethical integration, therefore, the truth claims of each religion reach a depth which, in the end, call each individual human being to a Yes or a No, and challenge her with an either-or. This is not only the case with the exclusivist prophetic religions of Semitic origin, but also with the more inclusive, mystical Indian religions and the wisdom-oriented religions of the Chinese tradition.... As much as a cultural and ethical dual citizenship is possible and should always be encouraged, religiously speaking, in the deepest, strictest sense of faith, dual citizenship should be excluded as a possibility—for all the great religions."

6. See Karl-Josef Kuschel, *Leben ist Brückenschlagen* (Stuttgart: Patmos, 2011), 33.

7. Hans Küng, *Theologie im Aufbruch: Eine ökumenische Grundlegung* (Munich: Piper, 1987), 306.

8. Orwell, "Looking Back on the Spanish War" (1943), 244–45.

9. Hans Küng, Klaus M. Leisinger, et al., *Manifest Globales Wirtschaftsethos* (Manifesto Global Economic Ethic) (Munich: dtv, 2010).

10. Hans Küng, *Was bleibt: Kerngedanken* (Munich: Piper, 2013), 93–94, 99, 100.

11. Bertrand Russell, "Bertrand Russell on His Meeting with Vladimir Lenin in 1920," https://www.youtube.com/watch?v=6TK9c-caEcw.

12. Hans Küng, *Kunst und Sinnfrage* (Zurich: Benziger, 1980), 37, 61.

13. See pp. 413–34 of my *Peking Eulogy* (2020) for a discussion of Ishiguro's *An Artist of the Floating World* in a "World Ethos" context.

14. See Hans Küng and Walter Jens, *Literature and Religion: Pascal, Gryphius, Lessing, Hölderlin, Novalis, Kierkegaard, Dostoyevsky, Kafka* (New York: Paragon House, 1991).

15. See "Christopher Hitchens on Rushdie," https://www.youtube.com/watch?v=gEVA4EAP_S0.

16. See Peter Hitchens, "Love Is the Opposite of Power," https://www.youtube.com/watch?v=FKUrFP3ys9w.

LIST OF CONTRIBUTORS

Francis X. Clooney, SJ, is the Parkman Professor of Divinity and Professor of Comparative Theology at Harvard University. After earning his doctorate in South Asian languages and civilizations (University of Chicago, 1984), he taught at Boston College for twenty-one years before moving to Harvard, where from 2010 to 2017 he was the Director of the Center for the Study of World Religions. Elected a Fellow of the British Academy in 2010, he was the President of the Catholic Theological Society of America during 2022–23. Recent books include *Reading the Hindu and Christian Classics: Why and How It Matters* (University of Virgina Press, 2019), and *Western Jesuit Scholars in India: Tracing Their Paths, Reassessing Their Goals* (Brill, 2020).

Anthony J. Godzieba is Professor Emeritus of Fundamental and Systematic/Constructive Theology at Villanova University, Editor Emeritus of *Horizons: The Journal of the College Theology Society*, and a coeditor of the series T&T Clark Explorations at the Crossroads of Theology and Aesthetics. His work in systematic, foundational, and philosophical theologies is published widely in various collections and in journals such as *Theological Studies, Louvain Studies*, and *The Heythrop Journal*. His most recent book is *A Theology of the Presence and Absence of God* (Liturgical, 2018).

Hermann J. Häring completed his doctorate on Rudolf Bultmann in 1970 and his habilitation on Augustine in 1978, both in Tübingen, where he worked with Hans Küng. In 1980 he became a professor of systematic theology at the University of Nijmegen in the Netherlands, and in 1999 became professor of theology and the philosophy of science. After his retirement in 2005 Dr.

Häring worked with Küng's Global Ethics project, and continued his work on church reform and interreligious dialogue (www.hjhaering.de). He is the author of *Hans Küng: Breaking Through* (2015).

Roger Haight is currently visiting professor at Union Theological Seminary, New York. He received his PhD from the University of Chicago in 1973 and has taught successively at four Jesuit graduate schools of theology: Loyola School of Theology at the Ateneo de Manila in the Philippines; at Jesuit School of Theology in Chicago; Regis College in the Toronto School of Theology, and Weston Jesuit School of Theology in Cambridge, MA. He is a past president of the Catholic Theological Society of America and recipient of the John Courtney Murray Award for theological achievement. Haight's work has attended to the nature of theology as a discipline, Christology, ecclesiology, grace, liberation theology, spirituality, and the dialogue of Christian theology with science and evolution.

Hille Haker holds the Richard McCormick, SJ, Endowed Chair in Catholic Ethics at Loyola University Chicago. Previously, she taught at Goethe University Frankfurt and Harvard Divinity School, Cambridge, MA. She holds a PhD and Habilitation in Catholic Ethics from the University of Tübingen, Germany. Her most recent book is *Towards a Critical Political Ethics: The Renewal of Catholic Social Ethics* (2020). Her research includes questions of moral identity and narrative ethics, a social ethics approach to biomedicine, health care chaplaincy, new technologies, Frankfurt School critical theory, and feminist ethics.

Jonathan Keir was a Postdoctoral Research Fellow at the University of Tübingen's Global Ethic Institute, where he completed the book *From Global Ethic to World Ethos? Building on Hans Küng's Legacy of Basic Trust in Life* (2018). He now works for the Karl Schlecht Foundation, a major donor to the Global Ethic Institute and Global Ethic Foundation.

Prof. Dr. Karl-Josef Kuschel, literary scholar and theologian, was a doctoral candidate, habilitation candidate and one of Hans Küng's closest collaborators at the Institute for Ecumenical Research at the University of Tübingen, as well as vice president

List of Contributors

of the Global Ethic Foundation, which Küng founded in 1995. From 1995 to 2013 he held the professorship for Theology, Culture, and Interreligious Dialogue at the Faculty of Catholic Theology in Tübingen. His work includes research and publications on the relationship between religion and literature as well as on interreligious dialogue. Among his most recent publications is *Christmas and the Qur'an* (2018).

Paul Lakeland is the Aloysius P. Kelley SJ Professor of Catholic Studies Emeritus at Fairfield University, where he taught for forty-two years. He is a past president of the Catholic Theological Society of America and was the 2020 recipient of the Association of Catholic Colleges and Universities' Monika Hellwig Award for outstanding contributions to Catholic intellectual life. His most recent book is *The Wounded Angel: Fiction and the Religious Imagination* (Liturgical, 2017).

Dr. Mary McAleese is Chancellor of Trinity College Dublin and was President of Ireland from 1997 to 2011. An academic civil and canon lawyer, she was formerly Reid Professor, Trinity College Dublin, Director of the Institute of Professional Legal Studies, Queen's University Belfast and Professor of Children, Law and Religion, University of Glasgow.

Johanna Rahner, Dr.theol., has been Professor for Dogmatics, History of Dogma, and Ecumenical Theology at the Faculty of Catholic Theology (University of Tübingen) since 2014 and also director of the Institute for Ecumenical and Interreligious Research at Tübingen. She received her Dr.theol. in 1997. Her publications include introductions to Catholic dogmatics and Christian eschatology.

Jakob Karl Rinderknecht is the Director of the Honors Program and an Associate Professor of Religious Studies at the University of the Incarnate Word (San Antonio, TX). His research concerns how embodiment and culture shape the Catholic Church in its internal and external relationships. Recent works include *Mapping the Differentiated Consensus of the Joint Declaration* (Palgrave, 2016, winner of the Harding Meyer Prize in Ecumenism) and a critical translation of Karl Rahner's *An Ecumenical Priesthood: The Spirit of God and the Structure of the Church* (Fortress, 2022).

HANS KÜNG

Susan A. Ross is Professor of Theology Emerita at Loyola University Chicago, a past president of the Catholic Theological Society of America, and a former editor of *Concilium: International Theological Journal*. She is the author of *Extravagant Affections: A Feminist Sacramental Theology* (Continuum), *For the Beauty of the Earth* (Paulist), and *Seeking Light and Beauty* (Liturgical).

HANS KÜNG: WORKS IN ENGLISH

This list includes only those texts available in English language editions. They are presented in chronological order of publication, with the most easily accessible editions indicated.

The Council and Reunion. London: Sheed and Ward, 1960.

Structures of the Church. New York: Thomas Nelson, 1962.

That the World May Believe. New York: Sheed and Ward, 1963.

The Living Church: Reflections on the Second Vatican Council. London: Sheed and Ward, 1963. In the U.S.A., published as *The Council in Action: Theological Reflections on the Second Vatican Council.* New York: Sheed and Ward, 1963.

Justification: The Doctrine of Karl Barth and a Catholic Reflection. London: Thomas Nelson, 1964. 40th anniversary edition, Louisville, KY: Westminster John Knox Press, 2004.

The Church. London: Burns and Oates, 1967.

Infallible? An Inquiry. London: Collins, 1971. Revised edition, *Infallible: An Unresolved Inquiry.* London: SCM, 1994.

On Being a Christian. New York: Image, 1974.

Why Priests? London: Collins, 1974.

What Must Remain in the Church. London: Collins Fontana, 1977.

HANS KÜNG

Signposts for the Future: Contemporary Issues Facing the Church. New York: Doubleday, 1978.

Does God Exist? An Answer for Today. New York: Doubleday, 1980.

Freud and the Problem of God. Enlarged edition. New Haven, CT: Yale University Press, 1980.

Art and the Question of Meaning. New York: Crossroad, 1981.

Eternal Life: Life after Death as a Medical, Philosophical and Theological Program. Garden City, NY: Doubleday, 1982.

Christianity and the World Religions: Paths of Dialogue with Islam, Hinduism, and Buddhism. Maryknoll, NY: Orbis, 1983.

The Incarnation of God: An Introduction to Hegel's Theological Thought as Prolegomena to a Future Christology. New York: Crossroad, 1987.

Theology for the Third Millennium: An Ecumenical View. Garden City, NY: Doubleday, 1988.

Christianity and Chinese Religions. Garden City, NY: Doubleday, 1989.

Global Responsibility: In Search of a New World Ethic. New York: Crossroad, 1991.

Judaism: Between Yesterday and Tomorrow. New York: Crossroad, 1992.

Credo. The Apostle's Creed Explained for Today. London: SCM, 1993.

Great Christian Thinkers. New York: Continuum, 1994.

Christianity: Its Essence and History. London: SCM, 1995.

A Global Ethic for Global Politics and Economics. Oxford: Oxford University Press, 1997.

Dying with Dignity: A Plea for Personal Responsibility. Cowritten with Walter Jens. New York: Continuum, 1998.

The Catholic Church: A Short History. New York: Modern Library, 2003.

My Struggle for Freedom: Memoirs. New York: Continuum, 2003.

Hans Küng: Works in English

Women and Christianity. London: Continuum, 2005.

Why I Am Still a Christian. New York: Continuum, 2005.

The Beginning of All Things—Science and Religion. Grand Rapids, MI: Eerdmans, 2007.

Islam: Past, Present and Future. London: OneWorld, 2007.

Disputed Truth: Memoirs II. New York: Continuum, 2008.